EUROPE
• AT COST •

A TRAVELLER'S GUIDE

EUROPE
• AT COST •

A TRAVELLER'S GUIDE

Klaus M. Peter

LITTLE HILLS PRESS

Photographs courtesy of the following organisations based in Sydney; The Greek National Tourist Organisation, German National Tourist Office, Swedish Consulate General, Irish Tourist Board, IBUSZ Hungarian Travel Company, Austrian National Tourist Office, Swiss National Tourist Office, Netherlands National Tourist Office, Consulate General of Belgium, and Little Hills Press.

Cover photograph courtesy of the Swiss National Tourist Office.

Typeset by Midland Typesetters, Victoria
Printed in Australia by Globe Press Pty. Ltd.
Production by Vantage Graphics

© 1985 K.M. Peter and Manfred Klemann, Singen
© Translation + Additions, 1988, Little Hills Press

Little Hills Press,
34 Bromham Road, Bedford MK40 2QD,
UNITED KINGDOM

Regent House, 37 Alexander St.,
Crows Nest, N.S.W.,2065
AUSTRALIA

ISBN 0 949773 43 3

DISCLAIMER

Whilst all care has been taken by the publisher and author to ensure that the information is accurate and up to date, the publisher does not take responsibility for the information published herein. The recommendations are those of the author, and as things get better or worse, places close and other open up some elements in the book may be inaccurate when you get there. Please write and tell us about it so we can update in subsequent editions.

CONTENTS

EUROPE

Glasgow
• Edinburgh

Dublin

London
Brighton

Bergen

Oslo
Goteborg

Falun
Uppsala
Helsinki
Stockholm

Odense
Copenhagen

Hamburg
The Amsterdam
Hague Rotterdam
Brussels
Ghent Cologne
Bruges

West
Berlin

Frankfurt
Luxembourg
Stuttgart
Prague
Vienna

Paris

Strasbourg
Zurich
Bern

Munich
Innsbruck

Sopron
Budapest

Constanta

Lyon

Milan
Venice

Belgrade

Bucharest

San Sebastian

Nice
Florence

Barcelona
Marseille
Rome

Lisbon
Madrid

Palma De Mallorca
Cagliari
Palermo

Athens

INTRODUCTION

EVERY PERSON DREAMS OF—TRAVEL.

Lets begin with an explanation

Travelling for pleasure, a change of environment, or just for relaxation has only become popular in relatively modern times. For a long time travel guides only considered the aspects of the clear perfection of buildings, the purity of large frescoes and the quiet attestation of ancient ruins as important aspects of travel.

They treated people with less academic interests arrogantly. But it is mainly this group who are really interested in travel and not 'the elite' who stay at the Hilton, Ritz or Waldorf hotels. Because of the large numbers of young people travelling, the new generation of travel guides cater for other aspects as well.

How should I Travel? (By coach and with a Rucksack?)

There are many alternative possibilities; you can trek along the european walking tracks; go cross country skiing along the groomed tracks (e.g. near Oslo); hire a bicycle (they are available for hire at a large number of railway stations in Europe); hire a boat and travel along the old industrial canals of Great Britain and France; take an organised cruise or a discovery trip on a yacht; or go pony trekking in Ireland. But you still can travel by more conventional means such as: by train, car, long distance bus, motorbike, or regular, charter or stand-by flights. The possibilities are almost endless. The best way to start travelling is to visit the various european cities and surrounding countryside. Because many travellers still have to take into account financial and time restrictions, the large european cities offer many impressive experiences that will prepare them for more intensive travelling.

Buy a Travel Guide and you're off

This travel guide attempts to introduce 45 important european cities and 11 other nearby towns. An important thing to remember when travelling is: a foreigner should always be an outside observer and therefore should be careful in his or her judgements–in his condemnation as well as his enthusiasm. Also he should not hesitate to wander a bit away from the usual tourist haunts e.g. K'damm in Berlin or Picadilly Circus in London, or the Colosseum or North Cape where the genuine centre isn't genuine any longer. This guide attempts to point out different aspects of life in the cities which it introduces: Cologne's cathedral is indeed an impresive work of art, and to-day's museums are worth visiting as they contain not only objects connected with royal and military history but also artifacts documenting the everyday life of various peoples, local folk-art and other aspects of the social history of a given region. However, a picture of Cologne or Copenhagen without their exotic local districts would not be complete. Wherever possible, this travel guide attempts to give this information.

The structure of the guide

The descriptions of the cities is preceded by a little information about the 21 countries from which the cities have been chosen. Under the countries is some data about the form of government, size, population, geography and a short account of the nation's history.

Next up-to-date information is listed: entry/currency/customs regulations, exchange rates, how to use the telephone, embassy addresses, emergency telephone numbers, information about the land e.g. accommodation booking addresses, speed limits, discount offers on public transport and location of the airports. In some cases special information is added.

The cities weren't selected by a strict formula and may not be the ones you would select but we feel that they offer a good cross section. In choosing the cities not only capitals and cities with large populations were considered, so some favorites e.g. Innsbruck and Lucerne as well as some simply beautiful places e.g. Edinburgh and Lyon, have been included whereas other cities like Liverpool and Manchester were left out. We also left out Geneva because it's dominated by sheiks, and Porto because anything that it has to offer is surpassed by Lisbon.

The sections on the individual cities contain an evaluated, general introduction including possible routes to the cities by car, train or air, as well as important addresses such as travel bureax and when available, youth information offices, both of which should be contacted as soon as possible after arrival as they have the most up-to-date information about accommodation and weekly and monthly cultural programmes. They are also usually staffed by helpful people who are only too pleased to talk to you.

After that information about the public transport system is given. An important tip: Get hold of some local alternative or tourist newspapers. They often contain valuable information. They are usually available at the tourist information office or kiosks. Information about places worth visiting, museums (including opening times), parks, 'In Places', squares, markets and other information is also given and where possible, is arranged into convenient routes. In some cases, we were also able to include some suggestions about cultural and social activities, entertainment, eating out, etc. Obviously, this is the sort of information likely to change at a short notice.

Suggestions concerning accommodation mostly focus on youth-hostels, hotels and camping-sites. The minimum cost for a double room in hotels/pensions is from US$25 upwards and in Scandinavia, the British Isles, France, Switzerland and the Low Countries, it can easily go much higher. One should not entertain false hopes as to which way these prices go. If you can't stay with friends and you haven't booked accommodation, you will soon find it very difficult. This can deprive a traveller of real contact with the realities of a place as much as living in a luxurious hotel.

Information needed before you leave home

Of all the countries chosen, visas are only required for France and the Eastern Bloc Countries. See description of the country concerned for further information. Vaccinations are not needed for any of these countries.

Duty Free Allowance for Common Market Countries:
200 cigarettes or 250gm tobacco, 1 litre spirits and 2 litres wine.

There are different time-zones in Europe:
In winter, the following countries use Central European Time (CET): Belgium, Denmark, Germany, France, Italy, Yugoslavia, Luxembourg, Holland, Norway, Austria, Sweden, Switzerland, Spain, Czechoslovakia, and Hungary.
In summer they use Eastern European Time (EET).
  During winter Eastern European Time is used by Finland, Greece and Romania and these countries use Moscow Time (MT), in summer.
  Great Britain, Ireland and Portugal use Greenwich Mean Time (GMT) in winter and British Summer Time (BST) in summer.
  Hope that's clear.

MONEY

In this book we attempt to help you to get the best possible value for your money in the most beautiful cities of Europe. Here are a couple of suggestions which may help you to handle your money better.
  Before departure it is advisable to drop into your bank and have a chat with the experts–they often have quite up-to-date hints.

Cash

In principle, you should only carry as much cash as you will need for that day because of the problem with thieves. In spite of this, we cannot avoid using cash. When you travel from country to country, you should buy a limited quantity of cash in the appropriate currency before you arrive in a particular country. But you should bear in mind, in some countries you will get a better exchange rate at your destination than beforehand. Most international airports have banks open to issue foreign exchange for as long as there are flights.
In almost all southern european countries, banks are open only in the mornings, and afterwards only the expensive exchange offices are open and they often won't change traveller's cheques.

Traveller's Cheques

Traveller-cheques are an almost ideal way of carrying money when you go overseas but keep in mind, it is very handy to have some cheques in small denominations ($10 or $20). As a safeguard the cheques have to be signed when they are issued and then again when cashed. A passport is required as further proof of identity. If the traveller's cheques are lost or stolen, your bank will replace them, less a service charge of 1%, which is often cancelled out by a higher exchange rate abroad.

How to carry your money

You should give this some thought before your departure. A money-bag worn around the neck is better than a money-belt which is often difficult to get at. It isn't a good idea to carry your wallet in your back pocket or in a lady's handbag as both are extremely vulnerable. It is much safer to carry your cash loose in your pockets. It is more difficult to steal.

Insurance

Because there have been so many claims for lost or stolen luggage, the premiums are becoming very high and it really only pays to insure expensive luggage.

For Australians and New Zealanders, in most cases Medicare will cover 85% of medical expenses incurred overseas, if you're not away longer than 2 years, but it will only be refunded on your return home. Hospital charges are NOT covered. You will need to take out some insurance for them. It is best to check with Medicare or your private health insurer before departure as sometimes the funds cover a certain amount of hospital charges. This also applies to American, Canadian and British citizens.

Unfortunately, it must be said, be on your guard and don't be too trusting and take as little as possible with you.

Ask you travel agent for brochures and up-to-date information about the countries you plan to visit and on arrival in a particular country ask for any further brochures etc. Maps showing roads and railway lines, lists of hotels, pensions, camping areas and restaurants are very useful, as are bus, train and plane timetables and they are all gratis.

International Student Identity Cards

Save you money all over Europe–often as much as 75% on museums and art galleries etc. and discount on rail travel and sometimes on air travel. Apply for one from your local university, college or tertiary institution. Most of the time the travel agent on campus will have forms.

STA Offices in Europe

Amsterdam, NBBS, Dam 17, Dam Square, Tel. 237 686
Athens, STS, 1 Gilellinon Street, Syntagma Square, Tel. 322 7993
Briston, 25 Queen Road, Clifton, Tel. 294 399
Canterbury, Student Union Building, University of Kent, Tel 67 436
Copenhagen, Dis Rejser, Skindergrade 28, DK-1159, Tel. 110 044

Dublin, USIT, 7 Anglesea Street, Tel. 778 117
London, 74 Old Brompton Road, SW 7, Tel. 581 1022
Paris, USIT, 6 Rue de Vaugirard, Tel. 326 3353
Switzerland, SSR, Leonhardsrasse 10, 8001, Zurich, Tel. 242 3000

STA Offices in New Zealand

Auckland, 64 High Street, Tel. 735 265
Wellington, 11-15 Dixon Street, Tel. 850 561

STA Offices in United States

Dallas, 6609 Hillcrest Avenue, Tel. 350 0097
Los Angeles, Suite 507, 2500 Wilshire Boulevard, Tel. 380 2184
New York, Suite 400, 17 East 45th Street, NY 10017, Tel. 986 9470
San Diego, 6447 El Cajon Boulevard, Tel. 286 1322
San Francisco, Suit 702, 166 Geary Street, Tel. 391 8407

STA Offices in Canada

Toronto, 44 St. Georges Street, Toronto, Ontario, Tel. 979 2406
Vancouver, 1516 Duranleau Street, Tel. 687 6033

STA Offices in Australia

Victoria, 220 Faraday Street, Carlton, Tel. 347 6911
South Australia, Level 4, Union House, Adelaide University, Tel. 223 620
Western Australia, Hackett Hall, University of WA, Crawley, Tel. 380 2302
N.S.W., 1A Lee Street, Railway Square, Sydney, Tel. 212 1255
Queensland, 40 Creek St., Brisbane, Tel. 221 9629
A.C.T., Arts Centre, A.N.U., Canberra, Tel. 470 800

TRAVELLING IN EUROPE

By car

N.B. in Europe traffic regulations vary greatly from country to country. Therefore, it is very sensible to find out about the most important differences before entering a foreign country. (Speed limits for each country are given later in this book). Although it is not obligatory, it is worthwhile to take an international driver's licence if you are planning to hire or buy a car. These are available from your Automobile Association. You will also need a green insurance-card as without it, some countries (e.g. Spain, Greece, and Portugal) require that extra insurance be taken out and that can be a strain on your holiday budget. It also helps no matter what complications arise. You will need to carry the usual obligatory objects such as a first-aid kit and warning triangle and in some countries you are also required to carry a fire extinguisher and a second warning triangle. A torch and a tow rope are essential equipment when travelling by car and because of the high incidence of car theft, it is a good idea to have a car alarm fitted. It is also recommended that you take out membership with an automobile club. Overseas clubs often have reciprocal arrangements and they offer good service in the event of an accident.

For example: The ADAC (German Automobile Association) has what is called an 'Auslands Schutzbrief' (a piece of paper which will ensure help if you have an accident in another country). If you are in possession of this and need help you can phone 089/22 22 22 day or night. The Schutzbrief ensures free of charge break down service, credit for expensive car repairs and also some help with extra costs in the event of an accident.

Also be careful when parking in the street in Europe. Apart from the parking signs being written in another language, various other methods are used to signify no parking e.g. coloured marks along the foothpaths. In some countries foreign cars which are incorrectly parked are simply towed away and it might be quite expensive and take quite a while, to recover your car.

Agencies arranging lifts

These are to be found in most large cities of as well as in most universities. A quite extensive list of them can be obtained by writing to:

Der Verband der Deutchen Mitfahrzentralen e.V.

Dieffenbachstr.39, D-1000 Berlin 61. (West Berlin)

A look through a local telephone directory might also be helpful. The abbrieviation for these agencies is MFG and the costs of lifts is usually approx. 6 Pf.(approx. 5 cents per kilometre). The agency charge is approx. $6.00. It is also worthwhile asking trucking companies for a lift, as often a driver will only be too happy to have company on a trip. Simply phone the transport companies along your intended route.

By air

The quickest and most expensive way unless you can make use of discount airfares offered in conjunction with overseas flights, or one of the good specials such as the camping-flights offered by the big travel agencies such as the German TUI or NUR (Neckermann) which specialize in package deals. They offer empty seats on some flights to 'standby' passangers who are required to book and pay for their accommodation before departure. In spite of that, such flights are good value. (They are sometimes called 'hit' or 'tip' flights).

From Germany some costing examples; Athens DM 450, Palma DM 400, London DM 280 return.

Cheap flights of this nature may also be offered by established travel agencies as well as by the so-called 'alternative' ones. In principle, it is worthwhile to drop into a cheap-flight travel office, the address of which are easiest to obtain from advertisements in local newspapers.

By train

Trains are very good in central Europe and the British Isles but they have a few shortcomings in southern Europe because of: an old network in Greece; bureaucracy in Spain; an energy shortage in Romania; and they are slow in southern Italy. They are very comfortable in northern Europe but the network there isn't dense enough because of the sparse population.

The luxury trains of the TEE class are becoming extinct and are being replaced by the fast inter-city-trains which operate according to strict timetables (they leave at the same time every hour making timetables unnecessary). On the other hand, the international express trains are often slow and seat reservation is advisable and sometimes mandatory. Long distance trains have sleeping-cars which are very expensive though the couchettes cost approx. US$15 per night (european average) or cheaper on local trains.

Many countries have special fares (listed in this book in chapters devoted to particular countries) which are cheaper than car hire or bus fares. The European Inter-rail Ticket is valid for all the countries in this guide (except Czechoslovakia)–Cost for under 16's US$250/470 SFr for 1 month.

There are many other cheap offers for young people and students such as Transalpine, Euro-train, etc..

AUSTRIA

Austria is a non-aligned nation but the Third Reich hasn't been forgotten and the people still have a complex about Germans. Americans it seems are more than welcome.

ENTRY/FOREIGN EXCHANGE/CUSTOM REGULATIONS: A valid passport is required. The amount of currency which may brought into the land is uncontrolled but the upper limit which may be taken out is 15,000 Austrian Schillings.

Duty Free Allowance:
200 cigarettes or 250gms tobacco, 2 litres of wine and 1 litre of spirits.

Currency/Exchange Rate: The currency of the land is the Austrian Schilling (O Sh.).

1 A$	=	9 Sh.
1US$	=	13 Sh.
1 C$	=	10 Sh
1NZ$	=	7 Sh
£1	=	20 Sh.

EMBASSIES:
Australia: 2-4 Mattielli Strasse, Vienna, Tel. 52 85 80.
Canada: Dr. Karl Lueger-Ring 10, Vienna, Tel. 63 66 26
N.Z.: Lugeck 1, Vienna, Tel. 52 66 36
U.K.: Reisner Strasse 40, Vienna, Tel. 73 15 75.
U.S.A.: 2 Friedrich-Schmidt Platz, Vienna, Tel. 31 55 11.

ACCOMMODATION:
Hotels, camping grounds: OFW, Margaretenstr. 1, 1040 Vienna,
Youth hostel: OJHV, Scottenring 28, 1010 Vienna;
There are many pensions and holidays at farmhouses etc. available on the plains.

EATING TIP:
Try the famous Vienna Schnitzel with chips available anywhere in the land. Other local dishes are also very satisfying and realistically priced.
Special: Salzberg Nockerln (a lemon flavoured souffle).

SPEED LIMITS:
In built up areas 50 km/h;,
outside built up areas 100 km/h;
motorways 130 km/h.
Toll is payable on the mountain pass roads, Alberg tunnel, the Brenner autobahn and Tauern autobahn.

RAILWAYS:

Tickets for 9/16/31 days for DM 210/286/453;
for the under 26's for 9/16 days 139/197 DM.

AIRPORTS:

International airports at Vienna, Salzburg, Klagenfurt and Graz.

INNSBRUCK

Innsbruck has the advantage of being the centre of a transport network.
It has a very varied cultural life style, and possesses a romantic old
town centre. It is surrounded by beautiful green areas and the mountain
world, and has the environment of a small town and different, natural,
down to earth inhabitants. When Innsbruck with a population of
118,000 is described as a large town inside the chain of the alps it must
share the description with Bolzano and Grenoble, but the Winter
Olympics town is a meeting place for young people all year round.
But–punks are turned away!

BY CAR: The Inntal (River Inn valley) autobahn (motorway) E17 from
Munich-Kufstein, the Brenner autobahn from Verona-Bolzano (tollway)
and the well built autobahn/long distance road from Arlberg Pass (toll
is charged for the tunnel but not for the Pass Road), and the road from
Switzerland/Baden-Wurtemberg all lead to Innsbruck. From Munich
you can take the shortest way along the main roads via Garmisch-
Patenkirchen or come via the Achen Sea. Parking areas are found around
the railway station or if you are coming from the west, in Innrain
Strasse, just before the pedestrian zone in the old town.

BY RAIL: The railway lines follow the same main routes. There are
very good train connection to the main through railway station, which
is to the south-east of the city and has all the usual services as well
as a young people's waiting room (Monday-Friday 11.00 a.m.-7.00 p.m.,
Saturday 10.00 a.m.-2.00 p.m.), where you can book accommodation and
obtain other information, Tel. 052 22/26362.

BY AIR: West of the town there is a small airport with flights to other
international airports such as Munich, Zurich, and Vienna. Okista
Jugend Flugreiseburo (travel agent) Tel. 81 777.

TOURIST INFORMATION: Burggraben 3, Tel. 25 715;
accommodation information is also available at the main railway
station, Tel. 23 766. They also hand out pamphlets such as 'Innsbruck
for Youth', and 'Tyroler Spezialities'. A local publisher has also brought

out a book, 'Stadt Fenster/Town Window' which looks critically at the town.

LOCAL TRANSPORT–Tram and bus ticket 13 OSh–its better to buy the 10 trip ticket strip for 86 OSh if you want to take a long tour.

POINTS OF INTEREST: You can see the city on foot quite comfortably. This walk should commence at the Salurner str. railway station. Go along Salurner str. to the Victory Arch of 1765. Go along the magnificent Maria Theresia street which starts here. If you look along the Maria Theresia street you will see the Annasaule (column) in the foreground and the old town in the background. It was erected in remembrance of a successful war against the Bavarians. This main street is always so busy, no matter which time of year it is, that the Landhaus (a baroque palace) almost gets lost; go right along Meraner str. to Bozner Platz and the Rudolfsbrunnen (fountain), erected in 1863 to celebrate Tyrol's 500 years as part of Austria. The old town starts at Market and Burggraben str., and to-day is reserved for pedestrians. You can hardly see the Goldene Dachl, a former royal lodge, for all the people. It has 2657 gold plated copper tiles which have been restored. The Goldene Dachl also houses the Olympic Museum which shows short films of highlights of the 1964 and 1976 Innsbruck games on three video recorders, daily 10.00 a.m.-5.00 p.m.

Something else which you should see after this is the Town Tower to the east built in gothic style, with a beautiful view (daily 10.00 a.m.-5.00 p.m.). The Ottoburg Haus is found on the town square and nowadays you can buy a drink of wine there. The cathedral is to the right of the 'Dachl' in Pfarr Gasse. It was built in baroque style around 1720. It adjoins the Hofburg (castle) whose main entry faces Rennweg. The rooms are magnificently furnished in 18th century style and can be visited (daily 9.00 a.m.-4.00 p.m., October-May only Monday-Saturday). The Great Hall is the most impressive.

On the opposite side of Burggrabens str. is the Landestheater, (theatre), the Leopoldsbrunnen (fountain) with a statue of a knight and the Court church with the Silver chapel. It was here that the war between the old rule and the People's Regent, Andres Hofer, took place. For the locals, even to-day it is a living symbol of their independence, although it resulted in the dividing of their folk groups into two states. It also contains the mausoleum with the empty grave of Kaiser Maximillian I and the most important renaissance sculptures of the german school: 28 larger than life bronze statues (The Black Mander) keep the kaiser company. Originally, statues of all the kaisers were supposed to stand here (daily 9.00 a.m.-5.00 p.m.).

In the direction of the theatre are the palace gardens. They are lit in summer and concerts are held opposite the Congress House. On the other side of Herzog Otto Strasse is the River Inn. Go along the Promenade and over the Innrain str. and you come to the university. From here on you need to take some form of public transport. On the lower half of Mt. Isel, at the south end of the city, is the basilica and the Wilten Church, Urzelle der Siedlung, who, according to the saga, was killed as a result of a fight between two giants.

On Mt. Isel–which is reached by crossing Brenner street and going along Berg Isel Weg (Tram 1)–is the olympic ski-jump, built on an historical field. Across the Inntal autobahn which follows the southern side of the mountain, is the Ambras castle with interesting rooms and collections and the castle chapel (May-September, Wednesday-Monday 10.00 a.m.-4.00 p.m.). If you want to look at the view even higher up, then take the chair lift from Rennweg (where the round painting is) up to Hungerburg (it is possible to go by car) and from there with the cable car up to Mt. Hafelekar (2234m). The intermediate station, Seegrube is 1905m. Cost: just under 33DM for the mountain and valley trip. You also can see the Karwendel Mountains to the north, which for the most part, are closed to car traffic.

MUSEUM TIPS: Tyroler Volkskunst Museum, Universitats str. 2 (daily 9.00 a.m.-12 noon, 2.00-5.00 p.m.); Tyroler Landesmuseum Ferdinandeum, Museum str. 15 (May-September daily 10.00 a.m.-5.00 p.m., closed in winter); Tyroler Landeskundliches Museum , Zeughaus, Zeughaus Gasse (May-September daily 10.00 a.m.-5.00 p.m.) Alpenvereins Museum, Wilhelm Greil str. 15 (Monday-Friday 9.00 a.m.-12 noon and 2.00 p.m.-5.00 p.m., October-May only Tuesday-Thursday); and the Alpen Zoo, Weiherburg has beautiful grounds (take the road to Hungerburg or the chair lift, daily 9.00 a.m.-6.00 p.m.)

FOOD: There is everything from fast food shops and self service to good local hotels and expensive restaurants. Tips: Uni Snack Hafele, Rechen Gasse, a cheap pub for young people; Beisl, Hofgasse; Self service: Neubock, Herzog Friedrich str. 30; Goldener Lowe, Seil Gasse 8, good value for money, in the old part of town and very original; good local food: Sailer, Adam Gasse 8; Weisses Rossl, Kiebach Gasse 8; homely italian: Pizzeria Romantica, Kiebach Gasse 11; exquisite: Belle Epoque, Zeughaus Gasse and Goldner Adler, Herzog Friedrich str. 6 also has mood music.

EVENING ENTERTAINMENT: For a three night stay you can get a Club Innsbruck pass, then the Bergwander bus is gratis, reductions on the chairlifts etc., tours and museums–general information as well as information on special events–very organised. You shouldn't miss out an evening at the theatre: Innsbrucker Keller Theater, Adolf Pichler Platz 8; Tyroler Volksbuhne Blaas, Maria Theresia str. 1, or Alt Innsbrucker Bauerntheater-Ritterspiele, Gasthaus Bierstindl, Kloster Gasse 6) or visit the popular Cafe 44, near the Victory Arch where you can eat Germknodel (dumplings) ; the young style Cafe Boheme, Seiler Gasse 5; or evenings: the Piano Bar, Herzog Friedrich str. 5; the Pub Anno 1900, right of the Victory Arch; Pinte, Pub/Cafe, Rechen Gasse (old student pub); Kultur Pubs: Komm, Josef Hirn str. 7; Treibhaus,

Anzengruber str. 1, Suburb of Pradl. Good cinema programmes: Cinematograph, Schopf str. 21 hands out the 'Calendarium' film programme. 'In' Discos: American Bar, Maria Theresia str. 10; Club Filou, Stifs Gasse 12. Concerts and Music programms are often held at the Kongresshaus, the Olympic ice rink, the conservatorium and at the castle.

ACCOMMODATION: usually at a premium! Youth hostel: Reichenauer str. 147, Tel. 05 222/46179; MK-Jugend Zentrum, Sill Gasse 8a, Tel. 31 311; Torsten Arneus Schwedenhaus, Rennweg 17b, Tel. 25 814. Camping: near the youth hostel Reichgenauer str. Private rooms: Plaickner, Kranebitter Allee 19, Tel. 05 222/858 742. Pensions: Riese Haymon, Haymon Gasse 4, Tel. 29837; Dollinger, Haller str. 7, Tel. 37351; Laurin, Gumpp str. 19, Tel. 41 104.

INNSBRUCK IN WINTER: Innsbruck's ski-ing area has the olympic town as its centre, and extends to the villages of Hungerburg, Igls, Mutters, Tulfes and Axams and includes their ski areas Seegrube, Patscherkofel, Mutterralm, Glungezer and Axamer Lizum. Height of the villages: Innsbruck 574m, ski-village 830-992m, ski runs to 2340m. The ski pass is valid for 34 lift complexes in this area with approx. 100km of runs, and includes the use of the buses in Innsbruck, Igls and Hungerberg as well as free entry into the public indoor swimming pools (e.g. Armraser str. 3 and Olympic Village, Kugelfangweg 46). Club members (membership free with 3 nights accommodation) can use the ski and Langlauf (x-country) buses in the area without charge (approx. 80km Loipen x-country ski runs). There are ski huts and mountain restaurants all over the area.

SOPRON

The old town of Sopron, called Odenburg by the Germans is definitely worth a side trip either from Budapest or from Vienna.

BY RAIL: You can take the main line of the Mav from Gyor to Sopron or you can go from Vienna (Wein, Sud) to Wr. Neustadt, and take the GySEV (Gyor, Sopron, Ebenfurth, Vasut) historical railway line which crosses the Austrian border to Sopron. (Important: apply for a visa beforehand).

TOURIST INFORMATION: Ferenczi u. 4, Tel. 99/12030 and Ibusz, Ogabona ter 8, Tel. 12 041, inexpensive rooms in private homes.

POINTS OF INTEREST: The town walls and the towers which date from roman times, the Maria Church, the cloister which is a girls' school to-day, the classical town hall, the town square, Beloiannisz Ter with its exceptional buildings, Fabrcius House, Storno House and Generals House. The whole of the old town is built in the shape of a horseshoe and is completely protected by the National Trust which is evidence of its flair. It has curvy lanes, narrow houses, small windows, archways, internal courtyards with flowers, paving, and ringing bells ... and after that go to a wine cellar, e.g. the Gyogygodor, Templom ut 2 or the Becsikapu borozo, Becsi ut, and drink a Kekfrankos which is the treasured wine of the people of Sopron.

MUSEUMS: The Franz Litz Museum in Matavas Kiraly and the Museum of Hungarian Castles, Templom utca 2. The Sopranos Festival is held from June to August (classical music). Hotel: Lokomotiv, Szabadsag k 1, Tel. 14 180.

The small gauge steam railway Fertoboz–Baratsag-Kastely branches off south of the GySEV in Nagycenk. Sopron office: Matyas kir. ut 19 or Tel. Budapest 388 144.

VIENNA–WIEN

Vienna is a genial town and the bastion of central Europe since the Turks were stopped in front of Vienna. Vienna has the insignia of a town of the world. (Pop. 1.53 million).

BY CAR: You can come along the western motorway, Munich, Salzburg, Linz or along the partly southern motorway, Klagenfurt/Graz.

Tourist information office with hotel reservations: Vienna autobahn rest stop on the Wien Zentrum (Vienna Centre) Exit. Park & ride with the U-Bahn (underground) to Schloss Schonbrunn (U4, West) or to Reumann Platz (U1, south).

BY RAIL: National and international trains from Switzerland and W. Germany arrive at the Westbahnhof; from Yugoslavia, Italy and the Balkans (Bukarest/Budapest) at the Sudbahnhof. Both railway stations have a tourist information office and have all the usual services, Tel. 1734/1735.

BY AIR: The international airport is Wien-Schwechat, 19km from the city centre and can be reached by trains which run every hour or by buses which run more frequently.

BY SHIP: You can also travel by ship to Vienna along the Danube (Donau). DDSG Information, Tel. 266 536.

TOURIST INFORMATION: The main office is in the Opern Passage,

B Level, Tel. 431 608; Austrian information, Margareten str. 1, Tel. 575 714. For youth information ask for the 'Live Wien' brochure.

TOURIST NEWSPAPERS: 'Falter' and the Falter programme liftout; New wave culture critic: 'Der Wiener'; Programme: 'Neuer Wochenspiegel'.

LOCAL TRANSPORT: It is improving with 100 new S-Bahn (city railway) trains having been ordered–and art doesn't have to take a back seat–different stations have different styles, don't forget to look at the the city railway pavilion at Karls Platz.

Good value: the Network card, 83 OSh for 3 days, because a single trip ticket costs 18 OSh. Always purchase tickets at news stands before boarding because there are no conductors. Tickets cost more from the automatic ticket vending machines.

POINTS OF INTEREST: Vienna is an example of town planning par excellence: not only because of the styles from earlier times but also because of Camillo Sitte, the electrification of the 19th century, the co-operatives and council flats. Examples of all of these have been documented by the State Planning Authority (Book with city tour by Lichtenberger, Elisabeth, 'Wien', 1978).

SIGHTS ON THE RING: East of the Votiv Church is the stock exchange on Schotten Ring, to the south are the main buildings of the university, the new gothic Town Hall (Tours, Monday-Friday only at 11.00 a.m.), opposite is the famous Burg Theatre (Tours Monday-Saturday at 9.00 a.m., 3.00 p.m., 4.00 p.m., Sunday 11.00 a.m.-3.00 p.m., or during performances). South of there is the much loved Volksgarten (people's gardens) with its Theseus Temple. Opposite is the Parliament House which is built like a greek temple (Tours Monday-Friday at 11.00 a.m. but not when Parliament is sitting) and lastly the old and new imperial palaces on Helden Platz, the seat of the Hapsburg family and centre of a world empire. To-day it is open to the public and contains the National Library and the Ethnological Museum (daily 10.00 a.m.-1.00 p.m.). The Old Hofburg with its Sweizerhof, Hofburgkapelle (chapel where the Vienna Boys Choir sings on Sundays at the 9.15 a.m. Mass from September-June) and treasure room which has been remodelled (there is a small exhibition in the fine arts museum).

Michaeler Platz in the direction of the city with Alf Loos house and the unsurpassed view of the sprawling old Hofburg. In the Hofburg is also the world famous Spanish Riding School which has performances at various times (Morning workout–Tuesday-Saturday 10.00 a.m.-12.00 noon). At the end of the Hofburg is the Albertina graphic collection (daily 10.00 a.m.-2.00 p.m.). Then turn left and go along Neuen Markt and you will come to the Kapuziner church and the kaisers' crypt (daily 9.30 a.m.-4.00 p.m.).

Go on through the Burgtor (gate) across The Ring to the natural history and fine arts museums both of which were started off with the kaisers' collections. In the middle of the park between the two buildings is the Maria Theresia memorial. In the Semper building are the important egyption collection and the coin collection in the Fine Arts Museum and the meteorite collection and the 25,000 year old 'Venus of Willendorf' at the Natural History Museum (Art: Tuesday-Sunday 10.00 a.m.-6.00 p.m. and Nat.Hist. Wednesday-Monday 9.00 a.m.-6.00 p.m.).

Along the Opern Ring behind the new Hofburg are the Hofburg gardens which have many memorials: Kaiser Franz Joseph, Mozart, Goethe, etc.

Go around the Academy of Creative Arts and the State Opera House (tours daily at 2.00 & 3.00 p.m., July-August 9.00 & 11.00 a.m., 1.00 & 3.00 p.m. or performances in the evening) to Kartner strasse, a pedestrian zone, which leads directly to the gothic St. Stephan's cathedral.

While we are talking about splendid buildings: Have a look at the unique Palais Esterhazy, Casino Cercle, where the international jet set play; don't forget the traditional Hotel Sacher which sells the original Sacher's Torte; and not very well known is the Glas Museum at No. 26.

In the cathedral which is called 'Steffl' by the Viennese, you can climb up the 137m high south tower-458 steps-(daily 10.30 a.m., 3.00 p.m.) or look at the cathedral and diocesan museum or even visit the catacombs (daily 10.00 & 11.30 a.m., 2.00 & 4.30 p.m.).

OTHER ATTRACTIONS: Near the cathedral is the Pestsaule and round the corner is St. Peter's church. Straight ahead is the Hohe Markt-the oldest market in Vienna where roman ruins have been excavated, and the Anker Figurene Clock whose figures parade at noon. Go along Rothenturm Strasse to the meat market and the Heiligenkreuzerhof and the Greek church.

On Karls Platz are the Kunstlerhaus, the technical college and St. Charles' church; on the west end of the small Sezessions building, the Austrian/Hungarian faction of the Parisian art nouveau, better known as Youth Style (city railway train stops), house fronts and the Anker Clock, the Majolika House, (left Wienzelle 40).

If you want to try it: CITY TOURS leave from the opera house (9.20 & 10.20 a.m., 2.20 p.m.) and cost 250 OSh, cheaper: opera house (10.30 & 11.45 a.m., 3.00 & 4.30 p.m.) for 130 OSh; more expensive by Flaker (horse drawn carriage).

IN THE SURROUNDING SUBURBS: the Steinhof church by Otto Wagner built in the gounds of the psychiatric hospital is the main work of the Sezession, 14, Baumgartner Hohe 1 (Bus 48a); Further out is the famous Schloss Schonbrun (daily 9.00 a.m.-12 noon & 1.00-4.00 p.m.) the former residence of the imperial family which has 1441 rooms. It has far reaching grounds in which are the Gloriette with a viewing platform, the Palm House built in steel and glass in 1883, the zoo and carriage museum with the kaisers' coaches in the schloss (Tuesday-

Sunday 10.00 a.m.-4.00 p.m.).

Another schloss: Belevedere built by Prinz Eugen and containing the Austrian gallery in both parts of the schloss (Tuesday-Sunday 10.00 a.m.-4.00 p.m., south of the Schwarzenberg Platz). In between is something special for botanists: the alpine garden and the botanical gardens as well as the park; numerous Beethoven memorial houses, such as the Pasqualati House, 1 Molker Bastei 8, also the A. Stifter Museum; as well as the two Hofs the Werkbund Siedlung (13, Veitnger gasse/Jagdschloss gasse–Tram 60) is an example of avant garde architecture; also the Haus des Philosophen Wittgenstein, 3, Kundmanns gasse 19 who was in on the planning (Bus 4a).

Because so much else is happening around it: the Prater, with its big wheel from where you get the best view of Vienna, particularly in the evenings; the Prater Museum near the planetarium (Saturday & Sunday 2.00-6.30p.m.); the small railway (with 391mm tracks). Interesting because it has been recently built: on the new U1, the UNO City, which since 1979 is a separate territory and sells UNO Postage stamps! Behind that the beautiful Danube Park with its 252m high Donau Turm (Danube tower); architectural trivia: (Loos) Karntneer Bar (1907), Karntner str. 10; Austrian Postsparkasse (bank) 1906, Georg Cock Platz 2; Kleines Cafe (1974), Franziskaner Platz 3; Restaurant Sazamt (1963), Reprecht Platz 1.

After so much, let's go to a little bit of green: beautiful old wine with 'Beisln': Bohmischer Prater (Tram 67, Bus 15A); Lainzer Tiergarten (zoo) wood and animal park, U4, Tram 60, Bux 60A; or the left bank of the Danube, part of the right is forestlike.

MUSEUM TIPS: The Bestattungs Museum, 4, Goldeg gasse 19, but you have to book, Tel. 651 631; the Ephesos Museum in the New Burg (Wednesday-Monday 10.00 a.m.-4.00 p.m.); most loved: Austrian Film Museum, Augustiner str. 1 (daily 8.00-10.00 p.m.); Freud's House, Berg gasse (daily 9.00 a.m.-1.00 p.m.); Museum of the World Language, Esperanto in the Hofburg (Monday, Wednesday & Friday 9.00 a.m.-3.30 p.m.); Memorials to the uprising in the former Gestapo headquarters, 1, Salzroe gasse 6 (Thursday, Friday 9.00 a.m.-12 noon, Monday-Friday 2.00-5.00 p.m.); Haus des Meeres in Esterhazy Park (daily 9.00 a.m.-6.00 p.m.); the Heeresgeschichtliche Museum; south of the Sud Bahnhof (railway station) (Saturday-Thursday 10.00 a.m.-4.00 p.m.); Historical Museum of Vienna,, 4, Karls Platz (Tuesday-Sunday 9.00 a.m.-4.30 p.m.); Museum of Modern Art, Palais Liechtenstein, 9, Fursten gasse 1 (Wednesday-Monday 10.00 a.m.-6.00 p.m.); Museum of the 20th Century, 3, Schweizergarten (Thursday-Tuesday 10.00 a.m.-4.00 p.m.); Pathology & Anatomical Museum, 9, Spital gasse 2, in the Narren Turm (Thursday 8.00,9.00,10.00 a.m. not in August); Tobacco Museum, 7, Messepalast (Tuesday-Friday 10.00 a.m.-3.00 p.m. Saturday & Sunday 9.00 a.m.-1.00 p.m.); Technical and Railway Museum, 14, Mariahilfer str. 212 (Tuesday-Sunday 9.00 a.m.-1.00 p.m.). Trams are also called Bim in Vienna and there is the Tramway Museum (Bahnhof Ottak Ring, May-September Sunday 9.00 a.m.-12 noon).

Pay a visit to the famous cemeteries: Zentral Friedhof (central cemetery-S/Bahn); Stammersdorfer, Tram 331 or Bus 31B.

N.B.: The numbers in front of the street names denote the particular district (Bezirk).

MARKETS: In Naschmarkt 6, Linke Wienzeile-on Saturdays the Flea Market, U 4; Markthalle 9, Nussdorfer str. 22; good self-service chain, 'Naschmarkt', Schwarzenberg Platz 14, Schotten gasse 1, Mariahilfer strasse 85;

ENTERTAINMENT: Ma Pitom, 1, Seitenstetten gasse 5, interesting area; Oxen Steak, 4, Prinz Eugen str. 2;

FOOD: Numerous sausage stands. Wiener Schnitzel: Schmidt, 7, Neubau gasse 52. Or try a coffee shop, enjoyed since Kolschitzky obtained turkish coffee in 1683: Hawelka, 1, Dorotheerg.6–artists' cafe; Zchwarzenberg, am S-Platz; Vienna, Fleischmarkt 20; with piano: Augustin, 15, Marz str. 67; Hummel, 8, Josefstadter str. 66.

Vegetarian: Wrenkh, 15 Hollerg 9; Siddharta, 1, Fleischmarkt 16. There are good taverns around the Westbahnhof (railway station) in Mariahilfer str.

And other pubs? Krah Krah, 1 Rabensteig 8; Wiener, 7, Hermann gasse 17; Bunter Vogel, 1, Biber str. 9; Oswald & Kalb, 1, Backer str. 14; Roter Engel, 1, Rabensteig 5; Ring, 1, Stuben Ring 20; Fruit juice shop, 1, Fuhrich gasse 12; Boonoonoos, 4, Margarenten str. 7; C Privee, 4, right Wienzeile 23; Alternative: Rotstilzchen, 4, Margareten str. 99. With Music: Jazzspelunke, 6, Duren gasse 3; Willy's Rumpelkammer, 16, Lerchenfelder Giurtel 17; Metropol, 17, Hernalser Haupt str. 55; Bluescafe, 3, Schlachthaus gasse 46; Krise, 1, Hegel gasse 8.

DISCOS: U 4,12, Schonbrunner str. 222; Wake Up, 1, Sailerstatte 5; Jack Daniels, 1, Kruger str. 6; Atrium und Wurlitzer, 4, Schwarzenberg Platz 10 at Papas Tapas; Camera, 7, Neubau gasse 2.

VIENNA SPECIALITIES: the Heurige (new wine pubs), very much for tourists in Grinzing, better towards Heiligenstadt or in the suburbs of Stammersdorf, Sievering or Jedlersdorf. TIP: Zwolf Apostel Keller, 1, Sonnenfels gasse 3; Zur Agnes, 19, Sieveringer str. 221; Casablanca, 15, Goldschlagg 2.

FESTIVALS: Summer music July/August; Festwochen May/June. Balls are held the whole year round in the suburbs (e.g. Florisdorf, Dobling, Mariahilf etc.) Cheaper cinemas are found in Mariahilfer str. In the Theater an der Wien, 6, left Wienzeile 6, Tel. 579 632 you can stand to see the show in the Stehplatze which is inexpensive, but you will only get these tickets if you stand there very early! CABARET

TIP: Platz, am 1, Peters Platz; Simpl, 1, Wollzeile 36; Dance Tip: New dance in the Szene Wien on Simmering.

ACCOMMODATION: There are a few youth hostels: Brigittenau, Tel. 338 294; Neubau, Tel. 936 315; Schlossberg gasse 8, T3l. 821 501.
Camping: West I, Huttelberg str. 40, Tel. 941 449; South, Tel. 869 218; West II, Tel. 942314.
Pensions: Bosch, Keil gasse 13, Esperanto, 4, Argentinier str. 53, Tel. 651 304; Quisiana, 6, Windmuhl gasse 6, Tel. 573 341; Merlingen, 8, Zelt gasse 3/13 Tel. 421 94 13; Wild, Lange gasse 10, Tel. 435 174; Falstaff, 9, Mullner gasse 5, Tel. 349 127.
You get a beautiful view of the city from Kahlenberg (Bus 38 S).

BELGIUM

The Kingdom of Belgium is a constitutional monarchy and is very densely populated. (Area-39,513 sq. km-Pop. 9.8 million). Belgium still has its boundaries from 1830 in spite of the cultural differences between the walloons and the flemish citizens.

Today Belgium, together with Holland and Luxembourg, is a part of the Benelux or Low Countries with practically no border-control between the members. The Headquarters of the E.E.C. are located in Belgium's capital, Brussels.

ENTRY/FOREIGN EXCHANGE/CUSTOMS REGULATIONS: A valid passport is required. There are no currency restrictions.

Duty free allowance:
200 cigarettes or 250gm tobacco and 1 litre spirits and 2 litres wine.

Currency/Exchange Rate: The currency of the land is the Belgian Franc (Bfr)

1A$	=	27 Bfr
1C$	=	29 Bfr
1NZ$	=	21 Bfr
1US$	=	40 Bfr
£1	=	60 Bfr

Belgian Francs are also used in Luxembourg (but not the other way around!).

TELEPHONE:
It is possible to dial direct to some other countries from specially marked telephone boxes. The local area code is then dialled without the 0.

Emergency Telephone Number: Police 901; Ambulance 900.

EMBASSIES:
Australia: 52 Avenue des Arts, Brussels Tel. 511 3997.
Canada: 6 rue de Loxum, Brussels, Tel. 513 7940
N.Z.: Boulevard du Regent 47-48, Brussels Tel. 512 1040
U.K.: Britannia House, 28 rue Joseph II, Brussels Tel. 219 1165.
U.S.A.: 27 Boulevard du Regent, Brussels, Tel. 513 3830.

SHOPPING HINTS:
Try the belgian beer, there are 355 brands not counting the home-made

varieties available in some villages. Among them the aromatic ones such as Leffe, Maredsous, Affligem, Postel, Duvel and Ketie.

ACCOMMODATION:

Hotels: BTR, PB 41,100 Brussel 23, Tel. 02/230 50 29;
Camping: Grassmarkt 61, Brussel, Tel. 02/512 30 30;
Youth hostels: VJHC,Van Stralen Str.40, 2000 Antwerp.
Important: Ask for a budget holiday brochure–cheap accommodation for young people.

SPEED LIMITS:

60 km/h in built up areas;
120 km/h on motorways; 90 km/h elswhere.

RAIL:

Monthly half-price ticket–450 BF;
B-Tourrail 5/8 days for 1460/1930 BF or 1100/1450 BF for under 25's;
Benelux-Tourrail with NS & CFL for 5 days travel in 17 days for under 25's between 15 March and 31 October for 90/123 BF..

BRUGES (BRUGGES)–GENT (GHENT)

Many towns of Europe are known by their superlatives: the highest cathedral, the biggest harbour, the oldest castle. Other towns are known for their colour and atmosphere. These two Flemish towns have many facets: the guild houses, business houses, markets and memorials and the assurance of free towns.

BY CAR: Belgium is covered by a dense network of motorways. To get to Bruges and Gent by car you can take the E5 from Cologne-Aachen-Liege-Brussels or the north/south Amsterdam-Paris road via Antwerp-Lille. Parking stations in Brugge: at Zilverpand, Dweers Str; at 'Biekorf', Nalden Str; in Gent park at: Dampoort, Antwerpenplein, or a little further out at Wilsonplein.

BY RAIL: The central railway station in Bruges is south of the old town, as is the central railway station, St. Pieters, in Gent (Tram 4 to the city), also in Gent is the harbour railway station, Dampoort, for trains to or from Antwerp. You can hire bicycles at the railway stations–a very practical form of transport in flat Flanders (Bruges: Tel. 050/332406, Gent: Tel. 091/22 44 44). It is necessary to book one day in advance! Cost: approx. 80 BF and 1000 BF Deposit.

BY AIR: Bruges and Gent lie between the international airport of Ostend and the even larger one at Brussels. There is a fast train connection from Brussels to the city centre and to Bruges/Gent. (Airport Tel. 02/751 8080).

BRUGES

It is a beautifully restored tourist centre and it's certainly worth a short stopover. 2000 houses have been renovated here. Bruges is probably one of the best preserved medieval towns in Europe. (Pop. 118000).

TOURIST INFORMATION: For tourist and information and hotel and pension reservations: Markt 7, Tel. 050/330711. 'Agenda' a calendar of events and the magazine 'Coast News' are also available here.

LOCAL TRANSPORT: buses. The central stop and information office is in J. van Oost str. The old part of town is fortified by canals built in the middle ages and most of it can be seen on foot. Because there are so many things worth seeing, a guided tour is recommended. You can book one at the tourist bureau (no fixed times–2 hrs/600 BF). If you can manage to get a few people together you could also take a 3 hour tour for approx. 850 BF. Don't miss out on a boat trip on the canals if you have the time (no fixed times–from Vismark, Huidenvetterspl or Nieuw Str., 100 BF.)–again if you can form a group it's cheaper approx. 50 BF per person. A ride in a horse drawn carriage is more romantic and exclusive but costs more (Markt Belfried from 400 BF).

POINTS OF INTEREST: The landmarks of the town are the halls from the middle ages and the Belfry, on Market Place, a tower which you can climb–366 steps (opening times the same as for everything which follows: daily 9.30 a.m.-12 noon and 2.00 p.m.-6.00 p.m.). Also on the Market Place is the Parliament House and behind there some small lanes for pedestrians only, and the Basilica of the Holy Blood and museum, and the Town Hall with its gothic hall. The area around the fish market is also very beautiful. Go along the Dijver Canal and you come to 'Europa Kolleg' a college for common market scientists. Next to it is the Groeninge Museum with its old flemish school collection. You can see here that it is not only in recent times that there have been non-conformists, already in the 15th century there was a flemish primitive style (Cost 50Bf–a little expensive, but worth seeing).

IMPORTANT: Opposite is the Gruuthuse Palace and museum of Flemish Craft, the late gothic church of Our Lady with its Madonna by Michelangelo and the mausoleums of Charles the Bold (killed in a battle with the Bern army) and Mary of Burgundy. Last, but not least, the Minnewater (Lake of Love) a romantic name for the former harbour on Wijngaardplein. There is a small park next to it. In the pedestrian zone in front of the harbour on the right is the Beguinage, where the Beguines lived until the economic depression at the end of the middle ages. It was an economic community of women who lived alone–men were not permitted to enter. This Beguinage was built in 1245 and to-day it is the home of Benedictine nuns. Because of this, you should visit the museum next to it (30 BF).

OTHER MUSEUMS: The Arentshuis, Dijver, with pictures of the old town (50 BF); Memling museum with its old chemist shop; St. Jans Hospital (50 BF); Museum for Flemish folklore, Balstraat (50 BF); and very important to the flemish handicraft industry, the lacemaking centre, a workshop where apprentices are trained in lacemaking. Opposite there is the Folklore Museum open only from 2.00-6.00 p.m.

FESTIVALS: The Flemish Festival of Traditional Music is held at the end of July until the beginning of August. All through the summer there are programmes at the Marionette Theatre, St. Jakobs Street 36; an enormous flea market is held in the middle of August; normal flea market is held on Saturday morning and Sunday morning at Dijver.

ACCOMMODATION: International youth hostel Europa, Bar. Ruzettelaan 143, Tel. 050/352679, Bus 2; Youth hostels: Huyze Elckerlyc, Hauwer str. 23, Tel. 33 62 26; Bauhaus, Lange str. 137, Tel. 050/336175; Home A. van Acker, Barrier str. 13, Tel. 38 3583; Snuffel Sleep-in, Ezel str. 49, Tel. 333133. Good Camping at St. Michiel, Tillegem str. 55, Tel. 050/38 08 19; Pensions can be booked through the tourist bureau.

GENT

There are numerous things worth seeing dating back to the middle ages when Gent was, after Paris, the most important town (Pop. 240,0000).

LOCAL TRANSPORT consists of buses supported by a few tram lines. A brochure of the routes 'Hret Gentse Stadsvervoer' is available. A tour of the city is recommended.

TOURIST BUREAU: Town Hall, Botermarkt, Tel. 091/241555. Information about all of east Flanders: Konigin Maria Hendrika Plein 64, Tel. 091/22163, Youth service, Gilde str. 8, Tel. 259 191.

POINTS OF INTEREST: There are plenty of tours on offer but the best one is the state run one which makes use of guides who have studied the town's history (600BF). Information: Belfort str. 9, Tel. 253641; From Saint Baafsplein horse drawn carriages 400 BF for only 35 min. A boat trip is also highly recommended (80BF) from Graslei; or an evening boat trip from Justitiepaleis (180BF). Before you go on tour of the town, or if you have very little time during a short stop over, you should see the multivision show at Gravensteen castle north of the city (April-September daily–60BF) and at the same time you can see the castle. Macabre: the Folter Museum, locally known as the Museum for Anti-Justice.

You shouldn't miss out on the walk from the Town Hall to St. Michael's bridge, past St. Nikolaus church, as it gives you a beautiful view over the town with its three different towers–St. Nickolaus, St. Bavo and the Belfry. In the cathedral of St. Bavo is 'The Mystic Lamb' painted by Van Eyck–cost, including the crypt 30BF; the cathedral is gratis. In front of the cathedral is the Belfry and the Cloth Hall, evidence of the worldwide power of the guilds in the middle ages. It is crowned by copper dragons over the former warning bell which was rung when the town needed to be defended. The audio-visual show 'Gent and King Charles I' takes place here. It is a sort of bell and light show (daily). From St. Michael's bridge go in the opposite direction to Korenlei on the tributary of the Leie. All along the opposite bank you will see the guild houses at Graslei. They are best viewed from the opposite side.

A little bit further on is the old harbour with its former meat halls and fish market. The castle of Gerhard the Devil, in Limburg str. a sign of nobility in this working class town. Particularly well known are the three Beguinen Courts–the Small, Violette St, the Great (Land van Waaslaan) which was built in 1872 in 17th century style; compare it with the Oud-Begijnhof St. Elizabeth which was built in the middle ages (from the castle go across Burg St, St. Elizabeth plein).

PUBS: Around Vrijdags Market: De wore Jakob, with Bavo at the Bar; Bier Academie with 250 sorts of beer, watch out for your shoes! Some more: De nieuwe zwarte Kat, Proveniensters str. 49; good food at the Central au Paris, opposite Raadskelder, Sint-Baafsplein; Epsilon Tea Room, Sint-Amant str. 118; Aula (Uni), Volder str. 24.

MUSEUMS: They all have the same opening hours Tuesday to Sunday 9.00 a.m.-12.30 p.m. and 1.30 p.m.-5.30 p.m., most are gratis. The Museum of Folklore, Kraanlei 65, 40BF.; Museum of Contemporary Art, N.d. Liemaeckerplein; Museum of Arts and Crafts, Jan Breydel str. 5; Archaeological Museum, Godshuizenlaan; Museum of Science and Technology, Korte Meer 9; Art and Culture Centre, St. Pietersplein 9; Botanical Gardens of the state university, Kl. Ledeganckstraat (Monday-Thursday, 2.00-5.00 p.m. and Saturday and Sunday 9.00 a.m.-12 noon).

The large university is the most popular meeting place for young people, but the bigger Citadel Park with the sports stadium next to the botanical gardens is also popular.

FESTIVALS in Gent: the Flanders Festival from the end of August until the beginning of October (traditional music by international orchestras) and the Gent flower show 'Floralien' every five years–the next one is due to be held in 1990. There are large flower plantations around the town.

MARKETS: Flower market daily from 7.00 a.m.-1.00 p.m., Kouter or E. Seghersplein; Vegetable market: Monday-Saturday 7.00 a.m.-1.00 p.m. at Groentenmarkt and on Sunday an art and craft market; a flea market on Friday and Saturday 7.00 a.m.-1.00 p.m. in Beverhoutplein.

ACCOMMODATION: International youth hostel, St. Pietersplein 12, Bus 5 or 7, Tel. 091/225 067; Camping; Blaarmeersen, Zuiderlaan 12, Tel. 091/215399. Tip: Ask at the tourist information office for information about 'Hotel Bonus Weekends'. Youth hostel in summer: Rijksuniversiteit, (national university) Stalhof 6, Tel. 091/220911. Stalhof 6, Tel. 091/220911.

BRUSSELS

A small walloonic-flemish city which has become an administrative centre of Europe with excellent railway connections and Common Market Offices. It is a charming city of contrasts and if you don't stop off here on your trip to the north-west you will certainly miss out on something. Brussels has two languages, for Flemings and Walloons. (Pop.1,000,200).

BY CAR: The motorways of Belgium radiate out from Brussels to all the important towns. There are tourist information offices on all the big border crossings. Brussels itself is circled by a broad ring-motorway. There are a large number of parking stations, conveniently situated: Botanique, at 29 Jardin Botanique; Rogier, Rue de Progres 68; Deux Portes, Porte de Namur/Blvd. Waterloo.

BY AIR: The international airport is approximately 10km north of Brussels.

BY RAIL: There is a fast train service to the Northern railway station and to Central station, Tel. 01/751 8080. There is also a fast railway line Paris/Brussels/Cologne. There are four railway stations: Gare du Midi/Suidstation (Southern station), Gare Centrale/Centralstation, Gare du Nord/Noordstation (Northern station), Quartier Leopold/Leopold-swijk (QL for short). All the railway stations are directly connected and the long distance trains stop at least at the Northern and Southern stations, so you will have no problems even if the timetable seems a

Belgium: Entrance to Beguinage in Bruges

Brussels: Town Hall

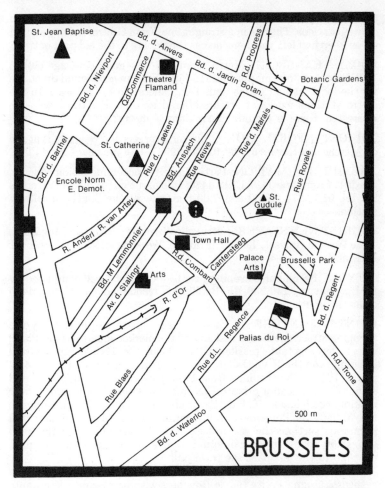

St. Jean Baptise

Bd. d. Anvers

Bd. d. Nievport

Q.d.Commerce

Theatre Flamand

Bd. d. Jardin Botan.

R.d. Progress

Botanic Gardens

Bd. d. Barthel

St. Catherine

Rue d. Laeken

Bd. Anspach

Rue Neuve

Rue d. Marais

Rue Royale

Encole Norm E. Demot.

R. Anderl

R. van Artev

Bd. M Lemmonier

St. Gudule

Town Hall

R.d Combard

Cantersteeg

Palace Arts

Brussells Park

Arts

Av. d. Stalingr

R. d'Or

Regence

Rue d.L.

Palias du Roi

Bd. d. Regent

R.d. Trone

Rue Blaes

500 m

Bd. d. Waterloo

BRUSSELS

bit crazy. You will find everything you will need in the momumental halls of the railway stations: shops, money exchanges, luggage lockers, train information. In the main hall of the Northern station on the left hand side is a railway information office and on the right up the stairs is the SNCB/NMBS railway museum, which besides having model trains has an interesting commentary (Monday-Friday, gratis). More interesting; Tram museum (30 carriages, 1894-1935 vintage), July/August, Sunday 2.00-6.00 p.m. 30 FB, Bus N; Museum of local transport, Wednesday, Saturday & Sunday 11.00 a.m.-7.00 p.m. Bus 36/42, Tram 39/44 sometimes you get to travel in old trams.

Catch the No. 3 metro or better still the underground tram (Nr.

52/55/58/62/81) to the city centre from the Northern or the Southern railway stations. They lie in a straight line. From Central railway station if you keep half left you come across the Square to the old part of town.

LOCAL TRANSPORT: Metro, tram and bus-good coverage (30BF, 130BF/24 hrs): Information Tel. 512 1790. You can get a small timetable for the local trains ('Trains dans l'agglomeration bruzelloise'). In the metro stations works of art are offered for sale. For those who are interested, there is a guide 'L'Art dans le metro'.

TOURIST INFORMATION: Office for Brussels and Belguim is at rue du Marche aux Herbes 61, Tel. 02/513 9090 before you near Grand Place.

YOUTH INFORMATION: Particularly for accommodation: Acotra, rue de la Montagne 38, Tel. 513 4480; Info-J, rue du Marche aux Herbes 27, Tel. 512 3274 (10.00 a.m.-7.00 p.m. also at the Southern railway station.

TOURIST NEWSPAPERS: 'Bruxelles/Brussel', 'Brussels Magazine', 'Deze Week in Brussel', 'Le Soir' (Fridays), 'Weekend knack', and 'Brabant Uitkrant'.

CITY TOURS and also evening beer tours are very well conducted by Le Bus Bavard, 140-250 BF. Booking is recommended Tel. 513 4480 or at the youth hotels.

POINTS OF INTEREST: There is also a bit to see: in the city the shopping street, rue Neuve and around the market square (Grand Place) where the vegetable market is also held; the 17th century Guild buildings and the Town Hall (tower 89m) Sunday-Friday 9.00 a.m.-4.30 p.m. 20FB. In the evenings from 10.00 p.m. there is a light & sound show. There is also a private Biermuseum: Gueuze Museum of beer making, rue Gheude 56, only Saturday 10.00 a.m.-5.00 p.m. Opposite the 'Maison du Roi' (Town Hall) containing a local museum, with a humorous section: the Wardrobe of the Manneken Pis! (daily 10.00 a.m.-12.00 noon). If you can stand to look at the fountain it is quite near (go to the left past the town hall).

Another small part of the old town is found on our way to the cathedral around Petite rue de Bouchers with its elegant restaurants and St. Hubert Arcade-If you thought Bern had the earliest arcades then you are wrong! (1847). The cathedral has been renovated. Around here the picture of the town has been spoilt, a lot of functional, even momumental administration buildings have been built in amongst the charming french buildings. In order to get away from the new functional architecture which is in vogue in Europe at present, the Government has taken the initative and formed a new body, ARAU which is responsible for architecture, town and traffic planning etc. (For information about tours and walks Tel. 513 4761). There are several art nouveau houses which are encouraged (JEK, a brochure about this is available from the tourist information office). Victor Horta's house (he was one of the early leaders in this field) is a good example of this (rue Americaine 25, Tuesday, Thursday, Saturday, Sunday 2.00-5.30 p.m. 40BF).

In the surburb of Quartier du Nord St. Josse, people made out of an emergency, a virtue: a lot of the bare concrete has been decorated with large paintings-the Manhattan Project. (blvd Jacqmain, Square Ambiorix; metro Rogier).

MUSEUMS: Tops for museum lovers-re-opened: Royal Museum for Schonen Kunste of Belguims (Tuesday-Sunday 10.00 a.m.-5.00 p.m. Place Royale); Military Museum (Tuesday-Saturday 9.00 a.m.-12 noon and 1.00-4.00 p.m., gratis, metro Merode); the same but only smaller: National Museum for Historical Figures (rue Trebackx 14, Tuesday-Friday, 10.00 a.m.-12 noon and 2.00-4.00 p.m., Bus 13/53); real action, mainly for children, but also very humorous, the Children's Museum (Wednesday, Saturday, Sunday 2.30-5.00 p.m., rue Tenbosch 32, Tram 32/81/93, 120FB). Brussel's lace which is famous throughout the world: (rue de la Violette 6, Sundays, Entry gratis, metro Gare Centrale). Inexpensive and humorous cinema: Kino Museum 9 rue Baron Horta 30 BF. Tel. 513 4155, Tram 94.

After so many sights now its time to relax: at the Parc Leopold near the Q.L. railway station; or in the south-in the Cabre Wood/Kamerenbos (railway station Boondael, Tram 32/94); on the other side: at the Park de Laeken with the Atomium (a structure in the shape of an iron molecule)-Tram 18/81. It was built for the World Fair in 1958 and in keeping with the euphoria of those times it has an exhibition of the peaceful use of atomic power.

If you are interested in seeing where the billions of primary produce subsidiaries are doled out, then look to the north from Leopold Park and you will see the headquarters of the Common Market. The headquarters of NATO is in Evere (railway bus BM). The fields and meadows of Waterloo are nearby (8.30 a.m.-7.00 p.m. daily). A round museum contains a panorama of the battle (9.30 a.m.-6.00 p.m., 50FB); Lion Heights, (8.30 a.m.-7.00 p.m. daily).

MARKETS: Flea market 7.00 a.m.-2.00 p.m., Pl du Jeu de Balles in the old fashioned suburb of Marolles (metro Porte de Hal); Vegetables: Pl St. Catherine (Metro de Brockere); Sunday morning-a large market near the Sud station: or buy a bicycle at the blvd. due Midi; Birds & flowers at the Grand Place.

RESTAURANTS: Caves d'Egmont, Grand Place; L'auberge des Chapeliers and New Mandarin, both rue des Chapeliers, near metro de Namur; La Houblonniere and Les Brassins around the Gare du Midi (international section) or at the Place St. Catherine (fish). Specialities; Moules aux Frites (mussels) and Vigaufra (waffles) as well as lollies (e.g. leonidas-especially the white ones).

ENTERTAINMENT: Cabaret: La Soupape, rue A. DeWitte 26, Tel. 649

58 88 and Ti-Rore, rue de Sablonniere, Tel. 219 2295; Concerts: Le
Travers, rue Traversiere 11; Le Botanique, Anspachlaan 114; Studio
DES, rue aux Fleurs 14; Bierodrome, Place F. Coq; Specialising in beer:
La Mort Subite, 5 rue Mont; Aux Herbes Potageres, 7; La Becasse, rue
Tabora 11; t'Spinnekopke, Place du Jardin aux Fleurs 1; Tarvetniers,
rue de Vauz; Youthful: de dolle Mol, rue des Eperonniers 51; Ryk de
Zinnen, rue des Pierres 14; Art nouveau: Falstaff, rue de Maus; Cirio,
rue de la Bourse 18; French: Goupil le Fol, rue de la Violette 22; with
250 sorts of beer: Le Jugement Dernier, Chaussee de Haecht 165;
Ultieme Hallucinatie, 316 rue Royale; Discos: Les Enfants Terrible,
avenue de la Toison d'Or 44; Vaudeville: 15 Galerie de la Reine; Le
Garage, rue Duquesnoy.

ACCOMMODATION: International youth hostel, Hoek Keizerslaan-
Hl. Geeststraat 2, Tel. 511 0326; Youth hostels are very well organized,
offer information and kitchen facilities: Chab, rue Traversiere 6, Tel.
2170258, metro Botanique; International Students' House, Chaussee
de Wavre 205, Tel. 648 8529; metro Porte de Namur; Sleepwell, rue de
la Blanchisserie 27, Tel. 218 5050, metro Rogier; Private accommodation
booking: La Rose des Vents, av. des Quatres Vents 9, Tel. 460 3459. If
you want to splurge: Hotel van Belle, Chaussee de Mons 39, Tel 521
3516, Tram 101 from Gare Du Sud, 3 stops, with a terrific breakfast.

CZECHOSLOVAKIA

The Czechoslovakian Socialistic Republic is made up of two parts CSR and SSR (Area 127,869 sq. km.–Pop. 15.4 million). Industrially it has developed very slowly since the second world war. The political and social crises that it has been through over the past 20 years has not assisted in the development of the country.

ENTRY/FOREIGN EXCHANGE/CUSTOMS REGUALTIONS: A visa is required for entry. This can only be obtained from the embassy beforehand (US$20 approx.). All photos–for passport and visa must be current! Individual travellers must exchange 30 DM per day at the border. Anything left over on the way out may be exchanged on the border. Czech currency cannot be brought into or taken out of the country, so work out how much money you will need beforehand. If you leave earlier than planned exchange back into western currency is only allowed for whole days and only with a form from the bank. Hotel reservation vouchers and trips paid for before are taken into account.

If you stay privately you must register with the police within 48 hours of arrival. You are permitted to bring in gifts up to 600 Kcs. value but are only permitted to take out 300 Kcs. duty free.

Be careful–the authorities may regard certain reading material as illicit.

Currency/Exchange Rate: The currency of the land is the Czech Krona (Kcs.). No Czechoslovakian currency may either be taken in or out of the country.

A$1 = 5 Kcs.
C$1 = 5.5 Kcs.
NZ$ = 6 Kcs.
£1   = 11 Kcs.
US$ = 7.5 Kcs.

If you don't change money on the black market your holiday is fairly expensive. Beloved souvenirs are cans of Coke, western cigarettes, silk stockings, cosmetics (only take small amounts in).

Emergency Telephone Number: 155.

EMBASSIES:

Australia: No Resident Representative–see Poland
Canada: Mickiweiczova 6, Prague 6, Tel. 32-69-41
N.Z.:   No Resident Representative–see Austria
U.K.:   Thunovska 14, Prague 1, Tel. 53-33-47/8/9
U.S.A.:   Trziste 15-12548 Praha, Prague, Tel. 53-66-41/8

BUYING TIPS:

Good prices for imported and local goods in the Tuzex shops using notes, vouchers or traveller's cheques. Very popular: Budweiser or Pilsener Urquell beer.

ACCOMMODATION:

Hotel, camping and youth accommodation: CEDOK, Prag 1, Naprikope 18, Tel. 114 251.

SPEED LIMITS:

In built up areas 60 km/h,
outside built up areas 90 km/h, expressways 110 km/h.

Petrol coupons are available from CEDOK, ADAC (automobile club) or on the border, not compulsory but a lot cheaper. Oil is available only by voucher (Super costs approx. US$0.80 per litre with vouchers).

RAILWAYS:

No cheap fares but inexpensive tariffs.

AIRPORTS:

International airports at Prague and Bratislavia.

PRAGUE-PRAHA

In the 19th century some of the european capitals tried to emulate if not surpass Paris, by erecting buildings of similar splendour. Prague, the 'Golden City', was one of these along with Vienna and Budapest. Unfortunately, in order to see this nowadays, you have to take a second or third look because many new suburbs have been built which you need to pass through on your way into the city. Many of the splendid facades have been damaged, not by the war, but by pollution and they often are hidden by scaffolding. (Pop. 1.19 million.)

BY CAR: You can come to Prague by various routes and the border crossings are: Schirnding if you come from northern W.Germany or Wurzburg; Waldhaus from Nurnberg/Amberg; Furth im Wald from Munich/Regensburg; or Eisenstein from Munich. The roads from all these border crossings go through Pilsen which is a popular rest stop because it is the home of Pilsner Urquell (famous czechoslavian beer), whereas the road via Passau/Philippsreut goes directly to Prague. Border crossings from Austria are Summerau from Linz or Gmund from Vienna. There are a whole row of large parking areas near the city centres. Remember that parking in the streets is prohibited.

1. St. Zid Habitov
2. Klementinum
3. Carolinum
4. Narodni Museum

500metres

PRAGUE

BY RAIL: You arrive at the main railway station which is opposite parkland and not far from the main street, Vaclavske Namesti–Wenceslas Square. To get there just turn left and go towards the museum. The main railway lines are those which come via Schirnding and Furth im Wald from Germany and via Gmund and Summerau from Austria. There are two trains via Schirnding but only one via Furth (from Munich), three trains via Gmund (from Vienna) and only short distance trains which require a lot of train changing via Summerau . Tel. 244 441.

BY AIR: The airport is at Ruzyne, approx. 20 km north-west. There is a bus connection to the city leaving from 25 Revolucni St., the office of CSA, Tel. 367 760.

TOURIST INFORMATION: There is a stand at the Hradcanski metro Station, Tel. 544 444. Main office, Pragotur, U Obecniho domu 2, Tel. 231 7100 with accommodation reservations or CEDOK, the government run travel agency, 18 Na prikope, Tel. 224 251. Youth information: CKM, Nore Mesto, 12 Zitna, Tel. 298 589.

LOCAL TRANSPORT: Now that the third metro line has been opened, important sights can be reached by the underground. Otherwise there are numerous tram lines and buses. The fare is 1 Kcs unless you wish to change and you must always buy your ticket before boarding. They are available from news stands, kiosks, hotels or tobacco shops.

CITY TOURS: A 3 hour tour leaves from Bikova ulice 6 (daily at 10.00 a.m. and also at 1.30 p.m. in summer). Prague by Night Tours (Wednesday & Friday at 7.00 p.m.); The Prager Party Tour offers a folklore programme at the Slovacian Chalet (round trip approx. US$10.50). You can also take a boat trip on the Vltava from Vltava Quay in the new town. It's a good way to see the town but don't take the round trip, return on the metro on the No. 3 line from Palacky Bridge.

POINTS OF INTEREST: Historical Prague is divided into four, really five, main areas: the Old Town with the old town ring bounded by the Vlatva River; the old Jewish Quarter, which is of such importance, runs from the Ring die Parizska down to the Svat. Cecha bridge; the Lesser Side which is the city area on the other side of the Vlatava; and lastly, Hradcany Castle which was built by Charles IV and the gothic St. Vitus' cathedral.

Between the railway station and the old town is the new town around Vaclavske Namesti (Wenceslas Square) which is really a wide boulevard. Prague has buildings from all eras but its new buildings are very functional and are a contrast to the beautiful old buildings. Some of the more important architectural styles are:

ROMAN–Martin's Rotunde on the Vysehrad cliffs, the original centre of the city where Queen Libussa said that a city should be built and St. George's church on the hill.

GOTHIC–a lot of early buildings such as the synagogue in the Jewish Quarter or later buildings such as the Powder Tower (1475) where the King's Palace formerly stood on the edge of the old town (Tues-Sun 9.00 a.m.-5.00 p.m.).

RENAISSANCE–Belvedere Castle and park and the singing fountains behind the castle.

BAROQUE–St. Nicholas' church built during the reign of the Hapsburgs and the catholic church during the Thirty Year War.

ROCOCO–the cathedral and the Archbishop's palace on the square in front of the castle. It was here that the old Cardinal Tomasek followed his own line against the Party. To-day it is used for exhibitions.

CLASSICAL–the suburbs of Karlin and Smichov (east of the old town and south of the Lesser Side).

HISTORICAL–the Bohmischen Savings Bank, to-day the Academy of Science, or the National Theatre at the 1st of May Bridge.

BOHEMIAN–the Prague House of Representatives near the Powder Tower; the main railway station and a lot of houses which you can find for yourself. From the FUNCTIONAL PERIOD the Terrace restaurant on the Barrandov Cliffs near Prague.

If you are fit you can see some of them on a walking tour: Start at the Powder Tower (from the railway station turn right, then go left along Hybernska), near the start there is an old lane, the Celetna ulice, which leads to the old town ring where not only the town hall with its tower stands but also the astronomical clock with its medieval figures amongst a sea of red flags. It is the meeting place of Czechs and tourists alike. The Jan Hus memorial is surrounded by government buildings. Make a detour along Teinhof St. to St. Jacob's church, or otherwise head towards the river to the Jewish Quarter with the synagogue and the Jewish cemetery. (Government run Jewish Museum–Sunday-Friday 9.00 a.m.-5.00 p.m.).

You can get a picture of how the city could look by seeing the renovated terrace houses. Another turn and you are in the old town: the Carolinum, a former theatre (from the ring road turn into Zelezna St.); the Bethlehem chapel (rebuilt 1954) where Hus held his revolutionary meetings. In these lanes Franz Kafka got his inspiration (his grave is in the new Jewish cemetery, metro Zelivskeho).

Now go across the Charles Bridge, the oldest bridge of the city with three towers and 30 statues and a view to Hradcany Castle. On the Lesser Side take a detour to the left to the exciting Kampa Quarter, then turn right to Waldstein Palace (Motescka, Tomasska, Valdsteinska) with its magnificent park and gardens which lead up to Hradcany Castle and are open to the public. Go across the Kleinseiter Ring with St. Nicholas church along Neruda Lane which climbs up to Hradschiner Square in front of the castle. In this area are St. Vitus Cathedral, Vladimir Palace, the Golden Lane with it's small, intriguing houses converted to shops which sell souvenirs and antiques (Kafka also lived here for a short time). Next to the Archbishop's palace is the National Gallery (Tuesday-Sunday 10.00 a.m.-6.00 p.m.). The former palace was expropriated by the regime for the Dept. of External Affairs. You can catch Tram 2 to the National Theatre if you like. A bit further on is Vaclavske Namesti (Wenceslas Square) with it's large hotels and beautiful arcades where the events of 'Prague's Spring' of 1968 took place. Be careful if you change your money on the black market as it's illegal. Above is the National Museum (Wednesday-Monday 9.00 a.m.-4.00 p.m.). Now turn left and you are back at the railway station again.

Memorials to the Workers' Movement: Klemens Gottwald Museum, Stare Mesto, 29 Rytirska and the Lenin Museum, 7 Hybernska.

ENTERTAINMENT: There is not only a lot happening at the Culture Centre (metro Gottwaldova) but Prague's pubs are legendary, and they are usually overcrowded but the atmosphere is great. However, it is more difficult to find good food. Some restaurants: U. Kalicha, new town, 14 Na bojisti; I. Fleku, near Wenceslas Square, 11 Kremencova with grade 13 dark beer and a cabaret; U Schnellu, 2 Tomasska; U Supa, 22 Celetna, with grade 14 beer, the strongest; Obecni dum, 1090 Namesti Republiky. There are also wine bars: U Golemna, 8 Maiselova; U Fausta, Nove Mesto, Karlovo nam. 4; Viola, 7 Narodni trida; U mecenase, 18 Malostranske namesti.

A few Taverns: U Prince, N. Staromestske; Chodske pohostinstvi,

Smichov, 5 Na Ujezde; Sumavan, Zizkov, 17 Ondrickova; Baltic Grill, 43 Wenceslas Square.

A SPECIAL THEATRE TIP: The Central Marionette Theatre, Loutka, 28 Nam. M. Gorkeho, Tel. 225 141.

ACCOMMODATION: Youth hostel, Spartakiadni, 5 Hlavni nadrazi, Tel. 355 165; Youth hotel: Krivan, 5 Nam. I.P. Pavlova, Tel. 293 341; It's best to book hotels through the tourist bureau or travel agents. Hotel Tip: Balkan, 28 Svornosti, Tel. 540 777.

DENMARK

Denmark is a constitutional monarchy with an area of 43,075 sq. km. and a population of 5.1 million not including Greenland and the Faroer Islands. To-day it is a member of the E.E.C.

Geographically, Denmark is divided into Jutland, Zealand, the Fyn Island Group, Lolland-Falster, Bornholm and many small islands such as Mon, Samso etc.

Denmark is popular with holiday makers because of its sandy beaches and sand dunes along the North Sea coast and the Baltic islands and bays. It's difficult to do any mountain climbing there though, because there are hardly any hills over 100m!

ENTRY/FOREIGN EXCHANGE/CURRENCY REGULATIONS: A valid passport is required. There is no limit on the amount of currency which can brought into the country but only 50 000 DKr. may be taken out.

Duty Free Allowance:
200 cigarettes or 250gm tobacco, 1 litre of spirits and 2 litres of wine.

Currency/Exchange Rates: The currency of the land is the Danish Kroner (Dkr.)

A$1	=	4.90kr
C$1	=	5.40kr
NZ$1	=	3.90kr
£1	=	11.00kr
US$	=	7.50kr

The buying power is not great because of the extremly high cost of living as in the other scandinavian countries.

TELEPHONE:

It is possible to dial some other countries direct. The 0 is then left off the local area code.

Emergency Telephone No.: 0-0-0 .

FOOD:

672 restaurants in Denmark offer a special menu, the Danmenu, for 65 Dkr in restaurants and 45 DKr. in cafeterias. They all display a special sign indicating this.

EMBASSIES:

Australia: Kristianiagade 21, Copenhagen, Tel. 262 244.
Canada: Kr. Bern, Kowsgade 1, 1105 Copenhagen, Tel. 122 299

N.Z.   No Resident Representative–see Belguim.
U.K.:   Kastelvej 36-40, Copenhagen, Tel. 264 600.
U.S.A.:   Dag Hammarskjolds Alle 24, Copenhagen, Tel. 423 144.

ACCOMMODATION:

Hotels, camping grounds and youth hostels: Turistrad, H.C. Andersons Boulevard 22, 1553 Copenhagen, Tel. 01/111325.
Special hotel cheques are available a discount prices for 120/170/210 DKr. per person per night.

SPEED LIMITS:

60 km/h in built up areas;
80 km/h outside built up areas; and 100 km/h on motorways.
Funen is the only island which is connected to the mainland by a bridge (near Fredericia) otherwise you have to use the car ferries which are expensive but there are reductions from Sunday-Thursday.

RAILWAYS:

Nordturist ticket for all of Scandinavia for 440 DKr. for 21 days.

AIRPORTS:

There is an international airport at Cophenhagen-Kastrup and air taxi services are available to 11 smaller airports.

COPENHAGEN

Your first impression: familiar and you can see it, because the buildings aren't too high and the squares aren't too wide, a city with charm and size: Copenhagen is the largest Scandinavian town (Pop. 1.37 million).

BY RAIL: The main railway station is on the opposite side of the through traffic tracks. In its modern main hall it has snack bars, shops and a combined train and travel information bureau. The luggage lockers are in the middle room and you can leave your luggage for three days (each day 5 DKr.). For young people with Inter-rail tickets, an Inter-rail centre has been opened. It is open from 7.00 a.m.-1.00 a.m. in summer and has information, music, restaurant, washing facilties–a great place.

BY CAR: You have to use a ferry once whether you come on the E4 from Hamburg/Lubeck via the Lolland islands, Falster and Seeland, or on the E3/E66 (Hamburg/Glensburg via Kolding, Odense and Halsskov.
   Both ferries, which leave every hour, cost approx. US$50 for the return

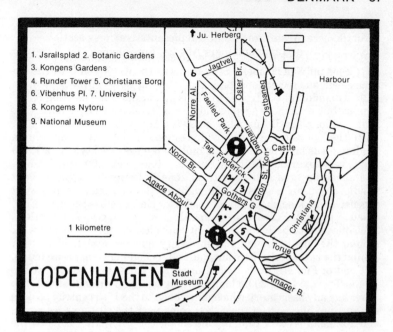

1. Jsrailsplad 2. Botanic Gardens
3. Kongens Gardens
4. Runder Tower 5. Christians Borg
6. Vibenhus Pl. 7. University
8. Kongems Nytoru
9. National Museum

Ju. Herberg

Harbour

Castle

Christiana

1 kilometre

COPENHAGEN Stadt Museum

trip for the car and 1 person, extra people US$16-20, but the Korsor Ferry is slightly cheaper.

BY AIR: From the international airport near Copenhagen there are daily connections to most large towns. Tel. 01/541 701–bus no. 9 goes to the city; if you want to go to one of the many islands then there are Air taxis.

TOURIST INFORMATION: H.C. Andersen boulevard l22, Tel. 01/111325 near the Tivoli Gardens. For young people: USE IT, Radhus str. 13, Tel. 01/156 518, daily 10.00 a.m-5.00 p.m., June-September until 8.00 p.m. near the Cosa Rose Pub!

TOURIST NEWSPAPERS: Copenhagen This Week and the Alternative Newspaper: Kobenhavn.

LOCAL TRANSPORT: From the railway station you can take a bus or a city train (Udden Stop) in spite of the route map not being complete. (Tickets 6-20 DKr. for single trips or 9 city tickets for 50 DKr., Tourist Billett 25 DKr for 24 hours; Cophehagen Card 60-150 DKr.).
Watch out: the city trains don't always stop. You could also hire a bicyle. It's quite usual in the north (Danwheel, Colbornsensgade 3; Rent a Bicycle, Istedgade 71, both on the left hand side of the railway station). Sight seeing buses leave from Radhuspladsen, 85 DKr. Harbour and canal trips from Gammel Strand 85-400 DKr. It's cheaper to take Bus

No. 3 but it doesn't have a commentary: Osterbro., Norrebro, Frederiksberg, Vesterbro, Valby, a representative cross section.

POINTS OF INTEREST: In order to see things around the city you don't need public transport: Straight away there is Tivoli Gardens (an amusement and recreational park and botanical garden–May-September 10.00 a.m.-midnight). Tivoli Gardens is an international meeting place. Similar, but with more people: Bakken in Dyrehaven, city train C line, Klampenborg, April-August from 2.00 p.m.

On the opposite side of Tivoli Gardens is the city hall square (Radhuspladsen). The city hall is built in renaissance style (cira 1900) and is very luxurious (Monday-Saturday 10.00 a.m.-3.00 p.m., 5 DKr.). The shopping area and pedestrian zone F. Berggade which is very middle european begins to the right of the city hall. It has very expensive fast food shops (one of the better places here is Stecker's Cafe, Salad Bar and Pizzeria in romantic new wave style). Luxurious boutiques are to be found in the city arcades. A more beautiful walk around the city is around the university quarter (go left at Nytorv, behind the cathedral) where antique and second-hand shops are found. The end of Fiol str. leads to Kultorvet and from there back past the Round Tower (5 DKr. 209m long walkway going up without steps). The tower has an observatory which dates back to the 17th centruy as does the surrounding part of town. You come past the city arcades again, and Kongens Nytorv Square, and along the pedestrian zone to the harbour area, Nyhavn, a small, almost genuine, harbour area with expensive restaurants. The hydrofoils to Malmo leave from the end of the canal (catch the bus back to the Railway Station: 28/41).

If you want to see a few special things: The main road on the left leads to the City Museum (Bymuseum Vesterbrogade, Tuesday-Saturday 10.00a.m.-4.00 p.m., gratis). Catch the city train to Osterport Station and take Lange Line's Bus no. 50 to the Lille Havfrue (Little Mermaid and the Kastellet Fortress), where tourists are found in hordes in the pavilion. Afterwards (from Osterport) sample a genuine brew at Tuborg Brewery (tours, 8.30 a.m.-2.30 p.m.; Strandvejen 50, City train Svanemollen) or the same at Carlsberg, Ny Carlsbergvej 140, Monday-Friday 9.00, 11.00 a.m., 2.30p.m. (Take a bottle opener with you).

MUSEUMS: The Workers' Museum, Romersgade 22 (Monday-Thursday 11.00 a.m.-4.00 p.m.); the Fyrskib, an old fire fighting ship at Nyhavn (Tuesday-Sunday 1.00-4.00p.m.); Hirschsprungske Collection, Stackholmsgade 20, danish art in a public park (Wednesday-Sunday 1.00-4.00 p.m.); Livgardens historical collection, Tothersgade 100, Museum der Liebgarde (only Tuesday & Sunday 11.00 a.m.-3.00 p.m.); Tussaud's Wax Works, this time danish (daily 10.00 a.m.-midnight) which cost 30 DKr. and is the most expensive. Museum of the Danish Freedom Fighters 1940-45, Churchill Park (Tuesday-Sunday 10.00 a.m.-4.00 p.m.), and the National Museum, Frederiksh. Kanal 12 (Tuesday-Sunday 10.00 a.m.-4.00 p.m.).

For Museums as well as train and bus travel there is the Copenhagen card which costs 60/110/150 DKr. for 1-3 days.

PARKS: First class parks are found all around the city: Orstedsparken; Botantical gardens; Rosenborg Park. If you want to go a bit further out then hire a bicycle and go to the Amager Faelled park south of Christians harbour, through the Valby park where the Rosenhave, (rose arbour) and the playground are very popular, through Vigerslev and Grondals to the Damhussoen Lake and the Utterslev Mose lake.

FOOD & DRINK are very expensive in Copenhagen, even though the price of alcohol is not as high as in Sweden. If you don't want to spend your 60 Kroner at McDonalds, then you can go anywhere and have the Danmenu (menu of the day) e.g. three places at Tivoli Gardens, the railway station restaurant, the sailing boat Isefjord at Nyhavn, Axelborg Bodega, Axeltorv 1, Illum (Department Store), Ostergade 52.

PUBS with Smorgasbord: Tokanten, Vandkunster 1; Sans Soucis, Madvigs Alle 15. Vegetarian: Det Gronne Kokken, Larsbjorn str. 10; Cranks Gronne Buffet, Gronnegade 12; Student restaurants: University Cafe, 2 Fiol STR.; Ambrosius, Hemmingsensgade 32; Asia, Farvergade.
Another few pubs: the Voertshuset Pinden, Reventiowsgade 4, just left of the railway station, the Casablanca with the Cinema Palace in Axeltorv, the Axelborg another good pub which is also there.
With Music: Parnas, Lille Kongensgade 16; Afro Club, Stengade 30; In the evenings: Smut Inn, Brydes Alle 36; Radhus Kroen, Longgang Str; Students: Pilegarden, Pile Str. 41; Skindbusksen, Lille Kongensgade 4; Disco: Charlie Brown, Standgade; Musikcafeen, Mag Str. 14; Grok Jazz Lorry, Allegade 7; Jazz: Montmatre, Noregade 41; Music groups: Jomfruburet, Fredderiksberggade; Saltlageret, Gammel Kongevej.

MARKETS: Fruit and vegetable and flea market at Israelsplads west of the Norreport railway station. Other flea markets are found at Horhusvej; and a street with secondhand goods is Ryesgade.

FREE TOWN CHRISTIANA: The island of anarchy, Christiana is in the middle of the city and has been independent since 1971. In the former army barracks freaks, dealers, dropouts, social workers and groups on the fringes of society have founded a commune.

ACCOMMODATION can be booked at Kiosk P at the railway station or at the USE IT office (see above).
Youth hostel: Bellahro, Herbergvejen 8, Tel. 01/289715, Bus 2; Amager Sjaellandsbroen 55, Tel. 522 908, Bus 16/37; Youth hotels (up to US$15 per person per night) Vesterbro, Ungdomsgard, Absalonsgade 8, Tel. 312 070, Bus 6/28, Sleep In, Osterbro, Skojtehal, Per Henrik Lings Alle 6, Tel. 26 50 59, Bus 1/6,;
Camping: Absalon, Korsdalsvej, Brondbyoster railway station (Tel. 41 06 00); Noerum, Ravnebakken, Tel. 801 957.

ODENSE

Odense is on the beautiful island of Funen and has a population of 170,000.

Right behind the railway station is the railway museum in Lokschuppen str. (10.00 a.m.-4.00 p.m.), in the opposite direction: go through the park and keep to the left of the pedestrian zone, past the tourist information office (Radhuset. Tel. 127 520 which also handles holidays in private homes) and you come to a small old town section with small flat houses, the Mint (Overgade 48) and Hans Christian Andersen's house (fairystory writer) H. Jensens Str. 39. The village-like atmosphere of Funen can be experienced in the open air village museum of Sejerskovej 50, Bus 2.

POINTS OF INTEREST: If you want to see everything at once: Sightseeing tours from the town hall, 3.00p.m. The Holmegaard glass building is art in its own way, Lille Glasvej 20, up from the Vestre Stationsvej. The boat trip on the Oden River is very picturesque (Filosofgangen, Bus 3). After that have a quiet drink at the Enventyr Bodengaden Pub, Overgade 18.

ACCOMMODATION:
Youth hostel: Kragsbjergvej 121, Tel. 09/130 425. Hotel: Hotel Kahema, Dronningensgade 5, 5000 Odense C, Tel. 09/122821, single room 145DKR / night.

FINLAND

Finland differs from the other three scandinavian countries in that it is a republic. It has an area of 338,127 sq. km. and a population of 4.8 million. Finland is not dominated by Russia like the east european buffer states and remains a neutral state between both blocs. Today about 7 per cent of the population are finnish Swedes and Finland is still a two language country.

It's best to visit Finland in July when the midnight sun shines.

ENTRY/FOREIGN EXCHANGE/CUSTOMS REGULATIONS: A valid passport is required. There is no limit on the amount of finnish currency which may be brought into the country but only 10,000 Finnish Markka may be taken out.

Duty Free Allowance:
1 litre of wine, 1 litre of spirits, 2 litres of beer, 200 cigarettes or 250 grms of tobacco.

Currency/Exchange Rate: The currency of the land is the Finnish Markka.

A$1   =   3.20 mka
C$1   =   3.50 mka
NZ$1   =   2.50 mka
£1   =   7.00 mka
US$1   =   5.00 mka

Emergency Telepone Number: 000

EMBASSIES:
Australia: No Resident Representative–see Sweden
Canada: Pohjois Esplanadi 25B, Tel. 171 141
N.Z.   N.Z. Ambassador in Moscow is accredited to Finland.
U.K.:   Uudenmaankatu 16-20, Tel. 647 922.
U.S.A.:   Itainen Puistotie 14a, Tel. 171 931

IMPORTANT:
Finland has mosquitoes in plague proportions, so remember to take the insect repellant.

TRIVIA:
Finland is the country where the sauna originated. There are about 1 million saunas in the country. Mixed public saunas are not usual.

Camping in the countryside is not allowed in principle but the authorities don't usually enforce this rule.

ACCOMMODATION:

Hotels, camping grounds and youth hostels: Finnish Tourist Board, P.O. Box 53, 00521 Helsinki 52, Tel. 90/144511.
Hotel vouchers, Finncheck, are available in summer.

SPEED LIMITS:

30 km/h in built up areas;
80 km/h outside built up areas; and 120 km/h on the motorways.
   It is obligatory to have the headlights on when driving even in the day.

RAILWAYS:

Finnrail ticket for 8, 15 or 22 days for 160/235/315 DM, 2nd Class.

AIRPORTS:

International airports are found at Helsinki, Tampere and Turku.

HELSINKI

Helsinki is primarily a town stamped by the east, more compatible with the baltic towns of Tallinn, Riga, Klaipeda which lie on the Soviet side and are more difficult to visit. Helsinki encompasses uncountable islands and waterways (Pop. 483,0000).
   The quickest overland route to Helsinki is via Stockholm, by train or car and then with Silja/Viking Ferries: (approx. 11hrs. Cost from 190 Fmk one way per person–cars cost the same as one person) to Turku from where you can drive on the E3 or take the train to Helsinki (good connections). You could take a ferry to Helsinki direct, or the same directly from Travemunde (Finnjet), is cheaper September-November.

BY CAR: When you go overland by car, you have to take into account the cost of the ferries in Denmark (by rail gratis) as well as an extra 1500 km drive from Stockholm to Helsinki via Bioden and Kemi around the Baltic–good roads.

BY RAIL: You have to change in Boden, Tornio and Kemo because Finland has a different rail gauge (Russian–1524mm).
   All the railway lines of the land come to the peninsular city terminal, built in the national romantic style (Tel. 65 94 11). The 8 tracks are not under cover, but there is a hall with fast food shops and adjoining the entry hall on the right, is the city information office (accommodation information also) and also a train information window. In front of the right side exit is a Finnish travel agency.

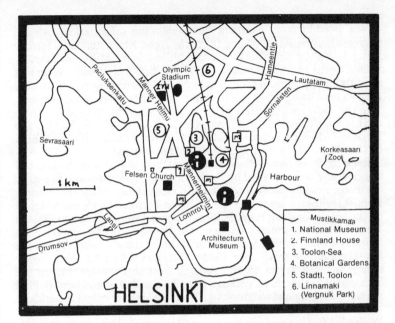

National Museum
1. National Museum
2. Finnland House
3. Toolon-Sea
4. Botanical Gardens
5. Stadtl. Toolon
6. Linnamaki
   (Vergnuk Park)

BY AIR: The international airport is at Vantaa, good bus and train connections, Tel. 8251.

TOURIST INFORMATION: The central tourist office is at Pohjoisespanadi 19, at the market/harbour, Tel. 169 37 57.

TOURIST NEWSPAPERS: Helsinki This Week, Helsinki To-day and Helsinki Journal.

LOCAL TRANSPORT: You can travel by bus, tram or underground–modern, but only 1 line (single trip 5 Fmk, ten trip ticket 44 Fmk, Tourist Ticket 26 Fmk for 24 hours). The Helsinki Ticket is cheaper, entitles you to discounts in restaurants, theatres and saunas, and can be used on all local transport, including boats and city tours. You can buy it when you get on, highly recommended (1/2/3 days for 45/60/75 Fmk). Accommodation with the Helsinki ticket: Class I-III up to 90/115/165 Fmk per person per night, weekends 14th June to 4th August, and Christmas to Easter. Tel. 90 171 133.

CITY TOURS: From the railway station Asema-aukio, 40-70 Fmk. Cheaper: simply take Tram 3T with commentary at the Tramstops.

POINTS OF INTEREST: Norra Esplanade has both the Finnish design and shopping centre. Now it is only a few steps to the harbour corner, the Kauppatori where there are also market halls and in summer, an evening market. Look at: the fountain with the mermaid, where an exclusive market is held, and right as well as left, are the terminals of the Scandinavian shipping lines (shipping information:, Ageba, Olympia-laitura, Tel. 66 91 93). Go to the right, Ehrenstomintie, further along is Kaivopuisto Park and the Mannerheini Museum, Porrast, Kalliolinantie 14 (Friday-Sunday 11.00 a.m.-3.00 p.m.); Mannerheim was an outstanding Finnish army and state leader, who cleverly steered the Finnish boat between Hitler and Stalin with a minimum loss of territory.

In the background is Helsinki's cathedral (Russian Orthodox), which can't be overlooked (Senat Place). Another very beautiful church is the Russian Orthodox Uspenski cathedral, in Katjanokka. It is dedicated to the Virgin Mary, and has small golden towers.

Back again to Senat Place and the cathedral which is the heart of the city, and was designed by the German architect, Johann C. Engel. Go along Pohjoiseplanadi to the main cross street, Mannerheimintie, from there take a tram (any 4's or 10) to Parliament House which is on the left. Walk along towards Toolon Bay and you will come to Finland House–where congresses are held. On the right is the city museum (Sunday-Friday 12.00 noon-4.00 p.m.), the National Museum is on the left–Finland in a small area! (daily 11.00 a.m.-4.00 p.m). Walk slowly along the lanes on the left and you will come to Tempelgatan, and the Tempeliaukio church, a synthesis of archaic and ultra-modern! Behind are the Runebergsgatan (gardens) (Tram 7) which are linked to parkland around the Olympic and swimming stadiums and ice rink (with tower). Walk a bit further and you'll come to Linnanmaki Park, for people who didn't stay long enough at the Tivoli Gardens . . .. Return with Tram 7 or Bus 24 (Toolontori) or simply walk through the suburbs, and rest a while in Sibelius Park, or take Bus 24 to the terminus and open air museum, Seurasaari, on an island which can be reached by walking across the dam. There are 84 buildings which illustrate finnish architecture. If you wish to find out more about this then visit the Architecture Museum, Kasarmikatu 24, Tram 4 (daily 10.00 a.m.-4.00 p.m.).

The sea fortress, Suomanlinna, (hourly ferries from the market square) is a bit out of the way, but is a museum, park and finnish culture centre rolled into one. Until 1972 it was occupied by the military, who have now moved to the island of Pikku Mustasaari; the second world war U-boat, Vesikko can be seen. With another water bus (Nora Esplanade to the end, then turn left along the canal) you come to the Maritime Museum, in Mustikkama along Korkeasaari. Also in Korkeasaari is the zoo (northern animals, daily 10.00 a.m.-7.00 p.m.).

Another few sights: The town hall, Seurahuone, on Market Square, was the cultural centrepoint in the 19th century; Observatory Hill which overlooks the harbour, is central and has a beautiful view; Katajanokka, the island on which the Uspenski catheral stands, was the birthplace of the town; The art noveau suburb, Eira (Bus 16); The Stock Exchange with its beautiful courtyard is in Fabianinkatu St; the student town, Otaniemi, north of Tapiola. The former artists' colony, Hvittrask, in

Luoma, Kirkkonummi (by train). The home of Sibelius in Ainola, Jarvenpaa (by train).

MUSEUMS: The old wooden house, Kristianinkatu 12 (Sunday-Friday 12 noon-4.00 p.m.); Military Museum, Maurinkatu 1, (Sunday-Friday 11.00 a.m.- 3.00 p.m.); National Maritime Museum, Hylkysaari (Saturday & Sunday 10.00 a.m.-3.00 p.m.); Finnish Sports Museum at the Olympic Stadium (Sunday-Tuesday 11.00 a.m.-5.00 p.m.), Technical Museum, Viikintie 1 (Tuesday-Sunday 12 noon-6.00 p.m.); Ateneum Art Museum, Kansakoulukatu 3, (daily 9.00 a.m.-5.00 p.m.).

ALSO: The epitomy of relaxation is naturally the Sauna. Unfortunately, in the last few years good saunas have become rare. Information from the Sauna Society, 'Sauna Seura', Vaskinjemi, Lauttasaari, Tel. 67 6877.

ENTERTAINMENT: It's not dull in the evenings: Young and old from Toolon gather at Pub 99, Mannerheimintie 58 (beer is about 10 Fmk everywhere); a similar pub is the Hallinkorva Pub a bit further along; a youthful Disco, Silver Night, is next to Pub 99; in the city the Jazz Place, Groovy (Grasviksgt, corner Albertinkatu) is quite good; Punks and Groups meet at the Lepakko Klub (Vasterleden); another popular pub is the Mikadon Salongit near Old Bakers Pub in Mannerheimintie Str, corner Lonnrotinkatu. Student Clubs: Ostrobotia, Museokatu 10; KY Exit, Pohjoinen Rautatiekatu; TF Disco, Otakaari 22 (which is in the suburb of Espoo); Piano Bar: Asemaravintola in the railway station. Discos: Alibi, Hietaniemenkatu 14; Harald's Kasarmikatu 40; Artist Pubs: Elite, Et. Hesperiankatu 22; Atelja, Arka iankatu 14, Kosmos, Kalevankatu 3.

OTHER TRAVEL TIPS: By ship, the day trip to Reval, Estland, USSR, 120 DM from Olympic Harbour; with the new train which carries cars on the section to Kolari (995km) to Lapland (only Fridays). By car to the Norweigan/Russian/Finnish border via, Imatra, Kuopio, Ruka, Luosto to Kirkenes.

FESTIVALS: On Midsummers Night Eve in Seurassai Park; on Helsinki Day, the 12th June; and at the end of August/beginning of September, music festivals are held in some open air stages in the parks.

ACCOMMODATION: Youth hostel at the Olympic stadium, Tel. 49 60 71; Espoo, Jamerantaival 7, Tel. 46 02 11, Bus 102,192. Camping; Rastila, Buss 90/96, Tel. 90/3165 51, Hotel: for Young People in summer, Academy, Hietaniemenkatu 14, Tel. 440171; Satakuntatalo, Lapinrinne 1 (the cheapest, with Sauna). Tel. 694 03 11.

FRANCE

The fifth French Republic was established under General De Gaulle. To-day France has a population 54.1 million and an area of 547,026 sq. km.

ENTRY/FOREIGN EXCHANGE/CUSTOMS REGULATIONS: A valid passport with visa is required and only 5,000 FF may be taken out of the country without a special permit.

Duty Free Allowance for people over 17 yrs of age:
1 litre of spirits, 2 litres of wine, 200 cigarettes or 250 gm tobacco and other goods to the value of up to 1,030 FF.

Currency/Exchange Rate: The currency of the land is the French Franc.

```
1 A $   =   4.00FF
1 C $   =   4.50FF
1 N Z $ =   3.20FF
£1      =   9.00FF
1 U S $ =   6.00FF
```

In spite of strong price controls always ask if there is any additional charge!

TELEPHONE:
After you have dialled the 19 wait for the tone before continuing and the local area code is then dialled without the 0.

EMBASSIES:
Australia: 4 Rue Jean Rey, Paris, Tel. 575 6200.
Canada: 35 Ave. Montaigne, Paris, Tel. 472 30101
N.Z.:   7 ter, rue Leonard de Vinci, 75116, Paris, Tel. 500 2411
U.K.:   109 Rue du Faubourg, St. Honore, Paris, Tel. 296 9142.
U.S.A.:   2 Avenue Montaigne, Paris, Tel. 723 0101.

ACCOMMODATION:
Hotels–only regional and town offices.
Youth hostels: FUAJ, 6 Rue Mesnil, 75116 Paris, Tel. 1/26 18 003;
Camping: FFCC, 78 Rue de Rieoli, 75004 Paris, Tel. 1/272 8408;
Holiday houses and holiday villages OVT, 67 rue de Dunkerque, 75009 Paris, Tel. 1/878 7121.

SPEED LIMITS:
60 km/h in built up areas;
90 km/h outside built up areas when its not raining and 80 km/h when it's raining;

100km/h on city motorways and 130 km/h on other motorways or 110 km/h during rain.
Toll is payable on almost all motorways.

RAIL:

All tickets even on the way out are issued by machines.

There are a wide variety of special priced tickets on offer:
France Vacances tickets for 7/15/30 days for US$85/180/275;
for young people there is a half-price ticket, Carre Jeune, or even better still the Carte Jeune for US$22;
also France Vacances Special valid for 8 days travel in any one month for US$175;
and Billet Sejour for at least 5 days and 1000km travel but is only valid on certain days.

AIRPORTS:

International airports at Paris, Nice, Marseille and Toulon.

AND: You should visit France at least once on the 14th July, their National Day

---

LYON

There is hardly a town of this size (Pop. 1.21 million) that is so internationally ignored as Lyon, the second largest town in France. It is centrally situated but because it doesn't have any mountains nearby, or isn't near the sea, or in a particularly pretty area, tourists usually pass it by. It has quite a few attractions that you shouldn't miss out on. Although the percentage of foreigners here (11.8%) is higher than in Marseille where there are a lot of north african immigrants (7.9%) it appears to be a genuine french town.

BY RAIL: Since August 1983 when the French Railways (SNCF) opened the first new fast express train line, Lyon appears to have moved closer to the 'world'. It now only takes 2 hours on the TGV train from Paris to Lyon's railway station–Part Dieu. The top speed of the train is 270km/h. From the Part Dieu take the metro to Saxe Gambetta, then the Trolley Bus 1 to the city centre, Place Bellecour. The Lyon-Perrache railway station is even more modern (the TGV comes to here). It is situated right on the north/south axis of the city centre between the Rhone and the Saone and has all the modern facilities that you would expect–shops, snack bars and cafes and a tourist information office (the main office is at Place Bellecour, Tel. 7/8422575). TGV Train (fast train) has connections to Paris, Lille, Geneva, Grenoble, Montpellier and

Toulon/Marseille, but you must book. Bookings are taken up until a few minutes before departure. It is the most comfortable and fastest way to get to these towns. It has aircraft type seats and a Bar carriage.

BY AIR: Lyon also has an international airport in the suburb of Satola in the south-east, but it only has flights to a few european cities in summer.

BY CAR: You can get to Lyon by road along the motorway from the north (Frankfurt-Karlsruhe) to Mulhouse A36 Beaune A6; from the east (Zurich-Genf) Chambery A41-A43 Lyon; from the south (Barcelona/Genoa) Orange A7- Lyon. In summer the motorways are usually overcrowded. Parking areas are found at the railway stations–the A7 goes directly to the Gare de Perache.

LOCAL TRANSPORT in Lyon is modern and varied. Metro (underground), trolley buses, buses and funicular–all of which may be used for the one fixed price. Single ticket 3FF; tourist card 2 days/37FF; 3 Days 53FF–good value for money: the 6 trip ticket.

POINTS OF INTEREST: You should visit the heights first. The old town is on the right bank of the River Saone and behind it is a hill dominated by the Basilique Notre Dame de Fourviere. Take the funicular–right line from St. Jean. The view of the town from behind the church is interesting. It's even better from the north-east tower. The T.V. tower to the north looks just like the Eiffel Tower. It was also built in the 19th century and is a brash opposite of the church which was built in the same era. If you look to the south from the hill you will see two roman theatres (Monday-Friday 8.00 a.m.-12 noon & 2.00-6.00 p.m. Saturday & Sunday shorter hours, gratis). During July & August special performances are held there. For further information on the subject visit the Gallic Roman Museum of Modern Architecture, 17 rue Cleberg (Wednesday-Sunday 9.30 a.m.-12 noon & 2.00-6.00 p.m., gratis). From Place de Minimes or St. Just, rue Trion you can travel on the left funicular line, same valley station. Now you've got your bearings you can look at the old town's lanes which start near St. Jean's Cathedral, a 12th century gothic cathedral which has tours conducted in different languages.

Now to the old town–the suburb of St. Jean. As well as the impressive houses in rue St. Jean, the Traboules are something unique. Lyon's own shield depicts passages going through houses and backyards, across bridges and small squares between the lanes, e.g. from 3 pl. St. Paul to 5 rue Juiverie, from 2 pl. du Gouvernement to 10 Quai Romain Rolland and others. Worth seeing around pl. St. Paul: the stairs at No. 10 rue Lainerie and two houses further on the gothic facade of the Mayet de Beauvoir building; the stock exchange building, 'La Loge du Change', pl. du Change. Lyon was one of the very early stock exchanges and trading centre; the pl. de la Trinite with houses from the middle ages (Cafe du Soleil); the historical museum of Lyons, Place du Petit College (Wednesday-Monday 10.00 a.m.-6.00 p.m., gratis) next to it, the Hotel de Gadagne and the Marionette Museum, open the same hours.

LOCAL FOOD: Arlette Hugon, 12 rue Pizay; Chez Sylvain, 4 rue Tupin; Le Garet, 7 rue du Garet.

BUT it pays to wander around the real city centre around Place Bellecour. Here in the pedestrian zones are lots of shops and small cafes. If you choose to walk the long route from south to north from the Perrache Sation you should walk via place Carnot, rue Victor Hugo, place Bellecour, then turn right to rue de la Charite and the terrific Hotel Dieu du Place and rue de la Republique to the Palais du Commerce and lastly to the Hotel de Ville, the most impressive town hall which has a central courtyard. You can go the same way on metro A. In the Palais St. Pierre, pl. des Terreaux behind the city hall you will find not only the art galley, Musee des Beaux Arts (Wednesday-Monday 10.45 a.m.-6.00 p.m., gratis), but also inside this Louis XIV building a beautiful courtyard where old and young meet.

Even further to the north (Metro Croix Rousse) is the Maison des Canuts (house of the silk weavers) 10 rue d'Ivry (Monday-Saturday 8.30 a.m.-12 noon and 2.30-6.30 p.m. 2FF). Also the Musee des Tissus, 34 rue de la Charite, (Tuesday-Sunday 10.00 a.m.-12 noon & 2.00-5.30 p.m., 10 ff, Students 5 FF, gratis on Wednesday).

FURTHER MUSEUMS: Musee des Arts Decoratifs, 30 rue de la Charite, as well as the Musee des Tissus; Musee des Hospices, (hospital museum) Hotel Dieu, Place de L'Hopital (Tuesday-Sunday 1.30-4.30 p.m., 2 FF); Musee de la Resistance (resistance museum) 5 rue Boileau, (Wednesday-Monday 10.45 am.-1.00 p.m. & 2.00-6.00 p.m., gratis); Musee de l'imprimerie et de la Banque (printery & bank) 13 rue de la Poulaillerie (Wednesday-Sunday 9.30 a.m.-12 noon & 2.00-6.00 p.m., gratis). In spring and summer on certain days of the week during the afternoons or the evenings there are guided tours–further information obtainable at the tourist information office (25-40FF). There are also organised boats trips on the Saone and Rhone from 10 Quai Servie or 10 Quai Pecherie, Tel. 830 5006.

The MODERN PART of Lyon is near the Perrache railway station but more around the Part-Dieu railway station, where the large companies have their offices e.g. the tower building of Credit Lyonnais and the bus and railway stations. A beautiful market is held every morning on the Quai St. Antonine, and in May & June on the Saone. It's even prettier to the north at the far reaching Park Tete d'Or with its large lake and the botanical gardens, which can be reached by the metro (Foch) and trolley Bus 4. The Palais des Congres and the Exhibition Grounds are also there. An even larger recreation area is the Miribel Jonage which can be reached from metro Laurent-Bonnevay with Bus 83 in the season. There are places for swimming and camping there.

IN THE DISTRICT: North of Lyon is the Schloss Rochetaillee with a national Automobile Museum (daily 8.00 a.m.-12 noon & 2.00-6.00 p.m. 13 FF). To the west is Charbonnieres les Bains, a monumental thermal pool with casino and health farm.

TIPS FOR RAILWAY BUFFS: In the summer season the Alpazur belonging to the Loisrail section of the SNCF, runs from Part Dieu station, Lyon, to Marseille and sometimes Nice. It is more or less just a hobby railroad now. On the stretch between Lyon and Nice it goes through the wild romantic sea alps (via Digne). Other Loisrail Connections from Lyon: the Ventadour to Bordeaux and from Part Dieu station the Rouget de l'isle to Strasbourg only in July and August, run by amateurs.

Two railway museums a bit further out: At Tournon on the southern line to Valence, the Chemins de Fer du Vivarais, a beautiful trip through valleys and ravines (steam diesel 1000mm, 33km, June-September daily, April-October on Sunday). And the Chemin de Fer Touristique du Breda from Pontcharra on the main line Lyon-Chambery-Grenoble is even better because of its locomotive park (Steam 1435mm, 11km June-September only Sundays).

NOW TO FOOD: Self Serice Athena Zola in the suburb of Villeurbanne, 163 Cours Emile Zola; Le Petit Bourg in the Centre Commercial near the Part Dieu railway station, Niveau 2; La Bartavelle, 17 rue Auguse Comte; near Perrache: Le Bistrot PPerrachois, 26 Cours de Verdun; Le Dolmen, Creperie, 46 rue Franklin or simply go to the pedestrian zone.

ACCOMMODATION: Youth hostel, Lyon, Venissieux, 51 rue Roger Salengro, open until 11.00 p.m., Tel. 7/8763923 from Perache Bus 53, Etats Unis Viviani. Youth information and accommodation bookings: Centre Regional d'Information Jeunesse CRIJ, 9 Quai des Celestins, Tel. 7/837 1528. Centre International de Sejour CISL, near Place du 8 Mai 1945, from Perrache, Bus 36. Hotels: de Geneve, 10 Quai Perrache, Tel. 8 371159; Morand, 99 rue de Crequi, Tel. 852 29 96; Columbia, 8 Pl. A. Briand, Tel. 860 54 65; Celtic, 5 Pl. St. Paul, Tel. 828 0112. Good value for money: Select hotel, 18 rue Bellecordiere, Tel. 8 42 27 78 and Select Home des Terreaux, 22 rue des Capucinas, Tel. 828 26 92.

MARSEILLE

Marseille with a population of 1 million is the largest harbour city in France. It is the main port on the Cote d'Azur and a large industrial town. It has a very modern, palatial railway station, St. Charles, Tel. 08 50 50.

Also near there is a public park and roman ruins, Termes des Cemenelum. In the newer suburbs, next to the Hotel Negresco which you can get to from the Promenade des Anglais, is the local museum, Musee Massena, Tuesday-Sunday 10.00 a.m.-12 noon & 2.00-5.00 p.m. Don't forget the harbour suburb, Lympia, which begins at Place Ile de Beaute. City tours on the tourist train from 1 l'Esplande Albert and new Place Massena or boat, Tel. 71 44 77.

BY CAR: You take the A7 from Lyon.

BY AIR: Airport-Marseille-Marignane, Tel. 42/89 90 10.

HARBOUR: Port Authorities, Tel. 91 90 66.

TOURIST INFORMATION: Office de Tourisme, 4 La Canebiere–the main road near the old harbour, Tel. 549 111. Youth information: rue de la Visitation, Tel. 499 155.

LOCAL TRANSPORT: There is a terrific network comprising metro, bus, tram and trolley bus. Timetables are available at the tourist information office.

POINTS OF INTEREST: The most interesting is the enormous dock area and the Vieux Port (old harbour) and surrounding old town. Also impressive: Musee des Docs Romain (roman harbour) 28 Pl Vivaus; the ancient cathedral, La Major, the oldest cathedral on the harbour and Notre Dame de la Garde situated on top of a 162m high cliff (lift) across the blvd. Andre Aune. The island fort Chateau d'If, an old defence fort made famous by Alexander Dumas in his 'Count of Monte Christo'. Modern architecture: the Cite Radieuse by Le Corbusier which can be reached along the blvd. Michelet. And a victory arch, the Porte d'Aix. Culinary Delight: Marseille is the home of Bouillabaise, a fish soup.

FESTIVALS: The Carnival procession is world famous as is the Nice Flower Festival in May; also the large Jazz Festival in July.

ACCOMMODATION: There are quite a few camping grounds on the outskirts of the city; Youth hostels, 47 ave. J. Vidal, Bonneveine, Tel. 73 21 81–from the railway station take the local train to Place Castellane, then Bus 44 or 19; Chateau de Boisluzy, ave. de Bois Luzy, Tel. 49 06 18. Take Bus 6 from the railway station. Cheap hotels are found around the railway station e.g. Beaulieu, 1 Pl. des Marseillaises, Tel. 907 059.

NICE

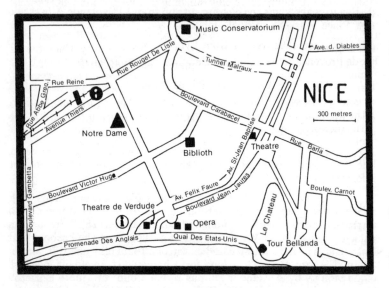

A modern coastal resort, an international city, a romantic old town, situated in the midst of a beautiful area. Theren't enough superlatives to describe it. It was only given to France in 1860 at the time of Italian unification. Even though a great number of europen aristocrats lost their money after the first world war, Nice still has retained its world rating. (Pop. 344,000.)

BY SEA: If you want to be elegant, then come to Nice with your own boat. Harbour information Tel. 93/89 40 85.

BY CAR: You can reach Nice very easily on the A8 expressway 'La Provencale' from Lyon to Aix-en-Provence via Nice to the Italian border. It is a beautiful drive along the Grande Corniche, the road built on historical paths by Napoleon. Coming from the east you drive past Mont Gros with its observatory, along the ave. des Diables Bleus to the city centre. The Moyeene Corniche is a tourist road along rue Barla and Place M. Barel from which you get many beautiful views. It's a romantic drive along the coast on the Corniche Inferieure from Place Ile de Beaute, Blvd. Carnot. In the city there are 27 organised parking areas. Gratis: Parc Autos Ferber, Promenade Corniglion Molinier, north of the airport where the tourist information, is and Bosquets, Ave. de la Californie.

BY AIR: The second largest airport in France is south-west of Nice. There are direct flights to 44 cities. A bus runs regularly to the airport from the Promenade des Anglais and the Place Massne, Tel. 93/213012. Long distance buses to Cannes, Menton Tel. 93/561211. The railway station on the main Marseille/Ventimiglia line is found north-west of the city centre. Tel. 87 50 50.

BY RAIL: Another two special tips for rail travellers: Between Nice and Digne in the coastal alps there is a private railway 'Chemins de Fer de Provence' (offically also called Kiefernzug). It winds through the romantic Var Valley. From Digne SNCF (French rail) connections to Marsailles and Lyons or Geneva. From Nice: Gare de Provence, Pl. G. de Gaulle. An unconventional route over the Italian border: Instead of the usual main road section Nice-Ventimiglia you can change in Nice to the Tenda railway which was reopened in 1979 (in Breil either go to Ventimiglia or even better still Cuneo/Torino or Savona).

TOURIST INFORMATION OFFICE is found at Ave. Thiers, at the railway station, Tel. 93/87 0707. Youth Information CIJ, Esplanades des Victoires, Tel. 93/80 93 93.

TOURIST NEWSPAPER: 'Semaine des Spectacles de la Cote D'Azur'.

POINTS OF INTEREST: The city is very luxurious and everything you have dreamed about: The Promenade des Anglais is 7km long and runs along the banks of the Baie des Anges and is lined with palm trees and flowers. The most expensive hotels and the casino are found here–Hotel Negresco–also expensive cafes with international clientele.
  At the intersection of the Promenade and the Quais des Etats Unis broad boulevards branch off to Place Massena. They are the connections between the old or lower part of town at the foot of Chateau Hill and the newer city centre around Av. Jean Medecin (in the direction of the railway station) and the Blvd. Victor Hugo. Lastly, there is the harbour area, Lympia, east of Le Chateau and west of Mont Boron. We recommend that you walk through the old town after you have first visited the promenade. Go along the Blvd. Jean Jaure from Promenade du Paillon to the 'Port Fosse' steps, then turn right into Rue du Marche past the Palais de Justice, Pl. du Palais, to the Marche aux Fleurs, (flower market), and the Fruits et Legumes (fruit & vegetables market) on Cours Saleya. The Galerie de Malacologie, is also found there at 3 Cours Saleya. It shows the fauna of the Mediterranean (Tuesday-Saturday 10.00 a.m.-6.30 p.m.); Pub: La Criee, 22 Cours Saleya; Le Pelican rose, 4 Cours Saleya, Bouillabaisse (fish soup).
  Some of the beautiful old buildings in the town: At the east of the markets, is a building which was the old Savoy Senate building until 1792, and later the Law Court until 1860. One street further on is Adam and Eve House. A little further on is the baroque Eglise de Jesus and across the street of the same name is the cathedral of St. Raparate on Place Rossetti which was named in honour of the martyr. Go through

the lanes-Halle aux Herbes, Place Entrale, rue du Collet until you get to the rue St. Augustin/rue Pairolliere-picturesque old town scenery. From here go along rue de la Providence which climbs up to Le Chateau a former fort from where you get a beautiful view. Around about the old town: Cultural information is obtainable at the Bureau Action Culturelle Municipale, 2 Pl. Massena, Tel. 62 12 12. On the north side are: Place Garibaldi, an early extension of the town; the Quai des Etats Unis die Opera; two art galleries 'des Ponchettes' with exhibitions of all sorts and the 'd'art Contenporain des Musees des Nice' (Tuesday-Sunday 10.30 a.m.-12 noon & 2.00-6.00 p.m.); bit further on is the Bellanda maritime museum on Place du 8 Mai 1945 (Wednesday-Monday 10.00 a.m.-12 noon & 2.00-5.00 p.m.).

But other suburbs also have their own atmosphere: The Russian church behind the railway station Gambetta Blvd. and Blvd. Tazarewich; near there in Ave d'Estienne d'Orves is the theatre Blimp, Tel. 964 040; In the snobby suburb of Cimiez, is the Chagall museum (which has a series of biblical paintings), ave. du Nr. Menard (Tuesday-Sunday 10.00 a.m.-12 noon & 2.00-5.30/7.00 p.m.).

FOOD in Nice is nicoise. A few of the many places (cheap and good value specials-for France): Le Felix Fauvre, 12 ave FF; Chez Davis, 11b rue Grimaldi; Chez Nino (100 beers), 50 rue Trachel; Self service: Cafe de Paris, 42 rue Pastorelli or on the rue Massena or in the old town.

ACCOMMODATION: Hotels: Darcy, 28 rue d'Angleterre, Tel. 93/88 67 06; Novelty, 26 rue d'Angleterre, Tel. 93/87 51 73; Bristol, 22 rue Paginini, Tel. 93/87 51 73.
The youth hostel, Bus 14 route Forestiere du Mont Alban, Tel. 93/89 23 64. Youth hotels: Relais Internaal de la Jeunesse, ave. Scuderi Bus 15, 22, Tel. 93/81 27 63 and Residence Les Collinettes, FJUAJ, 3 ave. R. Schuman, Bus 71, 17, Tel. 89 23 64.
Camping: Terry Lingostiere. Further accommodation is available in the neighbouring villages.

PARIS

If there were to be a capital of Europe then it would have to be Paris. Whereas London caters for young people, Paris always develops a new way of life. Even though the 20 inner suburbs (arrondissements) are influenced by customs from other lands, Paris remains very french. (Pop. 2,319,387 million).

BY RAIL: Paris has numerous small railway stations and six important terminal railway stations: Gare de l'Est (for trains to Alsace and

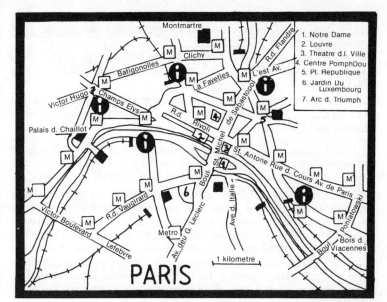

PARIS

1. Notre Dame
2. Louvre
3. Theatre d.l. Ville
4. Centre PomphDou
5. Pl. Republique
6. Jardin Du Luxembourg
7. Arc d. Triumph

southern Germany), Gare du Nord (Great Britain, Benelux countries and northern Germany), Gare St. Lazare (western France), Gare Montparnasse (south-western France), Gare d'Austerlitz (central France, Spain & Portugal), Gare de Lyon (Lyon, Marseille & Italy) where the TGV trains (super trains) arrive & depart.

At Gare du Nord there is a tourist information office and a AJF office (young peoples' accommodation) on Platform 19. On Platform 1 there is a railway information office.

At Gare de l'Est there is a tourist information office, Tel. 1/208 49 90–for all train information Tel. 261 50 50. Gare de Lyon, Tel. 1/345 92 22.

BY CAR: Motorways come from all directions to Paris and join the motorway ring around the city called the Peripherique. Quite a few exits connect with the main through roads to the city centre. The Peripherique is very dangerous because of the large volume of traffic continually entering and exiting. In the city itself, it is chaotic, lots of traffic lights, one way streets, no parking zones and expensive parking stations. If you really want to drive into the city centre then work out your route before hand from a good map and have your passenger direct you, because hesitant drivers are not tolerated. There are a few inexpensive parking areas on the Peripherique: Porte d'italie; Bagnolet (near the entry of the A3 from the east); Porte de la Villette, from where you can catch the metro.

BY AIR: The large international airports of Paris are:
Orly–14km to the south either take the A6, Bus 215/183A, or the train

RER C to Quai de'Orsay or Austerlitz (it's faster) Tel. 1/884 52 52. Charles de Gaulle–23 km to the north, by car take the A1, bus 350, or train RER B, Tel. 862 2280.

Both have city tourist information offices and helicopter services to the heliport at Porte de Sevres which is really a long way from the city centre.

TOURIST INFORMATION: Main office: 127 Champs Elysee, Tel. 723 61 72; metro Charles de Gaule, Tel. 720 57 58; UCRIF, Young peoples' information, Gare du Nord, Tel. 874 68 69.

TOURIST NEWSPAPERS: Passion, Magazine (english); L'officiell des spectacles (weekly programme), Pariscope (french weekly programme, the best of all), Paris Selection (tourist information).

LOCAL TRANSPORT: You will quickly work out the apparent confusion of the railway stations if you remember that they all are connected to a metro station of the same name. If you plan to travel through Paris then you should allow about 1 hour. Otherwise, when you are in Paris travel on the metro. The metro makes use of different technical systems but all are included in the price. (Interesting: rubber wheel system; fast system 3 RER Lines; artistic: Louvre Station; modern style: several e.g. Palais Royal; art nouveau: Reaumer-Sebastopol).

As well as the metro, there are buses which have crazy routes and are only interesting from the metro termini. On with the trains: the metro lines run between two terminal stations on opposite sides of the city after which they are named (always good to remember). In the larger stations there are route maps where the shortest way can be lit up. The pocket maps of the RATP are more practical and can be obtained at the larger railway stations. These maps double as a street map. Tickets 4.20 FF, Tourist Ticket 'Paris Sesame' 2/4/7 days for 48/72/120 FF good for 1st class travel, a good buy is the 'carnet' for 10/25/55FF. The 'Carte Orange' which is the normal weekly ticket, is very cheap, depending upon the zone, from 40FF.

BICYCLE HIRE: Paris Velo, 2 Rue du Fer a Moulin, Tel. 337 59 22, metro Censier Daubenton; Bicycle tours: Bicy-Club de France, Place de la Porte Champerret (metro station of same name), Tel. 7 66 55 92. City Tours: Paris Vision, from 100 FF, 214 rue de Rivoli.

MUSEUMS: The Government run museums are open Tuesday-Sunday 10.00 a.m.-5.40 p.m., gratis on Sunday except for special exhibitions. You can obtain museum guides and information about actual exhibitions at the tourist information office, Tel. 278 73 81.

POINTS OF INTEREST: Rather obvious is the Arc de Triumphe which is right near the main tourist information office, built by Napoleon to celebrate his own victories but in the meantime, taken into their hearts by the French. For 13 FF you can go up it, 10.00 a.m.-5.00 p.m. The

Amsterdam

South Holland: Near the Ulist River

Salzburg: Gardens of Mirabell Palace

Champs Elysee turns into the Avenue de la Grande Armee where the modern Palais de Congres is and on the left, the Bois de Boulgone, a beautiful park–not recommended after dark. The RER (train) goes from here to La Defense, a spectacular area with highrise buildings (Banlieu Ticket). It's better to go south from the Place de Charles de Gaulle (Ave. Kleber) to the Palais de Chailot which is well known because of the view from there to the Eiffel Tower which is depicted on numerous postcards. Among other things, the Museum of Mankind and the Cinema Museum are found in the Palais de Chaillot. The architecture of the building shows that the monumental fascist style was not only built in Italy and Germany–turn left to 11 Ave President to the Musee de'Art Moderne de la Ville de Paris which is particularly good.

One metro station further on (Alma Marceau), on the other side of the Seine is where our tour of dirty Paris begins at Place de la Resistance: the sewers of Paris (Monday & Wednesday 2.00-5.00 p.m.). Whole towns used to smell like it does down the sewers but thanks to modern technology, that is a thing of the past.

The Eiffel Tower still dominates Paris in spite of all attempts to surpass it (e.g. Tour Montparnasse in a straight line behind at the station of the same name). You can climb up or ride (9.00 a.m.-11.00 p.m., expensive, but there is a post office which sells special postage stamps–Tours 9.30 a.m.-11.20 p.m., 56 stories).

Firstly, high up in the air and now into the depths: a bit to the south, metro Denfert-Rochereau, are the Catacombs, later filled with bones removed from 30 cemeteries which were closed down. (Tuesday-Sunday 2.00-4.00 p.m.). You get a view across Marsfeld under the Eiffel Tower to the Ecole Militaire if it's not obscured by tourists.

To the left of the Ecole Militaire on Place Vauban are the impressive Hotel and Dome des Invalides erected by Louis XIV for soldiers and where Napoleon has rested since 1840. The Army Museum is also there (daily 10.00 a.m.-6.00 p.m., also light & sound display April-September at 11.00 p.m.). Go behind the Invalides through a small park across the Alexandre II bridge and you come to a few small palaces and then the area opens out to the Place de la Concorde (with the obelisk, which was given to Paris in 1836). On this square, during the bloody part of the revolution, 1119 people were guillotined, among them Danton. If you go a little way along the rue Royale between the Crillon and Madeleine Palace, you will see the Madeleine. From the outside it's a very quiet temple but it's a catholic church on the inside! Now turn right and you will be in the Jardin des Tuileries. Right at the start on the left is a small temple, Jeu de Paume, which contains a first class collection of impressionist paintings. It's well worth a visit (Wednesday-Monday 9.45 a.m.-5.15 p.m.). Behind there is the Louvre and in between is another small victory arch. On a rainy day you can spend all day at the Louvre (Wednesday-Monday 9.45 a.m.-6.30 p.m.). 6 collections from antiquity until you have had enough. The Mona Lisa is behind glass. On the left is the Palais Royal and the Comedie Francaise where

Moliere appeared. In the courtyard of the palace is a wonderful park. Now take a slow approach to the heart of Paris: walk along the bank of the Seine and on the right you will see the Ile de la Cite the absolute middle of France. Among other buildings here is Notre Dame.

As you go across the Pont d'Arcole which spans the Seine's arm, you will see on the left the Town Hall (free tours every Monday at 10.30 a.m.). In 1871 it was the barracks of the Paris Commune who fought their last battles in the 20th arrondissement. Also in the 20th arrondissement around metro Belleville and metro Menilmontant is the international quarter with its worldwide charm. On the Ile de la Cite in the cathedral of Notre Dame there is an archaeological vault/tomb and museum. South from there is where you go for an interesting evening, the Latin Quarter (legendary Boul). St. Michel's on the Seine is on the right and the small lanes of old Paris are straight ahead.

Next to the Ile de la Cite is the Ile St. Louis which is usually overlooked but it is where you can buy the best ice cream and sorbert at Berthillon.

Pub Tip: Flore de I'Ilw, 2 Rue J. du Bellay.

Artists' colony: metro Sully Morland. If you go straight ahead past the Town Hall, you will come to another place where the action is: the Centre Pompidou, which is being enlarged, a meeting place of artists. The Musee de l'Art Moderne (12 noon-10.00 p.m.) is fantastic. It is a huge place with lots of lanes, a witch's cauldron. A little behind and to the right is the Forum des Halles, which is of interest to shoppers. It was formerly the markets. At the Centre Pompidou, cnr. Rambuteau is a good self service supermarket Mejodine.

In the area around Place de la Republique and Arts et Metier, are beautiful houses and across from the Abbey St. Martin des Champs is an area teeming with life: Barbes (metro B-Rochechouart). Medina is the oriental old town section of Paris Marais (metro St. Paul), beautiful old quarter. The Montmatre quarter has the white Sacre Coeur. Take the metro to Anvers, then the funicular or walk up the steps which are crowded with young people from all over the world. At the top artists display their paintings. The Montmartre cemetery and a tiny vineyard are right near the metro Abesses.

PUB TIPS: Gilbus, 18 Rue du Faubourg du Temple, metro Republique (absolutely tops with live music); Caveau de la Huchette, Street No. 5, metro St. Michel, a first class jazz address; Fortunee, Rue de Petit Port/Rue Galande (good pubs, and sometimes in the church of St. Sever opposite, good concerts are held).

Jazz: Le Furstemberg, 27 Rue de Buci; a great fruit juice bar: Afruitdisiaque, Rue Vielle du Temple/Rue Rivoli; Bar: Au Pere Tranquille, Forum Les Halles, rue Pierre Lescot–expensive and exclusive but the No. 1 culture place; Hollywood Savoy, near metro Bourse; New Wave, the public disco baths: Les Bains Douches, 7 rue Bourg l'Abbe,; Roller disco: La Main Jaune, Palace de la Porte Champeret, metro

station of the same name; Theatre Cafe: Le Cafe d'Edgar Quinet, metro
Raspail; Threatre: Bouffes du Nord, metro La Chapelle.

There is a big music Festival held at the end of June which you should
try to see; the big concerts are held at the Olympia, metro Opera; You
can shop at the Drugstore day and night, metro Odeon, metro Charles
de Gaulle, metro Franklin D. Roosevelt; at Montmatre there are excellent
pubs: Anvers, right at the funicular; Au Tire Bouchon, rue Norvins.
A good area for pubs is Montparnasse (metro of the same name) and
Vavin on rue Moufftard is the largest pub in Europe: Pub St. Germain
des Pres, 17 rue de l'Ancienne Comedie, metro Odeon, cinema Mondays
only 18 FF.

Swimming Pools: Gare de Lyon, Ledru Rollin, metro Quai de la Rapee;
beautiful and old: Pontoise, 19 Rue de Pontoise, metro Cardinal Lemoine.

MARKETS: metro Ile de la Cite, Sunday mornings, bird and flower
market; Lepic, metro Blanche (vegetables); Marche d'Aligre, metro
Ledru Rollin, Marche aux Puces de Clingnancourt, metro Porte de
Clignancouer; Street Market: rue Moufftard, metro Monge.

DAY TRIPS: The castle and park at Versailles. (take RER C train). The
bascilica of St. Denis, M13.

ACCOMMODATION: Youth Hostel, IYHF, Choisy le Roi, 125 Av. de
Villeneuve St. Georges Tel. 890 92 30, a long way out; better: Accueil
des Jeunes UCRIF, 21 rue Beranger, Tel. 277 08 65 or BVJ, rue JJ
Rousseau, Tel. 236 8828/261 6643; both have many youth hotels on their
books.

There are plenty of inexpensive hotels in Paris (tourist information
office).

STRASBOURG

The capital of Alsace which, when France was divided up amongst the
sons of Charlmagne, became a part of the weak middle kingdom and
was a bone of contention between France and Germany for over a
thousand years. This land has its own strong culture, a germanic dialect
and its own lifestyle. To-day, the town has rediscovered its own culture
and because of its central location, it is becoming the headquarters of
european institutions. (Pop. 253,000).

BY CAR: It is easy to reach Strasbourg from the south or the north
because there is an expressway exit (Abfart Appenweier) from the A5
Basel/Frankfurt motorway, and from the west the motorway A4 comes
from Paris, Reims, Metz directly to Strasbourg. If you are coming from

the east then you can still come on the A5 or the A8 from Munich/Stuttgart/Karlsruhe. There are numerous parking places in and around the old town, e.g. in front of the Europa Bridge, Centre Administratif de Ville et Communite, Route du Rhin or opposite the Place du M. de Lattre de Tassigny.

BY RAIL: The main railway station is west of the old town. There are very good long distance train connections from Frankfurt, Basel, Karlsruhe and Metz (approx. hourly) and Paris, Lyons, Saarbrucken and Bern (approx. 2 hourly). The railway line which ran along the left hand bank of the Rhine between Strasbourg and Mainz has been cut in modern times. The Gare Centrale is an old railway station which has been modernised. It's snack bars are expensive. Information: Tel. 22 50 50. The main tourist information office is on the square in front of the railway station, Place de la Gare, Tel. 32 51 49.

BY AIR: The airport is south-west of the centre at Strasbourg Entzheim, and has some international connections e.g. Brussels, Gent, London, Lyons, Nice, Paris, Rome and Zurich. Information: 88/784099.

BY SHIP: The passenger ships which travel along the Rhine between Basel and Rotterdam dock at the Gare Fluvial at Quai des Belges. The harbour authorities, Port Autonome, are at 25 rue de la Nuee Bleue, Tel. 88/32 49 15. The dock area which is south-east of the city centre is also of interest to other visitors because of the Parc de la Citadelle in which are found the ruins of the Vauban Fort built in 1685.

TOURIST INFORMTION: The city office is at 10 Place Gutenberg, Tel. 88/325707. City programme: Strasbourg Actualities.

LOCAL TRANSPORT: Buses. The single trip ticket costs 5.30FF and the Carnet–5 trips 17.50 FF. For footweary tourists the mini-train from Munsterplatz is just the thing–April-October from 9.00 a.m. to evening, 14.70 FF.

POINTS OF INTEREST: As a rule, tourists usually wander through the extensive old town first, with its unusual facades through which flow people from every country. But modern Strasbourg is also worth seeing. It is the headquarters of the European Court of Human Rights, the European Science Bureau, and the European Youth Centre, and the European Parliament sits here (Avenue del'Europe). Only groups may see over it but individuals can join the tours, Europarat (Monday-Friday 9.00 a.m.-12 noon, 2.30-5.00 p.m.). Even if Parliament is sitting it is possible to visit, if you first phone 88/37 4574 or 77. Opposite is the large english garden, Orangerie, which was opened in 1837 and contains a pavilion. On the lake in the south-east is an old alsatian building and the Buerehiesel Restaurant (expensive–menus from A$36).

On the right a bit further on near the venerable, old Palais de l'Universite are the botanical gardens and the zoological museum, 29 Blvd. de la Victoire, Bus 7, Wednesday-Monday 2.00-6.00 p.m., gratis.

Adjoining is a modern residential suburb, mostly concrete. The old town is dominated by the Munster (cathedral), which is completely finished even though it has only one tower (142m, but you can only climb up to a platform at 66m, cost 5.50FF). The view is magnificent. The interior of the cathedral is bathed in a particularly beautiful light which falls from the rose window above the portal. The astronomical clock built in 1574 is also worth seeing. Admittance to the cathedral after 12.30 p.m. The Musee de l'Oeuvre, Notre Dame, 3 Place du Chateau (Wednesday-Monday 2.00-6.00 p.m., 3.50FF) is outstanding.

On the left of the square in front of the Munster is the Kammerzell building which has an exclusive restaurant. On the southern corner of the square is the largest department store, Magmod, which has parking and a cafeteria. Between the Munster and Kleber Squares is Gutenberg Square and then rue des Grands Arcades with tree lined walkways. If you just wander through these old town lanes you will be able to soak up the atmosphere. Don't miss out on La Petite France (little France)–well preserved old houses bordering the canal.

We can recommend a guesthouse on the Ill River a bit further on: A l'ancienne Douane, 6 rue de la Douane. La Petite France is framed by four defence towers which you can climb up to the viewing terrace 9.00 a.m.-midnight (33FF–go up one evening) and the covered bridges across the four arms of the River Ill which, together with the two main arms, the Ill and the Fosse du Faux Rempart circle the whole of the old town. If you have a bit of time then you should take a boat trip. Round trip cruises on the Ill and along the small canals go through the old town, La Petite France and the Europa Palast and leave from Chateau des Rohans (opposite the cathedral) from the middle of March to the beginning of November at 2.30 p.m. In the high season (April to September) there are extra trips and also evenings trips with commentary in french, english and german (13-15FF).

For those who are technically minded there are trips on the Rhine and to the Rhine harbour which go through the Strasbourg Lock and leave from the Promenade Dauphin (near the Centre Administratif Ville et Comm) from April to September, Wednesday, Saturday & Sunday 32-45 FF).

The area around Place Broglie and the Hotel de Ville (town hall) is more modern. Worth looking at are: the Banque de France building, where in April 1792 Rouget de l'Isle first performed the Marseillaise. The song was taken up by the warlike Peoples Army of the Rhine (from Marseille) and later became the French National Anthem.

A bit further on is Place de la Republique, formerly Kaiser Platz with relics of its time under prussian rule: The Alsatian-Lorraine Parliament House building and the Kaisers' Palace. Then walk along Av. de la Liberte to Quay Koch where people like to sit in summer.

The old town MUSEUMS offer an encompassing view of alsatian culture (Wednesday-Monday 2.00-6.00 p.m., from April-October also

10.00 a.m.-12 noon, 3.50 & 2 FF): The Chateau des Rohans, a copy of the Paris Town Hall built during Louis XIV's reign, contains the Museum of Fine Arts and Arts Decoratifs (Entry 5 FF) and the archeological museum. The Musee Alsacien, 23 Quai St. Nicolas, Pont du Corbeau and Galerie Alsacienne, 5 Pl. du Chateau; as well as the Musee Historique in the Grande Boucherie, Alsatian: Grosse Metzig, on the square of the same name where Strasbourg's war history is on display. Special offer: from June to the middle of September some of the museums stay open until 8.30 p.m. and offer conducted tours.

Another speciality in Strasbourg is the light & sound show in the evenings at the Munster (cathedral). Even though light & sound shows have become commonplace in Europe, this one is worth seeing because of its special effects–7FF.

CONCERTS: in July and August the Trachtenkapellen (brass bands dressed in national costumes) give concerts in La Petite France and on the Place du Marche aux Cochons de Lait auf (8.30 p.m.), in the Music Pavilion des Contades Parks Els. Music Vereine (music societies–June-September Thursday at 8.30 p.m.); in the Pavilion Josephine, Orangerie Park groups perform a wide variety of music (June-August, 8.30 p.m.). All of these concerts are free. As well as these folklore concerts are held in the courtyard of the Chateau des Rohan (June-August); Schifferstechen on the Ill (July-August, Monday & Friday 8.30 p.m.).

ENTERTAINMENT: For good food and a friendly atmosphere go to a Winstub (wine bar) or a Beerstub/Brasserie (tavern). They cater for different price ranges but most are expensive. A small sample: Vieux Chateaux, 10 rue de la Rapoe; London Tavern, 31 rue du Vieux Marche aux Vins; A la Bague, D'Or, 7 rue de L'Eglise; Armes de Strasbour, 9 Pl. Gutenberg; Wine Bars: Strissel, 5 Pl. de la Grande Boucherie; Au Pont St. Martin, 13 rue des Moulins; and if you are interested in seeing how beer is made: Meteor in Hochfelden (Wed. 2.30 p.m.) and Kronenbourg, 68 Route d'Oberhausbergen (Monday-Friday at 9.00, 10.00 a.m., 2.00 & 3.00 p.m.).

DISTRICT: We could give you thousands of tips but here are a few: A weekend in Alsace is always first class! The Route du Vin, (wine road) starts at Strasbourg and goes via Nolsheim, Obernai, Barr, and Chatenois. It's always wise to allow yourself plenty of time. The rebuilt Kaiser William II's Haute Konigsburg (castle) is worth seeing as it gives you some idea of how all the other ruins used to look (Selestat, Kintzheim).

ACCOMMODATION: Youth hostel, 9 rue de l'auberge des Jeunesse, Tel. 88/30 26 46, Bus 3/13/23; Foyer Notre Dame, Tel. 88/323 47 36; Foyer due Jeune Travailleur, 24 rue de Macon, Tel. 88/39 69 01.
Hotel: Le Colmar, 1 rue du Marie Kuss, Tel. 88/32 18 60; Trianon, 8 Petite rue de la Course, Tel. 32 63 97; Eden, 16 rue d'Obernai, Tel. 32 41 99.
Camping: Montagne Vert und Baggersee (Illkirch-Grafenstaden).

For car buffs: the Car Museum in Mulhouse, 192 Av. de Colmar, Tel. 89/42 29 17 and for railway buffs: the Railway Museum, Mulhouse Dornach, 2 rue Alfred de Glehn, Tel. 89/434420.

GREAT BRITAIN

Great Britain has a population of 55.83 million and an area of 244,046 sq. km., which includes the regions of England, Wales and Scotland as well as Northern Ireland.

The climate of the British Isles is plagued by cool winds and rain so always have something warm with you.

ENTRY/FOREIGN EXCHANGE/CUSTOMS REGULATIONS: A valid passport is required. Currency is not controlled.

Duty Free Allowance:
200 cigarettes or 250g tobacco and 1 litre of spirits and 2 litres of wine.

Currency/Exchange Rates: The currency (which was decimalized in 1971) is the English Pound Sterling.

1A$	=	£0.45
1C$	=	£0.50
1NZ$	=	£0.36
1US$	=	£0.68

England was inexpensive once but prices have risen in conjuction with inflation.

FOOD:
After the fish & chip shops, chinese restaurants, take away shops, the pubs are very good value. Many offer cheap counter lunches featuring typical english food.

The pubs are a friendly meeting place for all sorts of people. (Closing time is 11.00 p.m.). A cover charged is usual at Discos and one must be tidily dressed.

TELEPHONE:
It is possible to dial most countries direct. The area code is dialled without the 0.

Emergency Telephone Number: 999

EMBASSIES:

Australia:	Australia House, The Strand, London, Tel. 438-8000
Canada:	1 Grosvenor Square, London, W1X, Tel. 629-9492
N.Z.	N.Z. House, The Haymarket, London, Tel. 930-8422
U.S.A.	24 Grosvenor Square, London, W1, Tel. 4999 9000.

ACCOMMODATION:
Lists of hotels, camping grounds, bed & breakfast, brochures 'Young

Visitors' are available from the British Tourist Authority, 64 St. James St., London S.W. 1 A1NF.
Youth hostels (Y.H.A.) Trevelyan House, 8 St. Stephen's Hill, Albans, Herts. AL12DY.

SPEED LIMITS:

In built up areas 30 mph;
outside built up areas 55 mph; motorways 70 mph.

RAILWAYS:

It is cheaper to buy rail passes in your own country.
Special tip: preserved railway museum tracks are found all over England.

AIRPORTS:

There is a good service to all places in the British Isles from London, Heathrow and Gatwick airports.

BRIGHTON

A famous charming coastal town. Its pubs and stony beach have fallen out of favour with the International Set. In spite of this, its proximity to London and to the Continent, affords you an opportunity to experience life at an English coastal resort.

BY RAIL: Brighton central station is a terminal railway station which is almost in the city centre. It offers services in all directions and a left luggage room (£1.50 per piece). The inter-city trains leave from London's Victoria Station for Brighton. It is less complicated when you come from the Continent to Dover or Folkestone to catch the Boat Train than to try to go along the coast via Ashford, Hastings, Eastbourne, Tel. 0273/25476.

BY CAR: From Dover/Folkestone take the A 259 which closely follows the coastline, north of Eastbourne change over to the A27, which is a more pleasant route and goes through Eastbourne, Seaford and Newhaven. Several parking areas are found in Trafalgar Street east of the railway station.

BY AIR: The nearest airport to Brighton is Gatwick which is on the main railway line between London and Brighton. From Heathrow you have to take the Underground to Victoria Station from where there is a train every hour to Brighton. Gatwick, 0293/31299, Heathrow 01/759 4321.

TOURIST INFORMATION: 54 Old Steine, Tel. 0273/23755. South West Branch, Cheviot House, 4 Monson Road, Tunbridge Wells, Tel. 0892/40766.

POINTS OF INTEREST: From the railway station walk down Queens Road to the clock tower and you are in the centre of town. On your right is the pedestrian zone, Western Road, which is also the shopping centre. On your left are North Street, and Old Steine/Grand Parade, a boulevard with a grassed area in the centre. In between are the small lanes, the very charming old part of Brighton with its winding streets. All streets lead to the sea.

Worth seeing is the Royal Pavilion in Old Steine St., a palace belonging to the royal family, which was built in a pseudo-Indian style and looks like Disneyland (daily 10.00 a.m.-5.00 p.m.). Before you head for the beach, perhaps you'd like to look at a museum: the Brighton Art Gallery & Museum, an illustrious varied collection (Church Street, Tuesday-Saturday 10.00 a.m.-5.45 p.m., Sunday 2.00-5.00 p.m., gratis). When it's too cool to swim, just wander around the attractions at the beach. There are two long piers built in the victorian era which are amusement arcades. A fire broke out on the western pier during the shooting of the WHO's rock opera, Tommy, and it has been closed ever since. The Palace Pier which is 500m long is good to walk along but it has third class amusements: ghost train, video games and the National Coin Operated Machine Museum. Race meetings are held at the Manor Hill racetrack. Tel. 451597.

If there were no amusement parks on the beach in England, something would be lacking and the amusement halls under the promenade and Peter Pan's Fairground cater for this necessity. Don't forget to see England's first electrical railway, the People's Seafront Railway which follows the coastline. It is better to swim at Prince Regents Swimming Pool, Church Street, than in the sea, or in the newly opened King Alfred Leisure Centre with its exotic plants and many forms of relaxation (Kingsway).

Brighton and the sea, a connection which is particularly noticeable at the Aquarium, Madeira Drive, in the underground galleries built in neo-gothic style and its dolphinarium. Another English speciality: Greyhound racing at the Greyhound Stadium (April to October, Tuesday, Thursday and Saturday).

When taking a tour around Brighton and the neighbouring Hove you get the impression that the streets are laid out like a chess board. Here are countless secondhand and fast food shops. You could get lost in the small lanes of old Brighton. In 1978 the second WHO Film, Quadrophenia, was shot in these lanes and on the sea front. It recreated the dramatic gang wars.

Built in the very latest style: Churchill Square and the Brighton Centre. Take a ride on the Peoples Railway and see the largest yacht harbour of Europe, Brighton Marina, with racing on summer weekends.

If you want to take a quiet walk away from the sea then go to Preston Manor Park with its famous manor house (open Wednesday-Sunday Bus No. 5, 5a). The Technical Museum of British Engineering, Nevill Road, Hove is open daily from 10.00 a.m.-5.00 p.m. Other museums: the Booth Museum of Natural History, Dyke Road (Friday-Wednesday 10.00 a.m.-5.00 p.m.), Hove Museum and Art Gallery, New Church Road (Tuesday-Saturday 10.00 a.m.-5.00 p.m.).

Another worthwhile walk is to Rottingdean Village to the east where there are bizarre cliffs (6 km.).

ENTERTAINMENT: Discos: Busbys, Kingswest, Kings Board; The Cavern, Ship St; Hungry Years, 8 Marine Parade; New Wave, although a little exclusive: Pink Coconut, West St.; Subterfuge, basement of Apollo Hotel; Pubs with music: Abinger, 142 Kings Road; Folk Music: Dorset Arms, North Road; Country Music: Devil's Dyke, Mixed Music: Electric Grape, Queens Road and Royal Escape, 10 Marine Parade; also The Kensington, Kensington Gardens; Rock'n'Roll: Lewes Road Inn, Lewes Road; Folk music: Marlborough, Princes Street; Open until midnight: Northern, York Place, Piano Bar; St. Aubyn's, 22 Victoria Terrace, Hove.

The Zap Club, Lower Promenade is a culture centre in every sense of the word. A Theatre Restaurant is the Nightingale in Surrey Street.

FESTIVALS: The Brighton Festival is held in May and offers varied cultural programmes; a Carnival is held in July and a Veteran Car Rally in November. A good market is held on Saturday mornings in Upper Gardener Street.

IN THE DISTRICT: The South Downlands, hilly coastal land, are of particular interest. On the local railway line, in an easterly direction lies: Lewes with its castle and former abbey; the Michelham Priory near Polegate, with its old Mill and Gardens, and don't forget the Battle Abbey where the Battle of Hastings took place in 1066. (While in Battle go into the coffee shop Pilgrim's Place). Another place you can reach from Brighton by bus, is Stanmer, a village in the chalk hills where time has stood still for hundreds of years. From Brighton catch the train to Worthing, Littlehampton, then change at the first station to the northern line to Arundel with its Wildfowl Trust, an enormous Wildfowl National Park with places where you can go to watch the birds (9.30 a.m.-5.30 p.m.) a magnificent castle and near Littlehampton, somewhat better sandy beaches.

KENT AND EAST SUSSEX RAILWAY: For those who love railways and who can't wait: the Dover/Folkestone/London stretch from Ashford railway station (Bus 400). It is a railway with a great tradition. Unfortunately it has now been shortened to 4 miles. They have steam locomotives and countless industrial locos which run through pastoral land to Wittersham Road station. From there you can walk a little further into the Marshland, where there is a small castle. You can also get to there from Rye, a beautiful smugglers' nest (Steam 1435mm, 6.4km) Tel. 05806/2943-open weekends all year round, and Wednesday and Thursday as well from June to August. Tourist information: Tenterden Town Hall Tel. 3572; Rye Station Approach, Tel 2293; Pension Tenterden; William Caxton Inn, West Cross, Tel. 3142, Accommodation: University of Kent, Canterbury, Cornwallis Building, Tel. 6 6822; Youth Hostel Association, Canterbury, New Dover Road, Tel. 6 2911.

BLUEBELL RAILWAY: A lot of movies have been shot here and today it has the most extensive railway collection in the south.

The line goes also through the green High Downlands and has a great collection in the Locomotive Depot and in the Museum (Steam 1435mm, 8 km). Open at weekends all year and daily during June to September. Tel. 082 572/2370.

ACCOMMODATION: Youth Hostel, Patcham Place, Tel. 556196. Bus 5A; Pension Alpine, Bedford Square 26, Tel. 73 28 70. Aquarium Guest House, Madeira Place 13, Tel. 60 57 61. Other cheap places are found at Madeira Place, Bedford Square and Montpellier Street; Camping: Sheepcote Valley, Tel. 60 55 92.

EDINBURGH–GLASGOW

Where you would expect only green Highlands and rough coastlines north of the border between England and Scotland, a town unfolds quite unexpectedly, Edinburgh. It is a town which offers both a rich historical past and a modern international city scene. (Pop. 419,000)

BY RAIL: Scotland is connected by two branch lines to the British Rail Inter-City network: the eastern one starts at Kings Cross and goes via York and Darlington (where the first steam train railway line started) to Edinburgh (just under 5 hours with the Inter City 125); the western one is the electric train from Euston Station via Lancaster to Glasgow. As well as these there are fast trains and night trains, the latter with comfortable sleepers (cheaper than on the Continent). In Edinburgh the main railway station is Waverley Station, Tel. 031/556 2451, which lies in a small valley in the middle of the City; Glasgow also has a central station and diagonally opposite it is Queen Street railway station where the trains leave for the north.

Queen Street and Waverley Stations are the starting off points for the two main lines and some branch lines which go into the unique Scottish countryside. Both have take-away shops, luggage rooms, information office and Waverley Station also has showers.

BY CAR: You can get to Scotland by taking the M1 from London, Edgeware Road, west of Marylebone to Northampton, then the M6, from Birmingham to Carlisle, then the A74 towards Glasgow. Before you get to Glasgow change to the M74, and then the M8 between Glasgow and Edinburgh. A central parking station in Edinburgh is found in Castle Terrace, directly below the castle or before that in the western approach road and also in Lothian Road.

BY AIR: You can fly by the Shuttle to Edinburgh and Glasgow from London. From Edinburgh Airport (Tel. 031/333 2167) on the western side there is a bus service to Waverley Bridge railway station. There is also a tourist information office there. The same goes for Glasgow Airport (Tel. 041/887 1111), which has a bus connection to central railway and the main bus station.

EDINBURGH

TOURIST INFORMATION: Office is situated at 3 Princes Street, Tel. 031/225 2424: For Scotland: 233 Ravelston Terrace, Tel. 332 24 33.

LOCAL TRANSPORT: Edinburgh is serviced by buses. Recommended: the Freedom Ticket, 24 hours/£1.25 or the Tourist Card with map of the town, reduced prices for museum entry and cheap overland bus prices; for night owls: 5 bus lines operate until 2.15 a.m.

TOURIST NEWSPAPERS: What's on in Edinburgh; Newspapers: The Scotsman and The Evening News.

POINTS OF INTEREST: There are three sections of the town which are worth seeing during a tour of the city which has been the Scottish capital since 1437. The Castle, and in front, the old town and to the north, the 'new' town (built during the 18th century). All three areas are easily reached from Central station. You can either go across Waverley/Cockburn Street or across North Bridge south of The High Street intersection and you will be in the centre of the old part of Edinburgh, the Royal Mile.

The Tron Kirk, on the square where formerly an official weighing machine stood. Some more buildings: The royal palace of Holyrood at the eastern end of the Royal Mile, where even to-day, the Queen stays when visiting Edinburgh. The former abbey was also the seat of the scottish kings. There are 111 portraits in the picture gallery among them one of Mary Stuart (open daily from 9.30 a.m.-5.17 p.m. cost £1.30). On the right is the restored White Horse Close, former post coach station, on the left the Museum of Childhood, an unusual museum

(Monday-Saturday 10.00 a.m.-6.00 p.m.); John Knox's House-founder of the Presbyterian Church-kept in its original state (Monday-Saturday 10.00 a.m.-6.00 p.m.); On the square are: St. Giles' cathedral built in gothic style which has a very colourful history; the city chambers which are still to-day home of the local Parliament and the government offices (Tuesday-Friday 10.00 a.m.-3.00 p.m., gratis); in Lady Stair's House, Lawnmarket, there is a collection of mementoes of the three famous personalities of Scottish literature, Robert Burns, Sir Walter Scott and R.L. Stevenson (Monday-Saturday 10.00 a.m.-5.00 p.m., gratis). Opposite Riddle's Court and Brodie's Close, is the home of the spiritual leader and town councillor, Brodie, who was convicted of robbery and was sentenced to death on one of his own inventions, the gallows in 1788. Brodie was the basis for Stevenson's Dr. Jekyll and Mr. Hyde; finally the lookout tower. Now we come to the Esplanade and the Castle. What makes the Royal Mile a typical old town are the Closes, small streets which run behind the houses and lead to inner courtyards. The castle is built on top of an extinct volcano, has been the royal residence since the 11th century, and offers a fantastic view. You can view the rooms, the scottish crown jewels, and the weapon collection daily (9.30 a.m.-5.00 p.m., £1.30).

Still in the old part of town south of the castle is the Lawnmarket, which has several interesting facades which have been restored. It was the square where formerly executions were carried out. Try the nearby pub the Black Bull.

The 'new' part of town is to the north bounded by Princes, George and Queen Streets. From the railway station go behind the Scott Memorial (287 stairs up to the viewing tower). This 'new' part of town was the result of an architect's competition and is very impressive because of its lines. Edinburgh has a lot of round and crescent shaped streets even in the newer suburbs; For further information: New Town information centre, 13a Dundas Street (Monday-Friday 9.00 a.m.-1.00 p.m. and 2.00-5.00 p.m.).

IMPORTANT MUSEUMS: The new Edinburgh Wax Museum, 142 High Street (daily 10.00 a.m.-5.00 p.m.); Huntly House for local stories, Cannongate (Monday-Saturday 10.00 a.m.-5.00 p.m.); the Scottish National Gallery of Modern Art, Belford Road (Monday-Saturday 10.00 a.m.-5.00 p.m.); City Art Centre, 1-4 Market Street, (Monday-Saturday 10.00 a.m.-5.00 p.m.) and the National Gallery of Scotland Mound (daily 10.00 a.m.-5.00 p.m.); Museals Action Centre, Brass Rubbing Centre, 163 Cannongate; Royal Observatory Visitors Centre, Blackford Hill (Monday-Friday 10.00 a.m.-4.00 p.m., Saturday and Sunday 12 noon-5.00 p.m.) It has the largest telescope in Scotland. Near the observatory on Calton Hill is 'Edinburgh's Folly' a replica of the Parthenon in Athens which remains unfinished. What Scotland was like then is shown in a multi-media-show at the Scottish Centre (only Saturday 10.00 a.m.-4.00 p.m., £1.30).

PARKS: Since 1583 the university and spiritual centre of learning has retained its genuine uniformity because of the parks and the open spaces, e.g. the Royal Botanical Gardens, Inverleith Road, to the north of the 'new' town. The gardens have palm trees and an Alpine House (gratis). The National Zoo in Corstorphine Road, is famous for its penguin colony (daily from 9.00 a.m.-6.00 p.m.). Swimming pools: Royal Commonwealth Swimming Pool & Sauna, Dalkeith Road (Monday-Friday 9.00 a.m.-9.00 p.m., Saturday and Sunday 10.00 a.m.-4.00 p.m.).

CONCERTS AND FESTIVALS: from June to September mainly in the Princes Street Gardens; larger concerts are held in Usher Hall; the biggest festival is held in August with indigenous and international music and theatre groups, as well as avant garde cinema; in April there is a Folk festival.

ENTERTAINMENT: The pubs provide good entertainment and there are a great number of these. A few: Old style: Abbotsford, 3 Rose St.; Guildford Arms, 1 West Reg. Pl; Trad. music: Marine Bar, 57 Bath St.; Young & exclusive: Antiquary, 72 St. Stephen St.; Young and touristy: Yellow Carvel, 6 Hunter Square; Athletics Arms, 1 Angle Park Terrace, one drinks McEwan's 80/- here, the best scottish beer; For students-good food: Bailie, 2 St. Stephen St.; Bay Horse, 63 Henderson St; Traditional: Bennet's Bar, 8 Leven St; Culture & cinema: Carlton Studios, 24 Carlton Road; Seamen: Captain's Bar, 4 South College St.; Central Bar, formerly a railway station, 7 Leith Walk; For summer evenings: Cramond Inn, Cramond; Homo-Bar: Kenilworth, 152 Roise St; Eccentric: Oxford Bar, 8 Young St.,; New wave: Refreshers, 112 Hanover St; Political: Forrest Hill, 25 Forrest Road; Waverley Bar, 3 St. Mary St., Folk; Roller disco: 3 West Tollcross; More discos: Valentino's 3a East Fountain Bridge; Bobby McGees 96a Rose St. lane north; Jack Kane Centre Community Wing.

ACCOMMODATION: Youth hostel: 7 Bruntsfield Crescent, Tel. 031/447 2994; 18 Eglinton Crescent, Tel. 031/337 1120; YWCA Hostels, 2 Randolph Crescent, Tel. 226 3842; 41 Lothian Road, Tel. 229 4850; plenty of bed & breakfast accommodation-bookings through the tourist information office.

GLASGOW

Scotland's largest town. In the international tourist trade it is often put at the top of the list of Scottish towns. This is probably due to the fact that many peope from here migrated to America or Australia. Also many Irish guest workers came to Glasgow looking for work because of the numerous industries. Glasgow is in parts unusual because it is an Irish-Scottish melting pot. (Pop. 762,000).

TOURIST INFORMATION & BED & BREAKFAST BOOKINGS:
35 St. Vincent Place, Tel. 041/227 4880.

Attractions in short: the Town Hall on the main square, George Square; St. Mungo's Cathedral with its large cemetery, Wishart St; The Art Gallery & Museum (daily 10.00 a.m.-5.00 p.m., gratis); Kelvin Grove Park; just as beautiful as the Burrell Collection (daily 10.00 a.m.-5.00 p.m.); in Pollock Country Park you can see genuine Highland cattle; The People's Palace, Glasgow Green, (a park, daily 10.00 a.m.-5.00 p.m., gratis); a Victorian house: Hutchesons Hall, 158 Ingram St, Tel. 552 8391 (depending upon numbers); Technical: Museum of Transport, 25 Albert Drive; don't miss out on: The Barras, the whirling city and market life around Gallows Gate (catch a bus with 'We stop at Barras' sign on it, via G-gate), and London Road where Mercat Cross is.

LOCAL TRANSPORT: Buses and underground railway which curiously doesn't run on Sundays. Brochures with 8 round trips obtainable from Underground stations. Many beautiful parks: Victoria Park with its fossils, Victoria Park Drive North and Queens Park, Victoria Road,; Disco Tips: Henry Afrikas, 15 York St.; Viva, 15 Union St; Warehouse, 75 Dunlop St; and a lot in Sauchie Hall Street.

YOUTH HOSTEL: 11 Woodlands Terrace, Tel. 041/332 3004.

LONDON

London is a melting pot of all races and classes. It is divided very nicely into districts with the city of London having a population of only 5,893, whereas Greater London has an actual population of approx 13 million.

BY RAIL: London has 8 large railway stations. The most important is Victoria station, where the boat trains arrive from and depart for Dover/Folkestone and Brighton. There are no luggage lockers there but it has a luggage room on the left of the main platform.

There is a train and ferry information office at Victoria Station and a quiet tourist bureau at the left exit, which gives out a little information about London and the British Isles. You can get better information from the bookshop but you have to pay for it. Tel. 01/730 3488; What's On, Tel. 01/246 8045.

From Waterloo, which has the largest number of tracks, trains leave for Southampton and Cornwall, but you can also go to Cornwall from

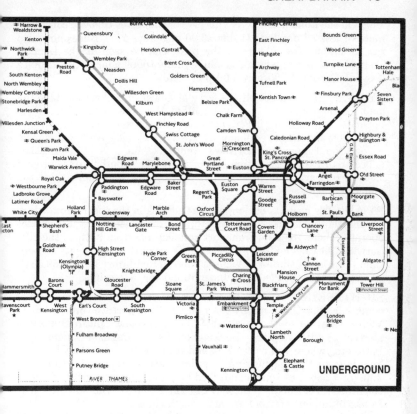

Paddington as well as to Wales, Birmingham, also in the west, whereas Euston, St. Pancras and Kings Cross which lie close to each other in the north, service the eastern, middle and western parts of England and also Scotland.

All railway stations are connected to underground stations of the same name. The locals call the underground, the tube. Also don't worry about it being the oldest underground railway in the world, it has been modernised. What the future, after 1990, will bring, is being developed by BREL, the locomotive consortium. At the railway stations you will also find London Transport Information Offices (Tel. 222 1234). In London you don't only use the underground as there are also very chic, red double decker buses (green in the outer suburbs). Fares have become more expensive: prices vary according to distance–but you won't pay less than 50p. You will find the prices and a map of the routes on the automatic ticket vending machines. The prices have now been frozen for three years. The underground lines all have names and a particular colour. One can go round in a circle on the London Circle Line all day long. On the London Explorer Bus (6V) or the Rover Bus you can travel more or less all day long (1 day £3.90 or 3 days £11). Buses now also run at night. How it was in the past, can be seen at the London Transport Museum where you can actually touch a lot of the exhibits (Covent Garden 10.00 a.m.-5.00 p.m., daily).

BY CAR: After you get off the ferry at Dover or Folkestone, take the main road and motorway A20/M20 Ashford, Maidstone to London. Driving in London is like driving in Paris because of the narrow streets, a lot of one-way streets and the large volume of traffic. Some good advice: Automobile Association, Fanum House, 5 New Coventry St., W.C.2, Tel. 01/9547373. It is better to park & ride from one of the outer suburban underground stations or leave the car at your hotel. Anyhow, you cannot beat the underground for speed.

BY AIR: The airports of London are Gatwick in the south, from where the charter flights operate and Heathrow, from where the regular airlines operate. There are good transport connections from both to the city. Gatwick: Tel. Crawley 0293/31299. From Gatwick there are plenty of trains from the Airport station to Victoria station; Heathrow: Tel. 01/759 4321. From there take the Piccadilly underground line to the city.

SIGHTSEEING TOURS by bus are offered by a great number of companies but those run by the London Transport Co., on the left at Victoria station are the cheapest (£3.50). The yellow Culture Bus which stops at 18 different places (Buckingham Palace, Trafalgar Square, Hyde Park, etc.) where you can get on and off as you please the whole day long is even cheaper making it an interesting proposition–from 9.00 a.m. for £2.50. The tours conducted by archaeologists commencing at the Museum of London, (Tuesday-Sunday 2.30 p.m., Thursday 7.30 p.m. from Monument station) are also worthwhile.

   The cheapest form of transport here like elsewhere, is the bicycle. In the narrow steets it's not too dangerous (from £3.60 for the day including insurance). Dial a Bike, 18 Gillingham St., Tel. 828 4040, close to Victoria Station–go down Wilton Road which is on the right. Taxis are also reasonable if there are four people.

TOURIST NEWSPAPERS: There's the famous 'What's On' and 'Time Out'. Also the 'City Limits' which contains everything from cultural reviews to the T.V. programmes, gratis. Also Nicholson's London Guide.

TOURIST INFORMATION: London Experience, Multi-media, Piccadilly, Trocadero Centre, Tel. 439 4938.

POINTS OF INTEREST: In London there is always something exciting happening. The centre of the city action is Soho and a little to the east, Leicester Square which has now been closed to traffic. Here you will find people from all over the world. Good cinemas are also found on Leicester Square (Odeon and Leicester Square Theatre). A cinema with a lot of atmosphere is the Classic, Tottenham Court Road.

Places further out are: Hyde Park with it's famous Speaker's Corner (U-station Marble Arch), Trafalgar Square with Nelson's Column, the National Gallery (10.00 a.m.-6.00 p.m. daily, gratis) and Admiralty Arch, as well as Kensington Market and Kensington Gardens in Kensington High Street. This is also where you meet the music people. There are not only punks, hippies and mods, but also mohicans, teddy boys, skinheads and others. Trends don't arrive here, they originate here. And something else: the young people of London don't just follow the last fashion trend, some of them are real Punks who live in condemned buildings.

From Kensington Markets, towards the city, is Hyde Park and on the right is Albert Hall, famous for its big concerts, which you can't miss. A bit further along is the Victoria & Albert Museum, Cromwell Road (U-station Kensington). English and Far East collections are displayed there.

If you still feel energetic you can walk to Green Park (Constitution Hill) and Buckingham Palace. Even further along The Mall is Admiralty Arch and on the right is Whitehall, where Parliament and No. 10 Downing Street are situated. The Changing of the Guard on foot takes place daily at 11.30 a.m., mounted from Whitehall Monday-Saturday 11.00 a.m., Sunday at noon. From here go across Westminster Bridge which spans the Thames to the Houses of Parliament and Westminster Abbey (both are open daily except on official occasions). In Central Hall opposite, are some of the crown jewels which were collected from all over the world (Monday-Saturday 10.00 a.m.-6.00 p.m. £1.60). A little further along the river bank is the Tate Gallery (daily, gratis, first class). Also important to traditional tourists, St. Paul's Cathedral where Lady Di and Prince Charles were married (U-station St. Pauls). If you walk along Cannon Street from there you come to a monument, built in memory of the Great Fire of London which started in a bakery in the 17th century. From there it is only a bit further to the Tower of London and the Tower Bridge (9.30 a.m.-5.00 p.m. daily-more expensive after 2 p.m.-once again some of the crown jewels). Opposite the bridge on the same side of the river is St. Catherine by the Tower, an old dock area with a few attractions, opposite H.M.S. Belfast, a 2nd world war cruiser which is now a museum (11.00 a.m.-6.00 p.m., daily).

Definitely a must: The British Museum, Russell St (U-station Russell Square); Museum of London, London Wall (U-station St. Pauls, Tuesday-Saturday 10.00 a.m.-6.00 p.m., gratis); Imperial War Museum, Lambeth Road (U-station Elephant & Castle, daily 10.00 a.m.-6.00 p.m., gratis). For more information ask at the Heritage Office.

The National Maritime Museum, Romney Road (B.R. Line West to Maze Hill, Tuesday-Sunday 10.00 a.m.-6.00 p.m.); the Royal Mews, containing royal coaches, Buckingham Palace Road (Victoria Station,

Wednesday & Thursday 2.00-4.00 p.m.); National History Museum, Cromwell Road, (South Kensington Station, daily 10.00 a.m.-6.00 p.m.) for everything about flora, fauna and ecology; like Paris, London also has a Museum of Mankind, Burlington Garden (Piccadilly Circus station, Monday-Sunday 10.00 a.m.-6.00 p.m.); something modern: Laserium, a one hour laser show, at the Planetarium, Marylebone Road (Baker St. Station, Evenings Tel. 486 1131).

CONCERTS: Hammersmith's Palace, Electric Ballroom, 184 Camden High St. Camden Town station; All Nation's Club, 4 Martello Road, or the Odeon in Shepherd's Bush Road (Hammersmith station). A good rock club is the Marquee, 90 Wardour St. (Piccadilly Circus station). For younger people: Six Bells, 195 Kings Road (South Kensington station), for English Folk fans: Islington Folk Club, 362 St. John St. (Kings Cross station) and irish folk bands at Two Brewers, 147 East Hill. You have to pay a cover charge at most places of approx. £3.50. For theatre bookings contact London Theatre Bookings, 42 Cranbourne St., Leicester Square, Tel. 4 39 33 71. The Society of West End Theatre sells stand-by-tickets — all tickets that haven't been sold by the day of the performance are sold at half-price also at Leicester Square.

PUBS: There are thousands of pubs in London and different areas cater for different types of people (for snobs in the west, for down to earth people in the east near the tower and south of the Thames for the genuine Cockneys, who speak their own dialect). In the pubs everyone mixes, young and old alike and you will always find someone to talk to. Some good pubs: Punch & Judy, opposite the opera house (Covent Garden station), also Tuttons and Placido Domino. Famous: Sherlock Holmes, Northumberland St., (Baker St. station). A popular place: Sound & Vision, Dean St. (Leicester Square station).

There is also a lot happening at Covent Garden (buskers & jubilee markets). Something similar is also found at Camden, Umfeld Euston/St.Pancras Railway stations; Camden Lock Markets (Camden Town station–Saturday & Sunday), the Camden Centre, Bidborough St. is a culture centre (St. Pancras station) and the Camden Plaza Cinema, 211 Camden High Street. The Palace, 1a Camden Road and also the Camden Unemployment Action Centre, 102 St. Pancras Way, run by the government.

More Interesting Clubs: Bananas, 201 Wardour St. (Oxford Circus station); for a good student evening: Le Beat Route, 17 Piccadilly (Piccadilly Circus station); Spats, 3 Oxford St. (Tottenham Court Rd. station).

MARKETS: Portobello Road (Notting Hill Gate station, Monday-Saturday 9.00 a.m.-5.00 p.m.) and Silver Vaults (Chancery Lane station, Monday-Saturday 9.00 a.m-5.30 p.m.) Petticoat Lane, Middlesex St. (Liverpool St. station, Sunday 9.00 a.m.-2.00 p.m.); Spitalfields, Commercial St. (Liverpool St. station, Monday-Saturday from 4.30 a.m.).

A MUST: Madame Tussaud's Wax Works (Baker St. station). Very expensive but absolutely crammed full. Something more natural, with statues of simpler people: London Dungeon, Tooley St (London Bridge station), 28 Tooley St. 10.00 a.m.-5.45 p.m.

For those who are genuinely interested in TECHNICAL THINGS: the Greater London Council Thames Flood Barriers which prevent the town flooding. (By train: Charing Cross to Carlton station).

PARKS: If, after you have seen Hyde Park and Green Park, you still want to see some more parks, then visit Kew Gardens, the Royal Botanical Gardens at Kew Rd., Kew. They are really beautiful. Or Hampstead Heath (North London Underground Line) the largest of the parks. Regent's Park contains the famous London Zoo, open daily 9.00 a.m. to dusk.

FOOD: There is no problem about food in London: as well as snack bars and fish'n chip shops there are the pubs (they have set hours for lunch) which serve counter lunches. Around Soho are a lot of chinese restaurants and take-aways. You can always buy something and eat it in a park, but you aren't allowed to sleep in parks as they are locked at night and closely watched.

ACCOMMODATION: At Victoria station there is always at lot of cheap accommodation offered by youth hotels. Most of them have their own bar and 'wild life' (e.g. Cafe Street Hostel, 76 Cafe Street, Tel. 352 7045, 20 minutes by foot from Victoria Station).
Youth Hostels: 5 altogether: 36 Cater Lane, Tel. 236 49 65; Holland Walk, Tel. 93 70 748, if they are full they will send you on to another one. The tourist information office also handles accommodation. You will find lots of bed & breakfast places close to the railway stations around Earls Court (Price £5-£9 is usual).

GREECE

Greece has an area of 191,944 sq.km. and a population of 9.7 million. It is characterised by its mediterranean climate and it has a very individual culture.

To-day, Greece is once again a democracy.

Geographically, Greece is divided into its mainland part which is a part of the Balkan Peninsular, the southerly Peloponnes Peninsular and the over 1400 islands in the Ionian and Aegean seas. In the Aegean Sea are the islands of Kykladen, Sporaden and Dodekanes, as well as many isolated islands such as Crete, Samos and Lesbos.

The almost endless 15,000 km long greek coastline, the hot mediterranean climate which is tempered in summer by the mild meltei wind, long mountain ranges, and last but not least the friendliness of the people are all things which attract a great number of tourists all year round.

ENTRY/FOREIGN EXCHANGE/CUSTOMS REGULATIONS: A valid passport is required. Only 3,000 Drachmas may be brought into or taken out of the country.

Duty Free Allowance:
200 cigarettes or 250 gms of tobacco, 1 litres of spirits, 2 litres of wine and 500 gms of coffee.

Currency/Exchange Rate: The currency of the land is the Drachma.

1A$	=	90dr
1C$	=	100dr
1NZ$	=	72dr
£1	=	200dr
1US$	=	135dr

The exchange rates are still quite favourable in spite of price increases due to the influx of tourists.

TELEPHONE:

It is possible to dial countries direct from orange telephone boxes. Local area codes must then be dialled without the 0.

Tourist/Police/Emergency Number: 171100

EMBASSIES:

Australia: 15 Messogheion Avenue, Athens, Tel. 3504611.
Canada: 4 Ioannou Gennadiou St., Athens, Tel. 7239511.
N.Z.:   An.Tsoha 15-17, Ambelokipi 115-21, Athens, Tel. 6410311

U.K.:   1 Plutarchou, Athens, Tel. 7236211.
U.S.A.:   91 Vasilias Sofias, Athens, Tel. 7212951.

SHOPPING HINTS:

Jewellery, pullovers, ceramics and sometimes leather goods.

ACCOMMODATION:

Hotels: 6 Aristidou St., Athens, Tel. 323-6962 or 323-7193;
Camping: NTOG, 2 Amerilos St., Tel 322-3111;
Youth hostel: OXNE, 4 Dragastsaniou St., Tel. 323-4107

SPEED LIMIT:

50 km/h in built up areas;
80 km/h outside built up areas; 100 km/h on the motorways.
   Toll is payable on the motorways but it is inexpensive.
   Green insurance card is mandatory.

RAILWAYS:

Inexpensive tariffs.
   There is a tourist card available for 10/20/30 days for 75/121/165
Drs.–even cheaper for groups of up to 5 people.
   The railway network in Greece is not very dense but there is quite
a good bus service.

AIRPORTS:

Athens has an international airport which has connections to 26 internal
airports.

ATHENS

Athens is an agglomeration, with a boiling kettle environment day and
night. Some claim it is a concrete jungle, but the 3.4 million inhabitants
of Athens spend a lot of time outdoors.

BY CAR AND RAIL: Basically, they are much the same; either down
through Italy and then by ferry or through the Balkan States. Both
stretches are difficult and very costly (with the exception of the Inter-
Rail-Ticket or Transalpino). The Italian route is perhaps more
comfortable and easier (modern trains, and motorways) to Brindisi/Bari
(Cost of Ferry approx 300 DM, passenger tariff approx. 140 DM.
Reduction for Students). It is cheaper to take your car only to
Igoumenitsa and from there drive through beautiful north western
Greece. The routes through the Balkans are the express train (Hellas

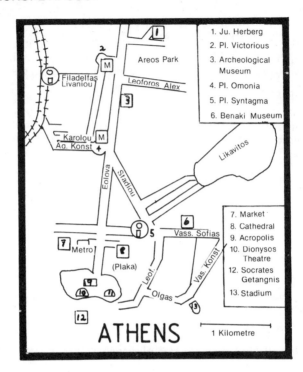

Legend (on map):
1. Ju. Herberg
2. Pl. Victorious
3. Archeological Museum
4. Pl. Omonia
5. Pl. Syntagma
6. Benaki Museum
7. Market
8. Cathedral
9. Acropolis
10. Dionysos Theatre
12. Socrates Getangnis
13. Stadium

ATHENS

1 Kilometre

from Dortmund, Athens from Munich). Because the trip takes almost two days a sleeper, or at least a reclining seat, is recommended. By car the route is over the bumpy E5: in Austria you have to pay a toll; in Yugoslavia it is badly constructed and very crowded. If you come by train you will arrive at the Larissa Railway station, which has the smallest number of platforms that any town ever called a railway station. Tel. 522 2491. It is joined to the Peloponnes small gauge railway station by an overhead bridge and this is where the trains arrive from Patras, the end station of the Italian trip.

BY AIR: The international terminal is the East Terminal of the Airport. Bus Nos. 18/21. Tel.975 6811; Domestic flights leave from the West Terminal–Bus Nos. 133/121.

LOCAL TRANSPORT: Taxis cost 20 Drs. Flagfall and 17/km in the City Zone. There is an extra charge of 20 Drs. from the railway station! Agree on a price before you get in if the meter isn't working. Between Midnight and 4.00 a.m. double tariff applies. After telling you all that, taxis really are the optimal way of getting around! You can also catch a bus from the railway station (20Drs.) to the city centre, Omonia Square, Syntagma Square, or the Plaka which is the old town. It is really important to get a map and timetable from the Bus Office as there are so many routes (Karageorgi Servias str. 2, Syntagma Square, Tel. 3 22 25 45). Metro: There is only one line, Kifissa-Piraeus and it is quite a hike from the railway station to Viktorias Square to get to it. The trains are rather out of date, note the wooden carriages. They are in the process of being replaced by new ones which should improve matters. The second stop on the single line is already Monastiraki, the centre of the old town where the daily, rather professional Flea Market is held. The side streets of the very old town are more interesting even though the whole of the old town is turning into a tourist centre (Taverns are expensive).

TOURIST INFORMATION available from the Tourist Police at the Larissa railway station, main hall on the left, and in the city centre in the National Bank on Syntagma Square. Tel. 32 22 5445.

TOURIST NEWSPAPERS: 'The Week in Athens', 'Athens News' and '80 Days Greece' are simple but informative papers for tourists containing the week's programme.

TOURS: You can get to know some of the town in a short time by taking a tour of the city-half day tours leave at 9.00 a.m. and include the National Museum-cost approx. 1400 Drs. run by Citam, Ermou 14 (Syntagma Square) and even cheaper still, 1250 Drs. from Stadiou str. 4.

POINTS OF INTEREST: Let us visit the old town, Plaka. Its flea market and main street, Ivestou (metro Monastiraki on the left) are very commercialized. As is the parallel shopping street, Ermou, between Syntagma (Constitution Square) and the Kerameikos Cemetery. On the western side of Syntagma Square is the former kings palace which is now the Parliament House. The Kerameikos cemetery has a museum (Wednesday-Monday 8.45 a.m.-3 p.m.). Athinas str., which runs at right angles to it, leads to Omonia Square which is pretty because it is a mixture of traditional and european Athens.

You can safely go into the side streets of the Plaka where there are rather expansive pavements; Kydathineon with it's cellar taverns, Lissiou with it's covered terrace taverns and narrow lanes or Tripodon street in the Anafiora Quarter (the traditional Bouzouki pubs are enjoyable). In the evenings everyone in the world seems to gather in the Plaka.

The ancient ruins and the extensive but almost as busy grounds should be visited early in the day. (The National Gardens, and behind them the Syntagma and Likavitos hills-good views-a funicular runs from Ploutarhou/Doras Distria). There is still quite an atmosphere here even though a lot has been removed by souvenir hunters, and what is left has been ruined by time, and smog.

The Acropolis is literally still the crowning glory of Athens. It is a landmark. It was built in the 5th centry A.D. The Parthenon Temple dedicated to the goddess Athena (upper half of the Plaka, entry on the western side) was reduced to ruins in 1647. The second temple is the Erechtheum where figures of women supported the roof and the Karyatiden were buried in the side hall. Further down the hill are the imposing ruins of the Theatre of Dionysus and the Odeum of Herodes Alticus–where, in summer, the Athens Festival is held. If you forgot to buy a book about Greek Culture at home, then you can buy one here or one of the many brochures which explain about the ruins in detail. The Temple of the flightless Athena-Nike is quietly beautiful. On the right is the Propylaea which formed the entry to the Sanctuary. In recent times more and more important figures and pieces of buildings have been brought into the Acropolis Museum and have been restored in the smog free environment. (Open daily 7.30 a.m.-4.45 p.m. Entry, including Museum 150 Drs.).

In ancient times before it was moved to Pnyx, the meeting place of the Assembly was. Angora from where there is a beautiful all round view–to the west is the Acropolis. Originally, the distance to all places in the land was measured from this point. Nowadays, distances are measured from Syntagma Square. Here, at this market place, Socrates engaged in his peripatetic method of education. (To-day the University is in Kratylon str.). Near Angora is the Temple of Hephaestos, which is outstandingly preserved.

Although the idea of free thought and democracy originated here things haven't gone as smoothly as you might expect (e.g. the Military Putsch in 1967 and the Dictatorship until 1974). Since the socialists came to power, the police now leave people who lean to the left alone, and instead harass the young punks.

On Filopapou Hill there is another theatre with a guided tour and light and sound show in summer. It is romantic to watch the sunrise or sunset from one of the hills.

South of the Acropolis in Dion. Areopagitou Street, are the Zappelon gardens on the left and Hadrians Arch and the Temple of the Olympian Zeus on the right. The Olympic Stadium appears to be antique, although it was only built for the revival of the modern olympics in 1896. Further 'new' buildings are the cathedral on Mitropoleous Square (look in at the very tiny byzantine chapel on the right); the Memorial of the Unknown Solder, with changing of the guard on Sundays; the university in Panepistomiou street. In the same street are the famous museum, Vassilissis Sofias No. 91, and the American Embassy, where demonstrations are often held.

MUSEUMS: The National Archaeological Museum, Tossilta street 1, (Tuesday-Sunday 8.00 a.m.-5.30 p.m.); the National Gallery Museum, Vass. Sophias av. 46 (Tuesday-Sunday 9.00 a.m.-3.00 p.m.); the National History Museum, Levidou str. 13, Metro Kifissia (Saturday-Thursday 9.00 a.m.-2.00 p.m.); Benaki Museum, Vass. Sophias Av. 22, (Tuesday-Sunday 8.00 a.m.-3.15 p.m.); Folk Museum, Plaka (Tuesday-Sunday 10.00 a.m.-2.00 p.m.); Ethnological Museum, Stadiou str. (Tuesday-Sunday 9.00 a.m.-1.00 p.m.)

FOOD: In Athens you can eat at numerous fast food places (e.g. 'munchies') but the Souflaki stands are better. You can buy something at the street markets, or at inexpensive and friendly shops which sell foodstufs and cakes. You can eat out of doors or at traditional taverns (expensive) where the menus are not written in english, but you can point out something that appeals to you from the big pots on the bar. The pubs are simple and cool, typical of a summer land, and the food served is cool to lukewarm. The Tasseqva, Livaniou street, 250 metres straight ahead from the railway station is very typical. Anna, Aghiou Louca streets near Platia Koliatsu; Sigalas, Platia Monastiraki 2; Corfu, Kriezotou street near Syntagma above left. Those in the parallel street Voukourestiou are somewhat better but cater more for tourists e.g. Vassilli. Near Omonia Square: Nea Olympis, Em Benaki 3; Rodeo Self Service, Satobriandou 17; Pefanis, Zinonos 12; near Syntagma Square: Meteora, Xenophontos Street; Syntrivani, Filellinon 5; Kentrikos, Kolokotroni 3; Delphi, Mikis/Metropoleous Street.

In the Plaka: Tav. Byron, Vakhou str. 1; Poulakis, Panos str. 6; Sigalas, Monastiraki Square 2; Eden, Flessa str. 3 (vegetarian); the international crowd meet at Souflaki-Bill's, Ermou 101, in the Plaka. Otherwise go into the Pubs where the locals go a bit off the beaten track. The people are usually very friendly there.

ENTERTAINMENT: Greek wine, who wouldn't think of it? It is still very inexpensive in the ordinary taverns and in the Pavillion in Dafni from June to September in casks (11km. from Athens, Bus 873, near Omonia). It is an acquired taste however. Although it is advertised in the brochures as 'Free' at this Wine Festival, it is only free after you have paid a fixed price. The central tourist office also organizes the Athens Tourist Festival (July to September) and the works which are presented at the Herodes Articus Odeon are most thought provoking (Contact: GZF, Spirou Miliou Passage 2, Athens, Tel. 322 1459). Concerts for young people are also held in Likavitor Park and at the Apollo Statium, Pizoupolis.

DISCOS: For only 330 Drs you can spend the whole evening at Pinochios, Adrianou Street. Picture Theatre Tip; in summer there are many open-air theatres showing english films.

STUDENTS AND YOUNG PEOPLE also gather on Dexameni and Exarchia Squares.

In the DISTRICT: Both end stations of the metro are interesting: Piraeus, the Harbour, and Kifissia, with a former king's villa, or the beach at Vouliagmeni, the thermal baths and south from there, where the water becomes cleaner again, at the Temple of Demeter, Eleusis. Last Tip. Rafina, a small harbour on the east coast-bus from Mavromateon Street, Areos Park, a bathing beach used by residents of Athens. Boat trips to the islands are cheaper from here than from Piraeus.

ACCOMMODATION: Youth Hostel, Kypselis street 57, Bookings: Oxne, 4 Dragatsaniou street, Athens. Tel. 822 58 60. In summer there are approximately 15 private youth or student hostels (no identity card required). You get to know a lot of people there and usually they have a nice bar. You can sleep on the roof or in the hall (depending upon the cleanliness). The Hotel Larisiakon is 100 m. from the railway station (Filadelfias 2, for 200-400 Drs.); in Pangrati is the Residence Pagration (Damareos street 75, Tel. 751 95 30) with T.V. and cooking facilities. For reservations in normal hotels contact Hotel Reservations (6 Aristidou st., Athens, Tel. 3233501). Around the railway station: Sofos, Hormovitou street 18, Tel. 8226402/5; Sans Rival, Paleologou street 2c, Tel. 5248675.

Camping grounds are mostly on the outskirts: A Voulas, Alkvonidon street 2, Voula, Tel. 89 52 712 (180 Drs. per person, approx. 20 km, you shouldn't swim there. Nea Kifissia, Kifissia (north-east of Athens) Tel. 801 6435/801 0202. Closer to Athens in the west at 190 Athinon ave, Dafni, Tel. 58 14114.

HUNGARY

The Peoples Republic of Hungary (Area, 93 032 m2; Population 10.72 million) encompasses to-day the homeland of the Maygyar who settled around 900 AD.

Hungary in the last ten years or so, has become fairly wealthy in comparison to Romania. This is attributable to political strategy. While Romania aligns itself with the rest of the communist bloc, Hungary follows suit as far as foreign policy is concerned, but it takes a liberal view in national economic policy. Hungarian shops and markets are plentifully stocked, though the Church is stifled. Jazz and rock music have a european flavour.

ENTRY/FOREIGN EXCHANGE/CUSTOMS REGULATIONS: Passports and visas are required. These are obtainable from the consulate or embassy. Cost approx. US$20 including postage, two photos must be included.

You are not required to exchange a set amount of western currency per day. 400 Ft per person per day may be brought into the country. You are permitted to bring in unlimited western currency. When leaving you can exchange up to 50% of the officially exchanged sum, so keep your dockets when you exchange. Tourists must register their address within 48 hours of entering the country. This is automatically done if accommodation has been rented through a travel agency.

Duty Free Allowance:
250 cigarettes or 250gm tobacco, 2 litres wine and 1 litre brandy.

Currency/Exchange Rate: The currency of the land is the Forinth (Ft.).

1A$	=	34Ft
1C$	=	40Ft
1NZ$	=	28Ft
£1	=	78Ft
1US$	=	50Ft

TELEPHONE:
It is possible to place calls to other countries from telephone box (10 Ft. Cost) or through the operator (dial 09).

Emergency Telephone Numbers: Police 07; Ambulance 04.

EMBASSIES:
Australia: Forum Hotel, Budapest V, Tel. 188-100
Canada: Budakeszi Ut 32, 1021 Budapest, Tel. 387-312/512
N.Z.   No Resident Representative–see Austria

U.K.   Harmincad Ut 6, Budapest V, Tel. 182-888
U.S.A.   V. Szabadsag Ter 12, Budapest, Tel. 126-450

SHOPPING TIPS:

Pop. records and books–see Budapest.

ACCOMMODATION:

The Ibusz Travel Bureau handles hotels, private pensions, camping grounds, youth information and package tours. They can be contacted through the Hungarian embassy or consulate in your country.

SPEED LIMITS:

In built up areas 60 km/h;
outside built up areas 80 km/h; motorways 100 km/h;
and the percentage of alcohol allowed is 0%.

RAILWAYS:

Inexpensive tariffs.

AIRPORTS:

International airport at Budapest. Flights from East Berlin, Schonefeld are cheaper.

BUDAPEST

The town dominates the small Hungary of to-day. Budapest is really one of the most beautiful towns in Europe. The Forinth (currency) is very strong, also it's appeal, its attractions, its culture and its food, are rich but not disgustingly so. (Pop. 2.06 Million).

BY RAIL: Budapest has four important railway stations, all of which are joined together. The Keleti pu (east station) is important because it's the junction for the international traffic, with its square in front. On your right on the side of the platform, is the train information office, waiting room and left luggage office (3Ft. per piece for 24 hours). The other railway stations: the Nyugati pu (west station built out of iron), which has departures to north-eastern Europe; the Deli pu on the Buda side of the river, has only a few trains leaving for other countries (Yugoslavia and Austria) but caters for the seasonal traffic to Balaton, and the Joszefvarosi pu caters for the Pussta Lines. Train information: Tel. 429 150, 227 860.

BY CAR: There is a well built road from Vienna-Bruck, via Hegyeshalom, Gyor, Tatabanya. or you can come from Vienna-

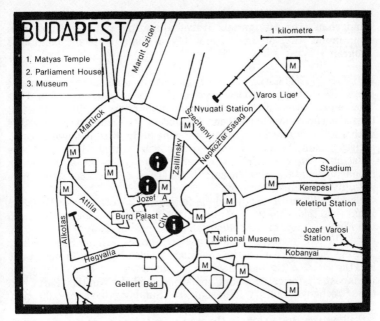

Eisenstadt via Sopron an old town near the Austrian border. It's a bit out of your way, but a beautiful trip. From there can go via Gyor to Budapest. Parking is just as limited here as in the cities of the west. A parking station in the centre of Pest is found in Martinelli Ter.

BY AIR: Budapest has an international airport (Ferihegy). Bus 93 travels between the airport and the city and then use the metro (Underground).

LOCAL TRANSPORT: Keleti pu and Deli pu are directly linked by the metro; Keleti and Joszefvaros pu are connected together by Trams 23, 24 and 36. From Keleti pu take the metro 2 stops and you are at the start of the city (Kossuth ut) from where all main streets radiate.

Now, if we mention buses and trolley buses then we have mentioned all the different sorts of city transport, which because of the normal width of the three underground lines which don't take into account the topography (compare Rome, Athens and Bucarest) provide a very good public transport network. The tariffs of 1 Ft and 1.50 Ft (bus) which have no competition are the cheapest (you buy the tickets at the railway stations, cafes or kiosks). A few trams run until 4.00 a.m.

TOURIST BUREAUX: Ibusz Offices are found at every railway station, Budapest Tourist: Roosevelt Ter 5, Tel. 17 35 55; Youth: Express, Semmelweisz u. 4, Tel. 111 430, good information and programmes. City Tours: Baderstadt, smaller city tours (ask at the Ibusz Office).

TOURIST NEWSPAPERS: The normal newspaper 'Budapester Rundschau', the Hungarian Travel Magazine and the Hungarian Programme Adviser; and a monthly in many different languages 'Program'.

POINTS OF INTEREST: Let's begin with an unusual tip: Marguerite Island (Margitsziget). In the north of the city a broad strip of land lies between the arms of the Danube, a symbol of the joining of the two towns' harbours (memorial near the Marguerite Bridge) and a paradise with a lot of hungarian specialities: wide parks with rose gardens, an artists' colony, two swimming pools (the Alfred Hajos and the Palatinus), an open-air cinema and stage, ruins of a dominican monastery and the new Thermal hotel (Tram 4/6); on the island there are only mini-buses, no cars.

Castle Hill on the Buda side is famous (M2 to the lively Moszkva Platz then take Bus 16) because of it's fantastic view of the town from the Fisher abbey, Matthais church and museum (daily 9.00 a.m.-7.00 p.m.), the old Town Hall, the House of Tancsics, Mihaly Str. 7, where Thomas Mann once lived, the pharmacy 'Golden Eagle' in Tarnock Lane and the great castle itself in which is housed the National Gallery, the Budapest Historical Museum, the Museum of the Workers' Party and the Szechenyi Library (Tuesday to Sunday 10.00a.m.-6.00 p.m. Saturdays gratis).

Still on the Buda side, to the north are the ruins of the old roman town of Aquincum which are quite interesting (HEV-Railway). There is a roman amphitheatre (Korvin Otto Strasse), the Hercules Villa (Megyfautca) and the museum in Lager Street (K. Otto cira 64; only until 2.00 p.m.) South of the castle hill is Gellert Hill (Tram 6, Bus 27) which you can't miss, primarily because of its Freedom Statue. You again get a beautiful view from the Citadelle and there is a park around the castle. If you want to go higher up, go to the Buda Mountains: e.g. Szechenyi Mountain with Tram 4/6, 56 and then funicular 'Fogaskereku'. At the top is a Pioneer (communist equivalent of the scout movement) Railway which is looked after by school children. A chairlift goes from Zugligeti Street 13 to the top of Janos Mountain which has a lookout tower (round trip is possible).

The real centre of the city is found on the other side of the river in Pest: go over one of the bridges, which have been built in varying architectural styles, and you are in the area bound by Felszabadulad Terrace, Martinelli Terrace, and Vorosmarti Terrace, where there are some traditional restaurants, the pedestrian zone, Vaciut, St. Stephan's church, the Parliament House (group tours only organized by Budapest Tourist). Also the Dedoute where since 1980 cultural exhibitions have again taken place, and lastly, the Paris Passage (Parizsi u./Petofi Sandor ut), which brings to mind an old world glory.

Go across Nepkoztarsasag Allee to Helden Square, where there is a semi-circle of statues–Hungary's kings, and leaders right up to the

Austria: Tirol area, village of Kitzbuehel in Winter

Greece: Hydra

Budapest: State Opera House

Freedom fighter Lajos Kossuth. Two museums are on the square: the museum of the Fine Arts and the Hungarian National with changing exhibitions. Behind the square are the national woods, Varosliget, a beautiful far reaching park with the zoo, circus, the Szechenyi health spa, the traffic museum, the farming museum which is housed in the castle Vajdahunyad, an amusement park 'Pester Prater' and the traditional tavern 'Gundel'. Further Museum Tips: The National Museum with the genuine St. Stephen's crown, which until 1978 was in the U.S.A.; Museum Korut, an ethnological museum, Kossuth L. Ter; the Gizi Bajor Memorial Museum for actors and actresses, Stromfeld Aurel u. 16; the Evangelical Land Museum, Deak Ter; the Semmelweis Museum of Medicine, Aprod u; the Museum for Trade and Industry: Fortuna u; the State Museum for War Stories, Toth Arpad Setany 40, and the Housing Museum, Fo Terr 4.

MARKETS: Overcrowded and a little expensive, the big market hall, Tolbuhin Ko. on the Szabadsag Bridge; a flea market at Nagykorosi ut 156 (Tram 13, Bus 54).

FOOD: One can eat well in cafes, restaurants and cafeterias. Apostolok, Kigyo u 4; Szeged, Bartok Bela u; Vasmacska, laktanyo u 3; Russian specialities: Bajkal, Semmelweis u 1, Bukarest, Bartok Bela Ut 48; Polish specialities: Karczma Polska, Marvany U 19; Cuban: Havanna, Jozsef Korut 46; Beer garden, gypsy music: Csiki, Angyal U 37; Notafa, Ady Endre ut 37, Fortuna, Hess Andreas Ter; Ezustsiraly, Napfeny U 7; Self service: Badacsony, Ulloi Ut 6; Grill International, Kosuth L. u 19; Izek Utcaja, Lenin Krt 47; Hallo, Majakovszkij U 65; Sugar, Ors vezer tere (shopping centre); Torkos, Mester U 12, Unio, Jozsel Krt 6; Zenit, Ferenc Krt 6. Nice also for good entertainment are the beer lounges: Berlini Suszterinas, Jozsef Krt 31; Becsi City, Sallai Imre U 18; Krisztina, Krisztine Krt 25; Hagi, Huszar U 7; Cafes: TE + EN, Bem rakpart 30, Hid, Ferenc krt; Ruszwurm,Szentharomsag U 7; Korona, Disz Ter 6; Vorosmarty Cukraszda, cake shops in the middle of the city on the Vaci u.

FOR EVENING ENTERTAINMENT; Budapest is famous for its music, even jazz and rock. In the Music Academy, Liszt Ferenc Ter 8, Concerts are often held (classical music); as well as in the Redoute in the City, Vigado Ter 1. Rock concerts are sometimes held in the MOM Culture House, Csorsz U 18; Meeting places for students: Numero Uno, Guszev u. 9; MKKE Klub, Kimitrov Ter 8; Var Klub near the Matthias church. Out of the ordinary: in the Laser Theatre of the Planetarium, a light and sound show, which is well worth seeing in any case, Nepliget, in Varosliget, Tel. 138 280; Open air rock concerts in the If Jusagi Park at Castle Hill; more traditional the dance hall, Favarosi Muvelosi Haz, Feheravi ut 47; Kassak Klub, Uzsoki Ut 57. A spring festival is held in March with all sorts of different cultural works; in autumn the Budapest Music weeks from the end of September to October.

BUYING TIPS: Hungarian Rock Group records are very good and inexpensive (Karthago, Edda and others–Rozsavolgyi, Martinelli Ter 5).

FOREIGN LANGUAGE BOOK SHOPS: Libri, Vaci u 32; Central Antiquariat, Muzeum krt 15; Book Shop, Rakoczi ut 14; Goroki, Vaci ut 33.

The Budapest baths are a magical dream: In Hungary natural springs and deep wells yield a half a million cubic metres of thermal water daily. As a result of this many people go to the baths to take a cure. One of the prettiest open air baths is the Csaszar Baths, Frankal Leo u. FU35 (Cost 12-30Ft) Central Office: Karolyi Mihaly u. 17. Tel. 185 896.

BOAT TRIPS ON THE DANUBE are also offered to tourists and because the town is beautiful on both sides, a boat trip is recommended. There are also boat trips with dancing on board. Anlegestelle Vigado ter; Tel. 181 223.

ACCOMMODATION: Youth hotel: Express Beethoven u. 7/9, Tel. 158 891; Ifjusag, Zivatar u. 1/3, Tel. 154 260; Strand, Pusztakuti u. 3, Tel. 686 637 (also camping); Lido, Nanasi ut 67, Tel. 886 865; or Express Office.
Camping: Hars-hegy, Harshegyi ut 5-7, Tel. 151 482; Romai furdo, Szentendrei ut 189, Tel. 151 482; Romai furdo, Szentendrei ut 189, Tel. 686 260;
Hotels and rooms in private homes, hopefully contact the travel bureaux and tourist information offices. Prices: 2 Star Hotels 400-800Ft/Double Room, Pensions 80-240Ft/Double Room, Hotels: Metropol, Rakoczi ut 58, Tel. 421 175; Nemzeti, Joszef krt 4, Tel. 339 239; Trio, Ordogorom u 20, Tel. 865 742; Wien, Budarosi ut 88, Tel. 665 400.

IRELAND (EIRE)

The Republic (70283 sq. km.) takes up most of the 'Emerald Isle' and has a population 3.48 Million.

In 1922 Ireland became a dominion and a sovereign independent democratic state in 1937 and left the British Commonwealth in 1948. The six north-eastern heavily populated counties (Ulster) stayed with England and became Northern Ireland although under the State Agreement, Eire now also has some rights in Ulster.

CLIMATE:

The climate of Ireland is affected by its windy sea position on one hand and by the warm gulf stream on the other.

ENTRY/FOREIGN EXCHANGE/CUSTOMS REGULATIONS: A valid passport is required. There is no restriction on the amount of irish currency brought into the country, but you are only allowed to take out 100 Irish Pounds.

Duty Free Allowance:
    200 cigarettes or 250gm. tobacco, 1 litre brandy and 2 litres of wine duty free. The importation of fresh meat, poultry and milk products is banned.

Currency/Exchange Rates: The currency of the country is the Irish Pound (IR £)

1A$	=	£0.48
1C$	=	£0.53
1NZ$	=	£0.38
£1	=	£1.05
1US$	=	£0.73

British Pounds and coins are accepted throughout the land without any problems but that is not true in reverse.

BUYING TIPS:

Linen and damask goods, and irish folk music records.

TELEPHONE:

To phone home the local area code is dialled without the 0. When the number answers press Button A; it is better to phone from a post office or hotel.

Emergency Telephone Number: 999.

EMBASSIES:

Australia: Fitzwilton House, Wilton Terrace, Dublin 2, Tel. 761
517/9
Canada: 65 St. Stephen's Green, Dublin, Tel. 781 988
N.Z.   No Resident Representative–see Great Britain
U.K: 33 Merrion Road, Dublin, Tel. 69 52 11.
U.S.A: 42 Elgin Road, Ballsbridge, Tel. 68 87 77.

ACCOMMODATION:

Hotels, bed & breakfast, camping grounds: Bord Failte, 14 Upper
O'Connell Street, Dublin, Tel. 747733.
Youth hostel: An Olge, 39 Mountjoy Square, Dublin 1, Telephone
01/745734.

SPEED LIMITS:

In built up areas 48 km/h;
outside built up areas 89 km/h.

RAILWAYS:

C.I.E. Rambler Tickets or better still train and bus ticket for 8/15 days
for US$30/45 approx.

AIRPORTS:

International airports in Dublin and Cork; & Shannon when arriving
from America.

Pubs are open longer than in England–until 11.30 p.m.

DUBLIN

Baile Atha Cliath is the correct name for the capital of Eire where
english architecture and the irish way of life are combined. The situation
is still the same to-day as it was in the past. It has an almost colonial
english style of government–Ireland only gained its independence in
1922 after separation from Ulster. It has a past of poverty though the
Irish are a culturally wealthy people.

BY AIR: The international airport is in the north and there is a frequent
bus service to the city centre. Airport Information: Tel. 01/377 747.

BY RAIL: The fast inter-city trains from London-Birmingham-
Holyhead connect with the ferries. An alternative route is from
Liverpool to Belfast/Northern Ireland.

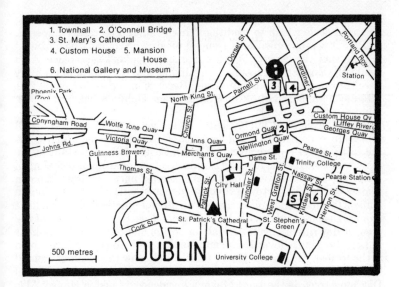

1. Townhall 2. O'Connell Bridge
3. St. Mary's Cathedral
4. Custom House 5. Mansion
                           House
6. National Gallery and Museum

BY SEA: There are also direct ferries from France: from Le Havre all year round; from Cherbourg from April to September. It is possible to take a car on all long distance ferries. The french lines arrive in Rossiare in the south-east of Ireland. If you are going to Dublin then it's better to go to Dublin Harbour or to Dun Loaghaire and catch the bus to the city centre.

The railway lines service the remaining three directions: Connolly (Amiens Street) for the north; Heuston (Kingsbridge) for the west; and Pearse (Westland Row) for the south. All the railway stations offer the usual facilities. Railway information Tel. 01/787 777.

TOURIST INFORMATION: Upper O'Connell Street, Tel. 747 733, where you can book rooms in Dublin and also anywhere else in Ireland. They have Tourist Trail signs.

Youth information: USIT Travel Shop Head Office, 7 Angelsea St., Dublin 2, Tel. 01/778 117. With an Internation Students Card you can get a 'Travelsave Stamp' IR £4.50 which allows you to obtain a 50% reduction on all the main routes and main forms of transport in Ireland (Train: CIE, NIR: CIE-Bus).

TOURIST NEWSPAPER: 'In Dublin'.

POINTS OF INTEREST: If you walk from any of the railway stations you will come to the River Liffey, which divides the town into two halves. Approximately in the middle, between the railway stations is O'Connell Street, the wide main Street which leads to the north where the city is found. Most of the city buildings aren't worth looking at but the G.P.O.

building is, as it mirrors the irish tragedy: It was built in classic middle european style which to traditional irish thinking is rather imperial. In 1916 it was occupied by a group of rebels who couldn't be informed in time that the general People's Uprising wouldn't take place. As a result, the English re-captured the building and the Freedom Fighters were thrown into Kilmainham Gaol. Because of the events of 1922, it is to-day a Memorial Museum (Kilmainham, Dublin 8, Tel. 01/755 990. Sunday 3.00-5.00 p.m.).

The side streets off O'Connell Street (Henry and Abbey sts. pedestrian zones) are examples of Irish flair. Across O'Connell Bridge which spans the Liffey River and up river, is Dublin Castle. It is important in the history of the city because the English reigned here uncontested until 1922. The Record Tower is part of the original norman castle. You can also see the State Apartments (reception rooms) and Holy Trinity Church (daily 2.00-5.00 p.m.) unless there is an official function. Now you have an impression of this castle let's compare it with the buildings of the present day rulers, the Town Hall (opposite) and the Irish Parliament in Leinster House (over Dame and Nassau sts.). In the College Green is the former Parliament House (until 1800), now the Bank of Ireland (Monday-Friday 10.00-12 noon and 1.30-5.00 p.m.). In the parallel Dawson Street, is the Lord Mayor's Residence, Mansion House. Also worth seeing in this area which, even to-day, is the showplace of Dublin, the English State Palace and Trinity College, the first university founded by Queen Elizabeth I, where famous writers such as Jonathan Swift, Oscar Wilde, Samuel Beckett and others studied. Even the nationalistic Irish came here, and the protestant upper class.

Also worthwhile seeing as well as the Library buildings, are some handwritten early christian writings from the early middle ages, when irish culture reached new heights. (Monday-Friday 9.30 a.m.-4.45 p.m.)

Some MUSEUMS, which are particularly typical of the area are: the state run Civic Museum, 58 South William St. (Tuesday-Saturday 10.00 a.m.-6.00 p.m., gratis); the Irish National Museum, Kildare St. (Tuesday-Saturday 10.00 a.m.-5.00 p.m.); the National Gallery, Merrison Square, (Monday-Saturday 10.00 a.m.-6.00 p.m., Sunday 2.00-5.00 p.m., gratis); the state run Fine Arts Museum, Hugh Lane (Tuesday-Saturday 9.30 a.m.-6.00p.m., gratis); the English style National Wax Museum, only with Irish personalities, Graby Row/Parnell Square; Museum of Childhood, The Palms, 20 Palmerston Park, Rathmines (only Sunday 2.00-5.30 p.m., daily in summer); The Joyce Museum (museum about the author, Joyce), James Joyce Tower, Sandycove, (May-September, Monday-Saturday 10.00 a.m.-5.15 p.m.) Tel. 01/809 265; 61 Harcourt Street is where Shaw lived and Bram Stoker, author of Dracula, lived at No. 16; Jonathan Swift's grave is found in St. Patrick's Cathedral. It was Swift who, in his sarcastic writings about the irish famine, lashed out at the English.

PARKS: St. Stephen's Green right in the city, where there are waterfalls and artificial lakes; the large Pheonix Park and Zoo to the west of the city; also in the west is the modern elite suburb with the Irish State President's Residence, the American Embassy, the Magazine Fort, a munitions fortress, as well as the Racing Track (zoo open daily 9.30 a.m.-6.00 p.m.). The Botanical Gardens are in Glasnevin (daily 9.00 a.m.-6.00 p.m.), and a Remembrance Garden for Irish Freedom Fighters is found at Parnell Square.

PUBS: Before we go on a pub crawl through the legendary pubs, we should plan a visit to the world famous Guinness Brewery. You can sample Guinness after you have viewed the Brewery and the free film. Because of this, children under 12 are not allowed on the tours. It is simple to find, catch bus 21 from Heuston Railway Station.

There are numerous pubs but we recommend that you visit the pubs with singing and the dance halls where traditional dancing is mixed in with Pop (mostly approx. IR£2.50-5.50 entrance, and then normal prices for drinks). Traditional irish music which is a little different from the commercialised Irish Folk Music, is found at the Meeting Place, Dorset Street; O'Donoghne's, Merrion Row, weekends at the Comhaltas Ceoltoiri Eireaan, Belgrave Square, the Irish Folk Music Centre or the Scoil Ard Ris, Griffith Ave.; Student Centre: Olympic Ballroom, Pleasant Street, D 8; Pubs with music: Baggot Inn, Merrion Row ; Jazz: Hurricans, Lower Leeson St; Hard rock: The Ivy Rooms, Parnell St; Rollerdrome, Harcourt St., a Roller disco; Culture Centre: SFX Centre, Upright Sherrard St., D 1; Something special: The Irish Cabaret: Abbey, Lower Abbey St., D1, Tel. 744 505; Ice rink, Dolphin's Barn; Disco: Gaiety Theatre South King Street, Tel. 771 717; Dublin Youth Theatre, Projects Arts Centre, East Essex St., D, Tel. 712 321; Tip: The Bad Ass Cafe, 9 Crown Alley. Some pubs also serve food.

Fast Food: Bewley's, Grafton Street and O'Connell Sts; vegetarian at The Runner Bean, Nassau Street. A good supermarket is found in Moore Street.

There are various festivals particularly Folk Music Festivals.

DISTRICT: for swimming go to Dalkey in the south or to Portmarnock in the north; Luncan and Leixlip are small up-river villages on the Liffey which are worth while seeing; from the southern suburb of Rathfarnham you can get to the Dublin Mountains; in Celbridge there is an example of an old irish castle (Castletown House, 20km); you get a beautiful view from Howth peninsula in front of Dublin Bay; the ruins of an abbey on Ireland's Eye island; there are similar ruins at Glendalough, even further to the south.

ACCOMMODATION: Youth hostels: 78 Morehampton Road, TEl. 01/680 325; Bus 10, 39 Mountjoy Square, Gel. 01/745 734; Camping: Cromlech Caravan & Camping Park, Tel. 01/ 826 882; there are also some inexpensive bed & breakfast places which can be booked through the tourist information office. The ones in the suburbs are cheaper because they are further from the city centre.

ITALY

The Republic of Italy encompasses the Apennian Peninsular (Boot), Sicily, Sardinia and is bordered in the north by the Alps. The population of just under 57 million live in an area of 301,252 sq. km.

The numerous art and architectural treasures as well as the mediterranean climate (dry summers and mild winters) along the coast and in the south, make Italy one of the oldest holiday lands of Europe. There is more industry and it is more densely populated in the north and whereas the west coast of the peninsular has harbours, the east coast only has flat beaches. The Mezzogiorno area in the south is the least developed and the most disadvantaged.

The tourist industry is of prime importance throughout the land. However, in spite of varying degrees of friendliness, the attitude that tourists are fair game and should be taken for a ride whenever possible still persists.

ENTRY REGULATIONS/CURRENCY/CUSTOMS: A valid passport is required.

Duty Free Allowance:
200 cigarettes or 250g tobacco, 1 litre spirits or 2 litres of wine and 250 gms of coffee.

Currency/Exchange Rate: The currency is the Lire. The rate of exchange is:

1A$	=	900 lr
1C$	=	990 lr
1NZ$	=	720 lr
£1	=	2000 lr
1US$	=	1380 lr

The purchasing power is good in country areas but prices are high in tourist centres.

TELEPHONE:

Firstly, you have to buy telephone tokens from a cigarette shop or from a special stand. Because there are hardly any coins in circulation and most of the rather old fashioned telephones only take Gettoni, they are also used as small change (100 Lire).

You can make international calls from almost all telephones, but you will need a little patience and it's cheaper after 10.00 p.m.

Emergency Telephone Number: 113.

EMBASSIES:

Australia: Via Alessandria 215, Rome, Tel. 832-721
Canada: Via Zara, 30, Rome, Tel. 844-1841
N.Z.   Via Zara 28, Rome, Tel. 851-225
U.K.:   Via XX Settembre 80, Rome, Tel. 475 544
U.S.A.:   Via Vittorio Veneto 199a, Rome, Tel. 4674.

SPECIAL INFORMATION:

Most banks only open in the mornings.

SHOPPING HINTS:

Leather goods, jewellery, spumante and cigarettes.

IMPORTANT:

Only shop/eat/stay where the prices are displayed and then keep your
eye on them! In the bars the drinks cost more if you sit at a table than
when you stand at the bar. Usually you have to buy a voucher from
the cashier first and then take it to the bar.

ACCOMMODATION:

Lists of hotels and camping grounds are available from: ENIT, 2 via
Marghera, Rome, Tel. 49711;
Youth hostel: AIAG, EUR-Palazzo Civilta del Lavoro, Quadrato della
Concordia, Tel. 591 3702.

SPEED LIMITS:

In built up areas 50 km/h;
outside built up areas 80-100 km/h; motorways 90-140km/h, and toll
is payable according to the distance travelled and the length of your
car–expensive.

RAILWAYS:

Kilometre book for 3,000 km valid for 2 months for 1-5 people for
US$90, good network.

AIRPORTS:

There are 25 large airports in Italy.

CAGLIARI

Cagliari is primarily a harbour town and the gateway to Sardinia. The
climate is one of the mildest in the Mediteranean. To-day the 230,000
inhabitants make a living by catching fishing, the tourist trade, and

industry. Unfortunately, this has also brought the usual pollution problems to Cagliari and even the traffic is regularly in a chaotic state.

BY SEA: It is recommended that you come to this island capital by sea: There are regular services from Genoa, Livorno, Civitavecchia, Naples and Palermo but they are rather expensive. The cost, including car, from Genoa is approximately US$150, from Civitavecchia approx. US$100. There are also ferries to the northern Sardinian villages of Olbia (Costa Smeralda) and Porto Torres. When you come from middle Europe, Cagliari is at the furthest end of the island. Tel. 070/654 664.

BY AIR: The airport near Elmas has regular flights to Zurich, Frankfurt and Dusseldorf; and the Sardinian Airline, Alisarda, which together with Alitalia, offer a service to all the major towns of the Boot of Italy. Buses run from Piazza Metteotti to the airport.

BY TRAIN: You can only get there by the inter-island service which is rather antique. The FS railway station is right on the harbour in the Via Rome. Trains go from there to Olbia and Sassari. There is a small gauge line from the FCS station, Piazza Republica, to Arbatax on the east coast. (Tel. 656 293 or 49 130).

LOCAL TRANSPORT: The town and district are serviced by buses. In Cagliari there are 14 bus lines. A pamphlet showing their routes and timetables is available free of charge from the tourist information office, EPT, Plazza Metteotti, right in front of the railway station. You can also get a map of the town from the provincial tourist office at 9 Plazza Deffenu. Tel. 070/663 207. city information, 97 via Maineli, Tel. 664 195.

POINTS OF INTEREST: It's best to commence a tour of the town at Castello, which is the name of the part of town around the castle as well as the name of the castle itself. To start with, this is the highest point and offers the best views. Its centre is the Viceroy's palace designed by the architect, Davisto, and built in 1769. To-day it contains the Prefecture and the local government offices of the province of Cagliari as well as those of the state of Sardinia. Next to the Viceroy's palace and looking on to the same square, is the palace of the Archbishop as well as the most important church of the town, the Cathedral, which is dedicated to Our Lady, and built in romanesque-pisanic style in 1257, but suffered numerous renovations, until in 1933, the architect, Giarizzo, changed the front into a pure romanesque style.

The National Archaeological museum is also located on Independence Square (Piazza Indipendenza)-(Tuesday-Sunday 8.30 a.m.-1.30 p.m.). It was built by the engineer, Dionigi Scano. It consists of a circular entry hall, and four large and three small rooms. The four large rooms contain sardinian artefacts and sculptures from the punic-roman period. Directly opposite is the tower of St. Pankratius, which is part of the fort and was built in 1305 by Johannes Capula.

The University of Cagliari is in the via Castello and is housed in an enormous building which has, as well as intellectual and natural science faculties, a geological and mineral museum. Further down the via Castello is the Elephant Tower, which is 30m high and was used as the town gaol for a long time. The old town area still has the Citadella dei Musei (Conservatorium of Music), a newer fort, which also houses part of the university and other local cultural organisiations. The roman amphitheatre is built into the cliffs where gladiators and lions did battle watched by approx. 20,000 blood thirsty people.

A lively anchor point in Cagliari is the area around the harbour. In the via Roma, the main street, which runs along the waterfront, you will find happy holiday makers drinking their first Capuccino a la Sardina in the cafes and kiosks. From the ferries come endless lines of traffic mostly foreign cars with surfboards on top. The roads to Iglesias and Oristano are regularly overcrowded.

Only a stone's throw from the harbour is the flame of the oil refinery with its raging black chimney, in the industrial area which is very close to the centre of the city and where thousands of litres of oil are stored in rusty tanks. That is the reality of Sardina. Large projects and industrial complexes threaten to ruin it.

But the more pleasant side of life still dominates this town, and the highlight of the year is definitely the Festival of St. Efisios. It grew out of a vow by the state administration, and during the festival a decorated ox cart with Nora in it, is pulled through town and at the same time people celebrate, drink, dance and no work is done. Other celebrations held during the year: The International Fair at the end of April; in July a Procession of Boats on the sea directly in front of the town.

After so many celebrations you will naturally need to rest and swim. The nearest beach is called Peotto and lies 6 km distant on S. Elia Peninsular. Catch Bus 9, or alternatively it's more comfortable to travel by QS along the beach. While this beach offers all the usual tourist infrastructure (restaurants, kiosks, and hire shops) it still appears to be quite clean. Whereas on the other side of town towards Pula, the beach is not much good for swimming because of pollution from industry and the oil refinery. The Parco Pineta M. Urpino is close to town and is surrounded by the Europa Street.

FOOD: Because of the expensive restaurant prices it is better to cater for yourself. Towards this end, visit the Mercado Coperto, viale Coco Ortu where amongst the brightly coloured advertisements, you will find all the fresh products you require for your day to day needs.

If you want to eat for a reasonable price you should get a list of restaurants which have a Tourist Menu from the tourist bureau. Usually a Tourist Menu costs around US$7. Restaurants which have decided to offer this, display a sign on the door or in the window. The list is not always up to date as some restaurants decide to drop out and others come in. Even without a list you can find them. The area around the harbour is full of restaurants, snack bars, pizziere, e.g.: Mura Corso, Vitt. Emanuele 189. Try something special: one of the numerous entrees of specially prepared squid salads, snails or assorted meat salads. For your main meal try fish.

IN THE PUBS: The town with its governmental offices and public servants, and soccer clubs, won't ever be more than second rate but it's not dead on the long summer nights. A row of cafes and bars are found along the Corso Emanuele and the via Roma, and snack bars are to be found in the harbour area. Business is booming at Assemini, the Las Vegas of Cagliari, a small town with discos which is found on the outer periphery.

ENTERTAINMENT: Now what is left for adventurous tourists who like to dance or for those who like their beer, who come on the ferries and who have to count their pennies but also want to have an experience they won't forget? They have to be satisfied with culture or go to the beach at Poetto.

ACCOMMODATION: The list of the Locandas, the cheapest possible accommodation is available at the tourist information office. And after that, off you go and good luck because these extremely small pensions are usually overcrowded. Two addresses for those who arrive late or on Sundays and who aren't able to visit the tourist bureau: Antares, Via Roma 149 and Melis, Viale S., Margherita 21. In Cagliari often student college accommodation is offered. By our calculations these are only flop hotels and cost approx US$40 for a double room, and if you are prepared to pay this much then you are better off at one of the private homes or Hotel Centrale, Via Sardengna 4, Tel. 654 783, Double Room approx. US$20.

THE DISTRICT around Cagliari is . . . Sardinia. If you are travelling around the island then it is recommended that you purchase a travel guide on Sardinia. We don't have enough space in this book to go into detail. We will just outline one typical holiday here:

Farm Holidays are offered by a co-operative of land owners which is found in the Province of Oristano. In these villages life revolves around work in the fields and making local craft items from baskets to carpets, from ceramics to embroidery. It is a traditional quiet lifestyle which is governed by nature and the seasons. Every village is different. Every patch of ground has its own particular beauty just as every sort of bread has its own taste. Because of past experience, the farmers conserve their farm produce in case of emergency. The tourist is offered half pension (dinner, bed & breakfast) and has no duties with the exception of an obligation to eat with the head of the family (padrone) in the evenings.

For INFORMATION and BOOKINGS contact: Co-operativa Allevatrici Sarde, Via Giotto 4, 09170 Oristano, Tel. 0783/78670.

FLORENCE-FIRENZE

Florence lies in the heartland of Tuscany, a pensioned off roman settlement which has been the seat of a bishop since the 4th century. Once the capital of a mighty city-state where the noble families had, very early in time, to turn over their influence to the citizens and bank magnates. Art and architecture has played an important part in Florence in all centuries,and reached a high point under the leadership of the Medici family in the 15th century. A Republic ruled by the Medicis survived until the 18th century when this state finally declined. Florence was for a short time the capital of Italy (1865-1871). To-day Florence is a centre for the tourists who come to Italy. (Pop. 453,000).

BY CAR: You can come across the Brenner Pass and go via Verona on the E6 straight ahead to Modena, where the E2 from Milan joins in. The E6 makes a semicircle around Florence and you should take the Florence/Firenze Norte Exit which leads to the central station area south of the Arno River. Parking areas are to be found near the main railway station and right behind the church on the Piazza St., Maria Novella. There are also parking stations in the city.

BY RAIL: The Santa Maria Novella station is more on the outskirts of the central business district and is the end station of the international trains. It is a very busy and well serviced railway station with direct links to and from Florence, former steep stretches have been straightened and new sections built including the Appenin-Basis Tunnel, length 18.5km. The main railway station with its marble exterior is firstly a work of art, but it also has all the services one needs at a railway station e.g. tourist information with accommodation bookings, ITA, Tel. 282 893; Train information Tel. 278 785.

BY AIR: There is no international airport near Florence, the nearest is Galilei Galileo near Pisa, with a bus connection to Florence, Tel. 050/25188.

TOURIST INFORMATION: Head office of Azienda Autonoma is at via Tournabuoni 15, TEL. 21 65 44; Regional information: EPT,. via A. Manzoni 16, Tel. 24 78 141 : recommended promotional material 'Florence for Young People'. Town programme: in the newspapers 'La Nazione' and 'La Citta' or in the 'Firenze Spettacolo' (monthly), new 'Firenze La Sera'.

LOCAL TRANSPORT: There is a poor bus service. The long distance buses to all corners of Tuscany depart from the square in front of the main railway station or from the Piazza San Maria Novella. Tickets may be purchased in bars or tobacco shops–the 7 day Tourist Bus Ticket

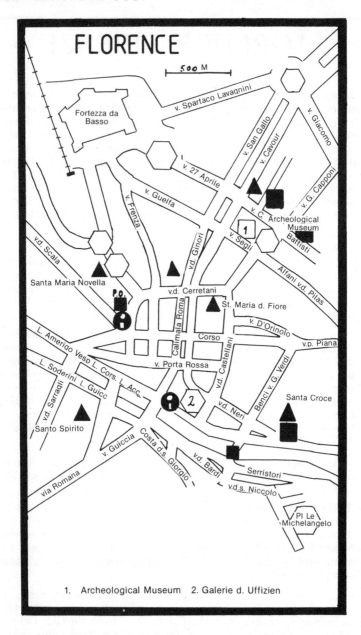

FLORENCE

500 M

1. Archeological Museum   2. Galerie d. Uffizien

is worthwhile only if you are planning long distance bus trips as you can see everthing in the city on foot.

POINTS OF INTEREST: The best place to commence a tour of the town is the railway station which is built in a functional style outwardly little different to the normal style of building in Italy. Straight opposite the hectic railway square is the Santa Maria Novella Church, where the town begins to show the other side of its face; It has a romanesque entry, a gothic interior and the upper part is built in renaissance style. It has peaceful inward facing cloisters and aisles in the shape of a cross with frescoes, but outside it is joined to the Piazza del'Unita Italiana and the Piazza St. Maria Novella, where travellers from all lands congregate, particularly in summer. If you go across the Piazza Unita and not directly along the via de Banchi, you can see the church of San Lorenzo and the Medici chapel on the way. It was built by Brunelleschi, who also built the cathedral, and it has works by Michelangelo inside. It is worth a visit because of the old and the new sacristies and library. Around the corner on the left is the Medici-Piccardi palace built in renaissance style with its beautiful courtyard and the roof frescos–recommended that the building, as far as possible, be viewed slowly from inside or from the courtyard (Medici-Piccardi: Thursday-Tuesday 9.00 a.m.-12.30 p.m., 3.00-5.00 p.m., gratis).

In the Piazza Madonna there is another market where you can buy all sorts of things. Now you should go along the via de Martelli to the square around the cathedral of Santa Maria del Fiore which was begun in 1296 and wasn't finished until the golden 15th century–1467. It is the second largest church in Italy–after St. Peter's in Rome–very impressive particularly its dome, a very distinctive feature when compared to the usual central european gothic spires. You can climb up the tower to the dome. There are highly prized works of art in the cathedral museum, Piazza del Duomo 9 (Monday-Saturday 9.30 a.m.-1.00 p.m. 3.00-5.00 p.m., Sunday 10.00 a.m.-1.00 p.m.). The dark, peaceful atmosphere of the cathedral is in contrast to the noise outside–traffic snarls, tourists and cafes. Also on the square is the Baptistry built around 1100 AD. one of the earliest romanesque buildings of Florence, with a gold-plated bronze door. Of the three doors, this is the most artistic and because of its sculptured figures is known as the 'Paradise Door'. Go along the via Calzaiuoli, an exclusive shopping street, and turn right into the via Speziali which leads to the Piazza della Republica, a modern meeting place, best known because of the Column of Plenty. Go straight along the via Calimala, where the 'Mercato Nuovo' general market is held. Turn left into the via de Lamb, on the corner is the Church Orsanmichele–with statues of the patron saints of the Guilds–turn right into the via Calzaiuoli and you come to: the Town Hall, Palazzo Vecchio, the Loggia and the famous Museum of the Uffizi, all on the Piazza Signoria.

The Loggia is a Hall decorated with figures (Perseus, with the Head of Medusa; kidnapping of Saberinnen), the Palace of the Signoria, now called Vecchio, is richly decorated and furnished and has a tower with a good view. Finally, the Uffizi, a museum with works by the florentine masters and an international master's collection as well (Tuesday-Saturday 9.00 a.m.-7.30 p.m., Sunday 9.00 a.m.-1.00 p.m.).

The Uffizi is spread out in side buildings until you get to the Ponte Vecchio (bridge over the Arno River). People live in the houses built on the bridge. They have developed a rather cosy appearance over the years. They were built on the bridge because of shortage of land in the middle ages. The Piazza Signoria and the long drawn out Piazza di Uffizi have sculptures by all important sculpturers of Florence and are pedestrian zones. They are naturally the place where most people congregate, particularly on hot summer evenings. . . The top place as far as the street life and salesmen are concerned.

Cross over the Ponte Vecchio to the south bank of the Arno and turn right along the via S. Jacopo, again a shopping street, to the via di S. Spiritu. This area is famous for its craft factories. On the left is the church of San Spiritu with its beautiful sacristry. Go back to the via Maggio and go along it to the Piazza S. Felice and the Palazzo Pitti. It was also built in the 15th Century and is politically important: It was the seat of the Pittis, the Medicis, the Lothringers and the italian kings. There are several museums: the Coach Museum, the Silver Museum (Wednesday-Friday 9.00 a.m.-2.00 p.m., Sunday 9.00 a.m.-1.00 p.m.), the Porcelain Museum (Tuesday, Friday, Saturday 9.00 a.m.-2.00 p.m., gratis), the Gallery of Modern Art, and The Medici Collection (Tuesday-Sunday 9.00 a.m.-2.00 p.m.). If you managed to see all that, then you are now allowed to go directly to the Boboli gardens which are next to the palace and rest for a while. It is a popular park and has an amphitheatre. If you want to continue with the tour, then go on to the fortress, Fortezza del Belvedere, which overlooks the park and offers first class views of the city: In one direction, you can look along the via di Belvedere and the via del Monte to the Piazza Michelangelo; the second view isn't really all that impressive, on the left is the church of San Salvatore al Monte, behind that is the fort and church of San Miniato al Monte–third and the most beautiful view, is best just after rain when the smog over the town has cleared.

FURTHER ATTRACTIONS: the Academy of Fine Arts, more paintings of the Florentine School and statue of David by Michelangelo, via Ricasoli 60 (Tuesday-Sunday 9.00 a.m.-2.00 p.m.); On the Piazza del la Santissia Annunziata is also the church of the same name, the Hospital of the Innocents for Children and the Archaeloogical Museum (Tuesday-Sunday 9.00 a.m.-2.00 p.m.) and to the left is the Piazza San Marco and church of the same name–statue by Savonarola–and monastery. Left of the Piazza del la Signora is the Piazza San Firenze with the Bargello Palace, which contains the National Museum Michelangelo Room (Tuesday-Sunday 9.00 a.m.-2.00p.m.). Opposite is the Badia church with its Campanila and to the right is Dante's house and museum (Thursday-Tuesday 9.30 a.m.-12.30 p.m. and 3.30 p.m.-6.30 p.m.). In front of the Piazza Santa Trinita in the via Tornabuoni is the Strozzi Palace with its beautiful courtyard and over the bridge of Santa Trinita on the right are the churches of San Frediano and Carmine. The Santa Croce church on the square of the same name, has the most famous graves.

Most of the museums are very expensive (3000L) but for Italians under 20 and over 60 are gratis, and also for foreigners on the 2nd and the last Sundays as well as the 1st and 3rd Saturdays in the month. A final museum tip: the Zoological Museum 'La Specola', via Romana 17 (Tuesday 9.00 a.m.-12.30 p.m. and Saturday 2.00 p.m.-5.00 p.m., Sunday 9.00 a.m.-12 noon, gratis).

FOOD: Buy it yourself at the Mercato Centrale at the station, as it's expensive in restaurants but a lot of places sell pizza in the street. Self service restaurants: Giannino in S. Lorenzo; Borgo, S. Lorenzo 31; Giovacchino, via Tosinghi 34r; Grande Italia, Piazza Stazione 25r; Il Grillo, P.S. Maria Novella; Cheap: Boboli, via Romano 45r; La Dolce Vita, via Passavanti 13r; Settebello, via Taddeo Alderotti 87; A little more expensive: Leo on Santa Croce, via Torta 7r; Mamma Gina, Borgo St. Jacopo 37r.

FESTIVALS: The historical town festival 'Calcio in Costume' is held on the 24th June.

DAY TRIPS: The coastal strip from Cinqueterre is very beautiful; the Chianti Region (Greve); and viareggio on the coast. Three panoramic roads to the north east to Fiesole, to Settignano, from Sesto to Trespiano and to the south the viale Torricelli and viale Galileo to P. Michelangelo.

ACCOMMODATION: Youth hostel, viale Augusto Righi 2-4, Tel. 601 451; Camping, Villa Camerata, near the Youth hostel, Tel. 610 300; Pension: Archibusieri, Vicolo Marcio 1, Tel. 282 480, right in front of the Ponte Vecchio; Giovanna /Nella/Pina, all three in the via Faenza 69, Tel. 261 353/284-256/212-231, about 2 mins. walk from the central railway station exit to the left. Hotel reservations: Borgognissanti 138r, Tel. 211 160.

MILAN-MILANO

Milan is more like a large city than Rome. It has chaotic traffic, new buildings, endless suburbs, banks and trade centres, and modern shopping streets. Milan is a city which can awaken two different feelings. Although you may not really want to go to a cement city, it does have the advantage of it being large, interesting and teeming with life in the midst of a beautiful area. (Pop. 1.63 million).

BY RAIL: The monumental terminal railway station had to be moved to allow the building of the gigantic via V. Pisani/Piazza del Republika. The railway station now has all the necessary services and a tourist information office. Tel. 222 441.

BY CAR: You are quickly in the city centre. There are three roads which come from three different mountain passes to the north: The Brenner motorway, the Simplon/Domodossola motorway from Sesto Callende, and the Gotthard Pass road and motorway from Bellinzone/Switzerland. The city is closed to vehicular traffic from 7.00-10.00 a.m.!!

BY AIR: The Forlanini Airport is only 10km from the city centre. Bus connection–No. 73, Tel. 62 81.

LOCAL TRANSPORT: There is a dense network of public transport–two underground lines in the shape of a cross and there are more being built. These are supplemented by trams. There are numerous bus lines. Ask for the 'Milano Transporti Panorama'. It should make things clearer. The Tram No. 1 runs to the city (Duomo, Scala).

TOURIST INFORMATION: EPT, 1 via Marconi, Tel. 809 662; Kommunal Information, Tel. 870 545 is in the Galleria Vittorio Emanuele, a beautiful old-fashioned shopping arcade with an iron/glass roof and dome built in 1865 which leads to the square in front of La Scala, the most famous opera house in Italy which seats 3,600. Don't forget to see the La Scala Museum, Piazza d. Scala/28 via Senato, Tel. 80 545 (open daily 9.00 a.m.-12 noon & 2.00-6.00 p.m.) (for the Province: 1 via Marconi, Tel. 808 813). The square in front of La Scala is joined to the square in front of the cathedral (Il Duomo) by the arcade. The cathedral has a museum (Tuesday-Sunday 9.30 a.m.-12.30 p.m. & 3.00-6.00 p.m.).

TOURIST NEWSPAPERS 'Viva Milano', Milano Mese', Spettacoli a Milano and 'Qui Milano', more for locals in italian.

POINTS OF INTEREST: In the city squares people from all countries mix in with the locals of Milan. It is quieter in the impressive Castello Sforzesco, which was first built in 1450 and only restored at the turn of the century. There are quite a few different collections there (Tuesday-Sunday 9.30 a.m.-12.30 p.m. & 2.30-5.30 p.m.) arts & crafts, copper etchings, library, coin collection, antique musical instruments and pre-history and Michelangelo's last unfinished sculpture. Directly behind the castle is the Park Semplone where you can see the Arco della Pace, a victory arch.

A few steps further on from the castle is the Ferrovia Nord Milano railway station run by the FBM (a private company). It has services to some of the nearby areas and still uses carriages made wholly from wood; a relic of the suburban railway time (cira 1920). In front of the station there is a market which sells everything.

MORE INTERESTING SIGHTS: the Palazzo di Brera with an overrated Pinakothek, mostly italian masters (28 via Brera, Tuesday-Sunday 9.00 a.m.-2.00 p.m.); not far away is the museum of the National Movement which covers the time around 1860 (23 via Borgonuovo, Tuesday-Sunday 9.30 a.m.-12.30 p.m.); the cemetery in the north-western part of the city has a lot of nice works of art, via Ceresio; the Palazzo of the kings and the archbishops right behind the cathedral; and some beautiful churches, such as San Satiro in the via Torino, to the right of Cathedral Square, Sant'Ambrogio, VS. Valeria with works of arts and a museum (Wednesday-Monday 10.00 a.m.-12.00 noon & 3.00-5.00 p.m.). Santa Maria delle Grazie, Corso Magenta, left of the Nord railway station, which houses the painting of 'The Last Supper' by Leonardo da Vinci in the old refectory; Sant'Eustorgio, Corso di Porta Ticinese, which has the relics of the holy Three Kings, and in the same street is the San Lorenzo Maggiore church with columns from the 2nd century; around the Porta Ticinese is an interesting part of the city (half right, Ripa de Porta de Ticinese). It has canals, typical houses and young people. The university area is behind the cathedral and the kings' palace in the direction of the Piazza Fontana/San Stefano, via San Antonio. Unbelievable: one can have a free latest style haircut at the hairdressing school, Tel. 742 0078.

MUSEUM TIPS: Museo Nazionale della Scienze e della Tecnica, Leonardo da Vinci, via S. Vittore 21 (Tuesday-Sunday); Galeria d'Arte Moderna, 16 via Palestro (Wednesday-Monday 9.30 a.m.-12.30 p.m. & 2.30-5.30 p.m.) also Risorgimento, via Borgonuova.

PUBS: Byblosnack, via Madonina. Disco: Plastic, 120 viale Umbria. New: Odissea due, 40 via Forze Amata. Galateria ecologica, 40 Croso Porta Ticinese (best ice cream); L'acerba, 4 via Orti (vegetarian); A Putia, 177 V. Fluvia Testi; Rinaldi Sicilliana, 30 via Frapolli; American Bar; Satchmo 3 via Roncaglia; Lunico, 9 via Bramante; La Pantera Rosa, 35 via Amedeo. Pub: Riverside, 150 Alz. Naviglio Grande.

ACCOMMODATION: Youth hostel, 2 via Martino Bassi from the railway station take Bus 90,91. Tel. 367 095; Camping: Autodromo di Monza, Parco Villa Reale, Tel. 039/387 771. Pensions approx. US$20 for a double room and can be booked at the tourist information office.

PALERMO

For people who have preconceived ideas about Italy and also those who have a fondness for the roman attitude to life, both will feel that Palermo lives up to their expectations. Here is a town that seems to bring out all the nuances of the italian way of life: the agglomeration of the half finished spread out cement city, the treasures of the past centuries that Goethe raved about, the magnificence and the bustle of the main streets only a few metres from where washing lines are strung high across the narrow streets.

The noisy, busy town is the main harbour of Sicily. It is overshadowed by the power of the Mafia who take a share of all profits but even so, the locals don't really seem to mind.

BY CAR: Palermo is more than 1,000km from Rome, but there are good connections. From Rome the E1 goes around Naples, through Salerno to Villa San Giovanni before Regio on the point of the boot. From there you can travel by ferry to Messina, and afterwards drive along a section of motorway which follows the northern coastline to Palermo.

BY RAIL: The railway ends at a rather small railway station where the zippy trains from Milan and Rome arrive. We recommend that you take the night train because of the beautiful morning trip along the north coast of Sicily. The railway station has all the important services. The tourist information office is near Platform 7, train information Tel. 24 12 66.

BY AIR: In summer there are good connections to all parts of Europe at Palermo Punta Raisi, Tel. 28 19 86.

BY SHIP: Of course you can come to the largest harbour of Sicily by ship. There is a connection to Cagliari (Sardinia), Naples and of course Genoa and Tunis. Information: Tel. 24 23 43.

TOURIST INFORMATION OFFICES: Main office, EPT, 34 Plazza Castelinuovo, Tel. 58 38 47 in the largest square of the city which is very long-go along the via Roma from the railway station to the end, then turn left. The regional tourist office is found at 9 Notarbartolo, Tel. 25 12 66. You can also make arrangements to hire a guide here who will tell you about the sights in your own language, or you can phone Milena Visconti, Tel. 53 33 50 or Emilia Gambino, Tel. 25 93 41. Tours of the city cost 12,000 L or 25,000 L (all day) at CIT Office, 453 via Roma, daily at 9.15 a.m. and 3.15 p.m., in winter at 2.15 p.m.

LOCAL TRANSPORT–bus. Information about routes and timetables can be obtained from the tourist information office.

POINTS OF INTEREST: A walking tour around the city starts at the railway station. (If you want to be exclusive you can take a horse-drawn carriage). Go down the via Roma, one of the main streets which has been done up for the tourists. Or else go along the parallel street on the left, the via Masqueda. You get to it by going through the lanes which lead off the via Roma. The via Masqueda gives you a truer picture of the town. One of the small street markets is held here. Foodstuffs, meat and fish are all sold here but the standard of hygiene is not high. From the via Maqueda turn left into the via Universita and you will see the large baroque church, San Giovanni degli Eremiti with red, half-ball domes which show an islamic influence. Opposite is the Corso Re Ruggero der Pareo d'Orleans, one of the many small parks where you can get away from the hustle and bustle of the city streets. Go around the corner to the right and you are at the beginning of the large Corso Vittorio Emanuelle. Towards the city is the castle which was built as a fortress by the saracens and extended by the normans. It is worth seeing because of the mosaics in the Capella Palatina (castle: Monday, Friday, Saturday 9.00 a.m.-12.30 p.m., chapel only Sunday and Holidays).

Go through the Porta Nuova of the Park Villa Bonanno (roman mosaics in the villa) and the Dioceasian Museum. Now you come to the most magnificent building of the city, the cathedral which is built in gothic-norman style and contains the graves of the german Hohenstaufen family as well as a treasure room (daily 7.00 a.m.-12 noon & 4.00-6.00 p.m.). Due to the dispute over William II's heir, the normans lost control of Sardinia and the german Staufische family claimed it. There is arabic influence in the architecture, and it became the centre of the town. Where the Corso crosses the via Maqueda is the byzantine church of Santa Maria dell'Ammiraglio, which was built in 1140. On the other side of the Piazza Pretoria with its lusty baroque fountains, is the baroque church of San Guiiseppe dei Padre Teatini, which is decorated with intricate marble.

Go along the via Marueda then turn left into via San Agostino and on the left is the gothic church of the same name built in the Middle Ages. Go through the small lanes to the right of the cathedral and you will come to the second most famous building in Palermo, the Teatro Massimo, built in 19th century neo-classical style, Tel. 58 36 00. Go further along the via Marqueda to the Piazza Verdi where the via Maqueda runs into the via Ruggeiro Settimo which leads to the main square, Piazza Castelnuovo where the overly large via Liberta begins. Around its intersection with via C. Lafarina there is a row of small parks and gardens, among them the English Park with the Peatro Popolare Zappala, Tel. 26 6881.

Then go back to the Piazza Castelnuova and the Teatro Massimo built in neo-classical style. The Garibaldi Festival building is also on the square, Tel. 58 43 34. Left of it is the Gallery of Modern Art (Tuesday-Sunday 9.00 a.m.-1.00 p.m.). Walk along the via Roma which runs off here back towards the railway station and you will come to two important museums firstly; the National Archaeological Museum cnr. via Bara/Piazza Olivella (Tuesday-Sunday 9.00 a.m.-1.30 p.m.); secondly, the Museum del Risorgimento, 1 Piazza San Domenico (Monday, Wednesday, Friday 9.00 a.m.-1.00 p.m.). In this old, rather run down part of town which goes down to the harbour, La Cala, are numerous churches and the large Vucciria market. The St. Francis of Assisi church in via Merlo stands out, also the Garaffo Fountain and the enormous magnolia in the Garibaldi Garden on the Corso Vittorio Emanuelle. Because the street follows such a straight line you can see the Santa Maria della Catena church and the town gate, Porta Felice. To the left is the start of the far reaching harbour and to the right, green zones such as the Villa a Mare followed by the very symmetrical Villa Giulia and finally back towards the railway station, the botanical gardens, 2 via Lincoln with an imposing neo-classical entrance gate.

You probably only can complete the above walking tour in one go if you are very fit, however, it doesn't cover all the interesting things. There is still the Regional Gallery of Sicily at 4 via Alloro (Tuesday-Sunday 9.00 a.m.-1.30 p.m., Bus 3/24) in the Palazzo Abatellis with a Pinakothek with art from the middle ages on display.

The Marionette Museum, 19 Piazza Marina (Monday, Wednesday, Friday 10.00 a.m.-12.30 p.m. & 5.00-7.00 p.m.). Traditional sicilian art is on display at the Ethnological Museum, Pitre, Accanto la Palazzina Chinese (daily 8.30 a.m.-1.00 p.m. & 3.00-5.00 p.m., Bus 14/15) and the Planetorium, 131 Corso Tukory (daily 12 noon-1.00 p.m.).

The Zisa Palace, seat of the norman king, William I, is in the via Ziusa, as well as other palaces in the west, such as the Cuba (Dice) by Boccaccio which is reflected in a lake in the middle of orange and lemon groves. Parco della Favorita adjoins the Sports Centre in the viale del Fante. The Ethnological Museum is also there.

A beautiful view of the city, harbour and sea can be obtained from Monte Pellegrino north-east of the city. Walk along the via Pietro Bonanno until you come to Castello Utveggio. On the way to Monte Pellegrino there is a turn off to the village of Santa Rosalia which has been dug into the cliffs. Inside is a grotto that is supposed to have healing water, with a gold covered statue of St. Rosalia.

A BEAUTIFUL CAR TRIP: Around Monte Pellegrino, firstly through the Park Favorita, back to the coast with its beach and fishing village of Lido di Mondello.

On the western outskirts of the town are the catacombs which you shouldn't miss; in the Catacombe dei Cappucini, via Cappucini (Monday-Saturday 9.00 a.m.-12 noon & 3.30-4.30 p.m., Bus 17) there are hundreds of bodies which, because of the air only decay very slowly. An impressive picture of death.

PUBS: In Palermo there are a whole range of pubs where you can eat inexpensively as well as inexpensive pensions, mostly around the railway station or in the via Roma.

DISTRICT: The villages of Monreale and Cefalu are worth seeing because of their cathedrals and their old towns even though they have been discovered by tourists. Cafalu, just before Palermo, is at the foot of massive chalk cliffs and has the Mandralisca Museum which is open daily from 9.00 a.m.-12 noon and 3.30-6.00 p.m. Monreale is closer, via Palermo (Bus 9). The churches there can only be compared to the most famous works of the masters.

ACCOMMODATION: No youth hostel.
Camping: Sferracavallo, via Pegaso, with Bungalows and Internation Trinacria, via Barcarello, Tel. 91/530 590.
Hotels: Ariston, 142 via M. Stabile, Tel. 588 973; Verdi, 417 via Mayqueda, Tel. 584 928; Corona, Tel. 231 340, Milton, Tel. 33 13 88; Vienna, Tel. 329 969 all in the via Roma 118 and 188; Novelli, Salita Santa Catarinal, Tel. 331 088. If you want to stay at a bit better place then try the Hotel Saussele, 12 via Vincenzo Errante, Tel. 237 524 or the Pension Esplanade in the surburb of Mondello Lido, Tel. 091/450 003.

ROME-ROMA

Built on seven hills and once the centre of the Roman Empire, and still the city which every traveller wants to visit. A hot city where the beautiful people like to go and often a little dangerous particularly for women. (Pop. 2.83 Million).

BY CAR: All roads lead to Rome. . . really. From Rome you can take the A6 which goes via Bologna and Florence but the road divides near Modena and from there the E6 goes via Verona and the Brenner Pass to Innsbruck and Munich and the E2 goes via Milan, Chiasso, Gotthard Pass to Lucerne, Basel, Frankfurt or Zurich/Stuttgart. There is a large ring road around Rome, the Grande Raccorde Anulare, which allows you to get to the city centre which ever way you like.

BY AIR: The International airport is Leonardo da Vinci at Fiumicino, Tel. 4687. There is a bus which runs from the airport to the Termini railway station.

BY RAIL: If you manage to catch a through train then you will arrive at the Termini railway station. (Don't get out at the Tiburtina railway station in the east if you can help it. If you don't have any option, then catch the city train to Termini railway station). There are luggage storage facilities right and left of the main platforms. All the usual

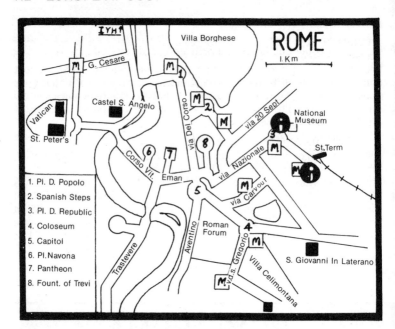

1. Pl. D. Popolo
2. Spanish Steps
3. Pl. D. Republic
4. Coloseum
5. Capitol
6. Pl. Navona
7. Pantheon
8. Fount. of Trevi

services are found in the main hall of the station. Train and ship information is on the right of the entry hall and information about other italian cities is available on the left, Tel. 47 75. Youth information: Punto d'Incontro,Tel. 474 3866.

TOURIST INFORMATION: At the Termini station and 11 via Parigi, Tel. 46 18 51. EPT, 6 via Parigi, Tel. 463 748; For students, 16 via Genova, Tel. 479 931.

TOURIST NEWSPAPERS: For young people AAM; Metro (programmes), La Settimana a Roma/This Week in Rome (for tourists); Roma in (advertisements).

LOCAL TRANSPORT: There are only two underground lines, the Ottaviano-Termini-Anangnine line (linea A) and the Termini-Laurentina line (linea B). Line B is due to be extended in the near future and new trains have been ordered. To make up for the lack of underground lines there are a lot of buses and trams which are also overcrowded even though there is a good service. You won't be able to work out where they all go if you don't buy the map 'Roma in Metro Bus' at a kiosk, unfortunately they are expensive and street directories don't show their routes. The only place you can get cheaper maps for L500 is at ATAC, Termini railway station, Plazza Cinquecento.

A tourist ticket which is valid for 3 days costs 5,500 L and is also valid for all museums. You can also buy a local transport ticket for 7 days for 3,000 L or a monthly ticket for 4,500 L. All these may be purchased at the ATAC Termini. Taxis are relatively cheap when there are a few people but have a complicated tariff system, so watch the meter.

POINTS OF INTEREST: There are organised city tours which visit the museums and leave from Plazza d. Rebublica (Tuesday-Sunday 9.15 a.m., cost L 17,000-22,000).

You will come across the attractions straight away:

The Forum Romanum (Line B, expensive entry fee and you can see most of it from the outside); nearby is the Colosseum (entry free) and the monument to Victor Emmanuel II; the Piazza Venezia (it may be demolished and it's practically a memorial to Italy's Independence Memorial) and the Palazzo Venezia once the Venetian agency and where Mussolini lived;

Next St. Peter's Square and St. Peter's Basilica and the Sistine Chapel (take metro line A from Termini to Ottaviano and walk south past the shops of Ottaviano or take the city train from Ostiense railway station to San Pietro station). The Castel Sant'Angelo dates back to roman times (on the Tiber River, Tuesday-Sunday 9.00 a.m.-1.00 p.m.).

The Catacombs (Priscilla's, 430 via Salaria, is supposed to be the most interesting). Other similar early christian hiding places are to be found in San Sebastiano at Porto S. Sebastiano and San Callisto south on the via Appia Antica (Thursday-Tuesday 8.30a.m.-12 noon and 2.30-6.00 p.m.).

The ruins of the Caracalla Baths (metro B); the Pantheon built in 27 B.C. (Piazza d. Rotonda); Ostia Antica (ancient harbour of Rome)–catch the train from Termini station to Ostiense and then the Acotral train or take a boat trip along the Tiber which leaves from the Ponte Marconi bridge at 9.30 a.m. (Lato Cinodromo) cost L 27,000.

The most important of the seven hills of Rome is Capitol Hill, north of the Forum Romanum, where in the courtyard of the Conservative building are the ruins of the colossal statue of Emperor Constantine and a statue of the wolf that suckled Romulus and Remus.

The Quirinale Palace which was the summer residence of the Popes, later the italian kings and to-day it's the President's residence, via Quirinale (Piazza Republica, Piazza Bernardo on the left).

The via Appica Antica, Appian Way, was the most important of the roman roads and has long rows of graves and other monuments along both sides of it. In the small church of Domine Quo Vadis, Jesus and St. Peter are said to have come face to face. The ruins of the theatre of Emperor Marcus Aurelius and the pyramid of Cecillia Metella (Bus 118) are interesting; the suburb of EUR which was Mussolini's pride and joy with a sports stadium and numerous small palaces attests to its former glory and its later decline (metro line B). Wander through the side streets as some of the building have stood since antiquity.

Now a few BEAUTIFUL CHURCHES: San Giovanni in Laterano (St.

John Lateran-metro Piazza le Appio) which dates back to the time of Emperor Constantine and is the highest ranked catholic church in the world.

Santa Maria Maggiore (St. Mary Major), the largest St. Mary's church from the same era, turn left at Termini station; a bit further on is San Pietro's in Vincoli (St. Peter in chains).

MUSEUMS: Don't miss out on: the Vatican Museum (take the lift to the top floor and work you way down)–daily 9.00 a.m.-2.00 p.m.; the Terme Museum, viale delle Terme, (Tuesday-Sunday 9.00 a.m.-2.00 p.m.); the Capitol Museum, Piazza del Campidoglio (Tuesday-Sunday 9.00 a.m.-2.00p.m.); National Gallery of Antique Art, Palazzo Barberini (Tuesday-Sunday 9.00 a.m.-2.00 p.m.). The most amazing is the Vatican Museum encompassing the Sistine Chapel, L5000 but free every third Sunday of the month–a must.

Now we come to the romantic SQUARES (Piazzas) where people gather: the Piazza Navona (baroque buildings); the Piazza della Rotonda (Pantheon, students); the Piazza del Popolo (galleries and antiques) and the Spanish Steps. Piazza Espana is now graced with a McDonalds restaurant with its ugly yellow and red 'M' sign–a source of much anger in the city, but embraced by the roman youth. From here one of the most exclusive and expensive shopping streets of the world starts, the via Condotti. International youth gather here as well as buskers, freaks, dealers, ice cream sellers, latin lovers etc. The Trevi Fountain is also very popular with the tourists.

The Piazzas are complemented by the PARKS, in particular, the Villa Borghese (which begins at the top of the Spanish Steps). It is a good place to picnic but NOT if you go in your swimming costume as the mounted police patrol the park. A smaller, more beautiful park is the Belvedere Tarpeo on the top of Capitol Hill. For lovers, the Gianicolo Park, Piazza Garibaldi (Bus 41). A nice market is found near the church of San Giovanni, in Laterano in the south east (vegetable market with a unique flavour). Don't swim until you are 100km north of Rome.

FOOD: While the pizzerias are often expensive, look around for a tavern which serves counter lunches. You can choose your lunch from the selection by just pointing, and the prices are reasonable and besides the locals are rather friendly away from the main tourist attractions. Sometimes they even have a 'Menu Touristico' e.g. the Salvatore, via Castelle Fiordo (around the corner from the Pension Primrose, Montebello St). Three squares with taverns serving meals: Piazza Navona, Piazza Farnese and Campo dei Fiori (university). Walk through the suburb of Trastevere west of the Tiber River and you will find good taverns day or night (Isola Tiberina, Ponte Garibaldi); Macrobiotic: Centro Macrobiotico Italiano, 14 via delle Vite.

PUBS/DISCOS: Because everything happens in the streets in Rome we can't tell you anything that will take your breath away. The oldest rock palace is the Piper, 9 via Tagliamento; La Luna, 16 via della Fontanella, New wave; the largest Disco also for teenagers is the Much More, 52 via Luciana; the Fantasie di Trastevere, 6 Santa Dorotea has a cultural programme, and something similar is offered by the Castel Sant'Angelos, 1 Lungotevere Castello. The Bandiera Gialla, via della Purificazione is an international meeting place.

Youth meeting places: Fonclea, 82a via Crescensio; Rotterdam da Erasmo, 12 via S'Maria dell Anima; Surreal Cafe, 39 a Vicolo del Leopardo; Sweet Movie, 146 via Rasella.

DISTRICT: Don't forget to visit Tivoli and the Villa d'Este with its park and its famous fountains and also the Villa Gregoriano which is situated in a beautiful scenic area.

ACCOMMODATION: Youth hostel, 61 viale delle Olimiadi (metro A, Bus 32, Tel. 396 4709). Centroi Giovanile, 10 via P. Pancrazio, Tel. 698 5332; International student home, Civis, 5 viala M.d.Affari Esteri, Tel. 396 2951.
Camping: Capitol, Ostea Antico, 45 via di Castelfusano, Tel. 560 2301; Flaminio, via Flamina km post 8, Tel. 32 79 006.
Hotels: Ponte Sisto, 64 via dei Pettinara, Tel. 6568 843 (and Piazza Sisto, caters for groups); Primose, via Montebello (from Termini station to the right); very nice: Fleury, 194 via Cavour, Tel. 474 43 45; Piazza di Spagna, via Mario de Fiori, Tel. 67 93 061; Sorriso, via Broccat, Tel. 67 98 661; Alba, 12 via Leonina, Tel. 48 4471; Villafranca, 9 via Villafranca, Tel. 49 1152; further cheaper, more basic hotels are found right and left of Termini railway station. A BAD TIP: Casa del Passaggero, 1 via del Viminale, Tel. 475 5776.

VENICE

One doesn't know any more if the town is flooded more by water or by tourists. (Pop. 355,000.) The relentless stream of tourists from all over the world is now more massive in the city of 400 bridges and 177 canals than it is anywhere else in the world. The industrial settlements and the oil refineries in the suburb of Mestre which not only provide a smoke screen for the driver, but are also responsible for the rapid sinking of the lagoon town, are absolute absurdities. Before your trip to Venice you might like to read Thomas Mann's 'Death in Venice'...

BY CAR: You can only drive across the 4km long car and rail bridge built during Mussolini's time to the Piazzale Roma, and from there on, there are no cars in Venice. From there vaparettos (motor boats) carry visitors along the Canale Grande and to St. Mark's Square. The Motoscafi are faster, but who wants to hurry. The gondolas are more romantic but expensive, and are only used by a small number of tourists nowadays-not like in the past. (Always agree on a price first! The official price from the railway station to St. Mark's Square is L 60,000). Other parking places: in the east on the dam-P2, S. Giuliano, boat 24; in the west-P3, Fusina, Boat 16. The town is an interesting stop for young people travelling by train on a trip to the Balkans or to southern Italy. In the last few years the railway station has become a popular stopover and meeting place for young people.

In summer, people from everywhere on their way to somewhere else, sit on the steps in front of the railway station. The first stop for rail travellers should be the EPT Office at the railway station. You can get a map of the city from them as well as detailed information about the attractions and public transport, Tel. 71 5016.

BY AIR: The international airport of Venice is the Marco Polo. Buses travel approx. every hour between the airport and the Piazzale Roma. For round about four times the price you can go by motorboat to St. Mark's Square. Tel. 700 355.

TOURIST INFORMATION OFFICES: As well as those at the railway station and airport, there is a central office at Rialto Palazzo Martinengo, Tel. 700 355. Student information: DORSODURO 3252, TEL. 705 660.

TOURIST NEWSPAPERS: 'A Guest in Venice'.

LOCAL TRANSPORT is by boat.

POINTS OF INTEREST: The number of palaces, churches and attractions is almost endless. During a short stay you should see: St. Mark's Basilica and Square including the evidence that the town is sinking; the fantastic Clock Tower; the Doges' Palace. St. Mark's was built in 828 in gothic style to house the tomb of St. Mark. The church was finished in it's present form in 1094. Although you can climb up the bell tower (daily 10.00 a.m.-7.30 p.m.) you shouldn't miss out on the Cathedral museum and its treasures. Almost as famous as St. Mark's is the Doges' Palace which can be visited daily from 8.30 a.m.-6.00 p.m. The Pozzi, the cells which were used as the gaol, shouldn't be missed. The Clock Tower (9.00 a.m.-12 noon and 2.00-5.00 p.m.); the pigeons on St. Mark's Square are fed by council employees and because of this one is prohibited from eating picnic lunches here because the birds might eat the paper bags, bread or soft drink cans-wherever did the Italians get that idea?

Further important attractions are found on both sides of the Canale Grande. Opposite St. Mark's is the Santa Maria della Salute Church and on the same side, the Academy of Fine Arts (Tuesday-Sunday 9.00 a.m.-2.00 p.m.) and the excellent Palaste Ca'Rezzonico, Ca'Foscari, Balbo.

Only 3 palaces along the Canale Grande are still owned by families listed in the Golden Book of the Town. Opposite is the Palazzo Grassi in which exhibitions are held. Lastly there is the second most famous attraction of Venice, the Rialto Bridge from here it's not far back to St. Mark's Square along the shopping street, Mercerie. On the bridge itself there is a market.

MUSEUMS: Maritime Museum, Arsenale 8 (open daily 9.00 a.m.-1.00 p.m.), Archaelogical Museum, S. Marco (Tuesday-Sunday 9.00 a.m.-2.00 p.m.). You can go to other islands: the Isola di San Michele where the cemetery is; Murano (glass museum -Thursday-Tuesday 10 a.m.-4.00 p.m.); Giorgio Maggiore, Giudecca or to Lido, the strip of land in front of the open sea that has many hotels, beaches etc. but they are not particularly clean.

FURTHER TIPS: The Paradiso Perduto in the southern part of Cannaregio is a good place to eat. The Carneval is turning more and more into a hippy meeting place.

ACCOMMODATION: The cheapest pensions are found in the suburb of Cannaregio, nearest to the railway station. The youth hostel is on the island of Giudecca, directly opposite St. Mark's Square (Tel. 041/38 211).

LUXEMBOURG

The Grand Duchy of Luxembourg with an area of 2,586 sq. km. and a population of 365,500, is one of the largest of the dwarf countries of Europe. In 1918 the Grand Duke Letzeubuerg considered uniting with Belgium. A close relationship still exists to-day between the two small countries which goes beyond the Benelux Agreement and the Common Market.

Although the Grand Duke still holds the office of Chief of State, to-day the land has a democratic constitution. Geographically, it is split into two sections: in the north are the middle heights of the Ardennes (mountain range) and in the south the fertile plains.

ENTRY/FOREIGN EXCHANGE/CUSTOMS REGULATIONS: A valid passport is required. Currency is unrestricted.

Duty free allowance:
200 cigarettes or 250gm tobacco, 1 litre brandy and 2 litres wine/champagne.

Currency/Exchange Rates: The currency of the land is the Luxembourg Franken/Franc.

1A$	=	26 flux
1C$	=	30 flux
1NZ$	=	20 flux
£1	=	58 flux
1US$	=	40 flux

The Luxembourgers have their own notes, but their currency is very closely coupled with the Belgium Franc. In Luxembourg Belgium Francs are accepted but not the reverse.

TELEPHONE:
To phone overseas the local code is dialled without the 0.

Emergency Telephone Number: 012

EMBASSIES:
Australia:	No Resident Representative–see Belgium
Canada:	No Resident Representative–see Belgium
N.Z.	No Resident Representative–see Belgium
U.K.:	28 Boulevard Royal, Luxembourg, Tel. 29 864.
U.S.A.:	22 E. Servais, Luxembourg, Tel. 40 123.

SHOPPING TIPS:
Miniature cast iron fire grates 'Taak', china and pottery. All of which

are very awkward to take with you around Europe. Luxembourger mosel (wine) and beer are highly recommended.

LANGUAGE:

It is difficult to find any dictionaries of the local dialect. French is spoken overall and but people aren't keen to let on that they understand German, although their dialect originally comes from Mosel/Frankish.

ACCOMMODATION:

Hotels, pensions, camping grounds: Office National du Tourisme, Boite Postale 1001, 1010 Luxembourg. Tel. 487 999.
Youth hostel: CAJL, Place d'Armess 18, 2346 Luxembourg. Tel. 25 588.

SPEED LIMIT:

In built up areas 60 km/h; outside built up areas 90 km/h; motorways 120 km/h.

RAILWAYS:

Tickets for all trains and buses: 1 day US$5, 1 month/US$35, 5 days in one month/$US13, and the 'Benelux-Tourrail' see Belgium/Holland.

AIRPORTS:

International airport at Luxembourg

LUXEMBOURG

The Village of Europe. But all the same it's unique and worthwhile seeing. If you are planning a short trip through Europe then you should plan a stopover. It has very deep river valleys, a wonderful museum and the Casemates, extensive underground passages which connect the old forts. Pop 79,600.

BY RAIL: The railway station, Luxembourg Gare, gives the whole of the southern part of town its name. It is a medium sized through railway station. The railway information office, Tel. 492 424, has small shops and snack bars, and banks are found to the right on Railway Square opposite. Also on the right is the tourist information office (Tel. 48 11 99). Through trains from Bern/Zurich, Strasbourg, Milan, Bussels, Maastricht and Koblenz pass here. For railway buffs, the Luxembourg railway station is very interesting as trains from Belgium, France and Germany come here as well as the local CFL trains. They have different ways of getting their electricity, so if you are interested in the different locomotives, this is the place to see them. In 1984 Luxembourg Railways had their 125 year celebration.

BY CAR: You can get to Luxembourg quite easily by car although there are areas still without expressways. From northern Germany and Koblenz use the A48 Koblenz-Trier autobahn which branches off to the west from the Hunsruck autobahn A61 and the Sauerland A3. The border crossing is Wasservilligerbruck and there is often a queue waiting to cross. Ways around it are: Near Trier branch off right to Bitburg, then left via Olk to Ralingen (Border) or via Minden to Echternacherbruck. In both cases take the E42 from Echternach to Luxembourg. From the south and also from Frankfurt, Alzey, Ludwigshafen take the A6 Kaiserlautern-Saarbrucken or the A8/B10 from Karlsruhe (Munich) via Zweibrucken. Before you come to Saarbrucken (from Karlsruhe simply straight ahead) take the A8 around the Saarland. The border crossings are Remich or Perl from the south, or Wormeldingenl from the north

  Large Parking Areas: At Glacis, R. Schumaner Square (from the north and west, it's the first crossing) or from the south (Blvd. d'Avranches) either go along the Blvd. de la Petryusse to Av. de la Liberte and left to Rousegaertchen or along the Viaduct to Knuedler Park, Place du Theatre.

BY AIR: Luxembourg also has an international airport, 6km east of the town, which is well known for its cheap flights. Buses leave for the railway station approx. every hour (Tel. 436 161). There is a tourist information office at the airport.

TOURIST INFORMATION: A second tourist information office is found on one side of the La Petrusse River Valley in the Town Hall on Place de'Armes in the centre of the city, Tel. 22808. Buses leave from the railway station (Bus 12/20) for the city centre. The city centre starts here in these small lanes.

TOURIST NEWSPAPERS: La semaine a Luxembourg (multi-language) Vade Mecum Culturel, Agenda Touristique (French).

POINTS OF INTEREST: The attractions are what ever you're interested in: A stroll across the wide-spanned bridges or along the river valleys will give you highly unexpected impressions of the town. There are several forts and bastions to remind you that in the middle ages Luxembourg was an important military power. Luxembourg was, until 11th May 1867, like a northerly Gibraltar.

  The Fortress, which was built by the often changing rulers of the town, include about 40,000 m^2 of underground passages, the casemates, which would be a safe place to be in a bomb attack. A signposted walk (red triangle on a white background) guides around the area. The fortress is a combination of a good natural position being enhanced by manmade structures. The walk begins at Place de la Constitution, towards the

Athens: The Acropolis

London: Financial Centre, Threadneedle St.

Ireland: Blessington Lakes

Dublin: Horseracing at Leopardstown

Switzerland: Zurich's Bahnhofstrasse

north end of viaduct Roosevelt; from the railway station it's straight along ave. de la Gare; from the city centre along the blvd. F.D. Roosevelt. The Petrusse River valley is crossed by the viaduct. On Constitution Square are the first casemates which have five different levels, the Petrusse (open daily, in winter only Saturday & Sunday). There is also a memorial to those Luxembourgers who fell in the world wars.

Again in the direction of the viaduct is the National Library and the Notre Dame Cathedral, both on the left. A bit further on is the Holy Ghost Citadelle, to-day the State Archives, built by Vauban, Ludwig XIV's master builder (1685). Along the way you get a good view of the valleys and the lower parts of town. The path is about half-way up the mountain and leads to the Corniche. You will see the large complex of the former Munster Abbey which was a gaol until 1984. There are again numerous fortlike buildings and at the Schloss Bridge is the entry to the second casemate, the Bock Casemate (open from March to the end of October). On the cliffs there are the excavated remains of the ancient Lutzelburg castle built in 963 around which the town grew. From here you can see the Maander valleys of the Alzette, the suburbs of Clausen and Pfaffenthal and the 'Drei Eicheln' the three big defence towers built during the Luxembourg-Austrian era. Along the street which leads to the valley, Montee de Claussen, rue du Fort Olizy is the youth hostel.

At one end of the Schloss Bridge is a Goethe memorial, on the left is St. Michael's church, and on the right is the seat of the government. Go past the fish markets to the museum which is next to the Grand Duke's palace and Luxembourg works of art are housed in a lot of inter-connected buildings. Among the treasures is a bronze mask from the 1st century. (Tuesday-Sunday 10.00 a.m.-12 noon, 2.00-6.00 p.m., gratis).

The sign-posted track goes past the three towers down into the valley, through the lower part of town and through part of the parklike areas along the Alzette and back up again. An amusement park with mini golf and the Petrusse Park are at the bottom of the climb up to Pont Adolphe and the ave. de la Liberte, which leads you back to the railway station.

This tour really leaves out the city centre, which is found around the Place de Armes where the Town Hall is, and which has a relief model of the whole fortress. There is also a concert pavilion there and street cafes which are very lively in summer.

Another really lively place is the Place Guillaume II. To the west in blvd. Royal is the central bus terminal. If you go along ave. Monterey or ave. Emile Reuter you will come to the green ring around the former fortress. In the park between the avenues is the central transmitter of Radio Luxembourg, the commercial radio-television station.

In the outer western suburbs is the Centre European, where the seat of the Supreme Court of the European Economic Community, the General Secretariat of the European Parliament, the European Investment Bank and other agencies are found. In the Hemicycle Eur building is a youth disco, Um Bock. The autobahn bridge 'Grossherzogin

Charlotte', which connects this area to the city centre, appears to be almost a little out of place.

If you feel like a little culture then go to the Thomas Mann Library, Luxembourg (42 blvd. Joseph II, Tel. 475 282, Monday-Thursday), or to the Art Gallery, ave. Emile Reuter, (Wednesday-Monday 3.00-7.00p.m., Saturday & Sunday 10.00 a.m.-12 noon) Cinema Centre: Place du Theatre, Tel. 479 62 644; Cine Utopia, ave. de la Fainzcerie, Tel. 472 109.

CITY TOURS: from the railway station Buskai 5, 9.30 a.m. 220 FL. You discover how old fashioned this town really is at the Schober Messe, a fair which last two weeks and starts on the second last Sunday in August.

FOOD AND ENTERTAINMENT: Very french, very expensive and very formal. Taverns: Target, Rue des Bains 17; La Taverne, ave. Marie Therese 5 (you can only get food until 8.00 p.m.). Cafes: Monopol, ave. de la Liberte 53, De Blinddarm, Rue Aldringen, next to PTT. Culture centre: Melusina, Rue de Treves (down, over Montee de Clausen); Pubs in the Old Town: Le Bistro Artscene, 11 Rue de Rost; Peckvillchen, 26/30 Rue de l'Eau; For young people: des Artistes, 22 Montee de Grund; Cafe Cockpit Inn, 43 blvd. Gen. Patton; Cafe Beim Malou, 47 rue de la Tour Jacob; Disco Humphreys, 36 blvd. d'Avrenches; Capucins, in the street of the same name; Theaterstuff, 49 Allee Scheffer; Garage, 42 rue des Etats Unis.

INTERESTING: As well as the European Centre there is the European Memorial which has both american and german soldiers' graves, 7 km east of the city close to the N2. There are over 15,000 solders buried here in this woodland cemetery.

THINGS TO SEE IN THE DISTRICT: If you can spend a little more time, then you should buy a day ticket on the Luxembourger Railway for 179 FL. Combined train/walking trips (Train-Pedestre) are offered. It's hard to travel north to south in the Grand Duchy and the main railway lines go in the other directions. The line via Mersch, Ettelbruck to Clervaux and Troisvierges is the longest of the land, and goes through the Ardennens where one of the most bitter battles of the last world war was fought.

ACCOMMODATION: Youth hostel: 2 rue du Fort Olisy. Tel. 26 889. Camping: Kockelscheuer,Tel. 47 1815. Hotels: in comparision, cheap: Windsor, 7 rue de Strasbourg, Tel. 484 801; De La Place, 11a Place Wallis. Tel. 488 567; Carlton, 9 rue de Strasbourg, Tel. 484 802.

NETHERLANDS

The Kingdom of the Netherlands is a constitutional monarchy with a parliamentary system and is one of the most densely populated countries in Europe but still has large areas of open space. (Area 40,844 sq. km-Pop. 14.3 million).

The land of cheese and dykes, windmills and tulips is perhaps sometimes over rated. The people are not always particularly friendly to foreigners. The geography of the land is notable for its lack of mountains and for the fact that much of its land is under sea level.

ENTRY/FOREIGN EXCHANGE/CUSTOMS REGULATION: A valid passport is required. No currency restrictions.

Duty Free Allowance:
200 cigarettes or 250g tobacco, 1 litre brandy and 2 litres wine. The border control is very lax as a result of the legalisation of soft drugs.

Currency/Exchange Rates: The local currency is the Dutch Guilder (gl).

A$1   = 1.45 g
C$1   = 1.60 gl
NZ$1 = 1.80 gl
£1   = 3.20 gl
US$ = 2.20 gl

The level of prices is more like those in Switzerland.

TELEPHONE:
It is possible to dial overseas direct. The local area code is dialled without the 0.

Emergency Telephone Number:
Different in every town. Amsterdam: Police 222 222; Ambulance 555 555.

EMBASSIES:
Australia: Koninginnegracht 23, The Hague, Tel. 630 983
Canada: Sophialaan 7, The Hague, Tel. 614 111
N.Z.   Mauritskade 25, The Hague, Tel. 469 324
U.K.:   Vermeerstraat 7, Amsterdam, Tel. 764 343.
U.S.A.:   Museumplein 19, Amsterdam, Tel. 790321.

FOOD:
About 600 restaurants in Holland (like in Denmark) offer a fixed price menu that costs approx. 17 gl. and is recognisable by the sign "Tourist

Menu'. You can also eat cheaply and well in the self-serve restaurants in the HEMA department stores (from 6 gl.).

INTERESTING INFORMATION:

At the VVV-Tourist Information Office you can buy a museum ticket which is valid for one year and costs 7.50 gl. for the under 25's, otherwise 20 gl.

ACCOMMODATION:

Hotels: Nationales Reservierungszentrum, Postfach (postbox) 3387, 1001 AD Amsterdam, Tel. 020/211 211.

Pensions, only those which are licensed, otherwise private handling is prohibited.

Camping is handled by the local VVV-Offices.

Youth hostel: NJHC, Prof. Tulpplein 4, 1018 GX, Amsterdam, Tel. 020/264 433.

SPEED LIMITS:

In built up areas 50km/h;
outside built up areas 80 km/h; motorways 100km/h. Plenty of motorways.

RAILWAYS:

Tickets for 3/7 days for US$40/US$55.

Extra tickets for local transport.

National local traffic ticket 14.80 gl. and also strip tickets which are even cheaper still.

Benelux-Tourrail for NS, SNCB, CFL for 5 in 17 days for 123/90 (under 25 years) from 15th March to 31st October.

AIRPORTS:

International airport near Amsterdam, smaller inland airports.

AMSTERDAM

A city of bizarre differences: picturesque old town canals and the cement city of the suburbs, absolutely liberal authorities, but no prospects for many young people to ever get a job, great freedom to live an alternative life style and culture but often total dependance upon drugs and prostitution. Tourists on drugs are not as welcome as they believe. The people here are still very reserved as far as the Germans are concerned. Population 687,000.

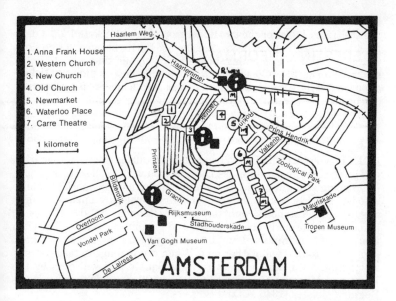

1. Anna Frank House
2. Western Church
3. New Church
4. Old Church
5. Newmarket
6. Waterloo Place
7. Carre Theatre

1 kilometre

AMSTERDAM

BY CAR: Amsterdam can be reached by motorway: from middle and southern Germany by the E36 from Duisburg-Emmerlich and on the E3-E71 from Hamburg-Osnabrueck-Enschede.

BY RAIL: Central station is the main through traffic railway station. It is located on the northern edge of the old town which is built on over 70 islands. For all general information Tel. 238 383.

BY AIR: The international airport of Amsterdam is Schiphol, approx. 16 km from town and can be reached with Bus 143 or Tram 4, a suburban train.

TOURIST INFORMATION: The head office is located on the square in front of central station, Stationsplein 10, Tel. 020/266 444, and city office is located at Leidseplein 15. Drug Emergency Telephone No. 265 115. Social Movement: Oranje Nassulaan 51, Tel. 736 869.

Also available there are Yearly Museum Tickets (M-Karte). It will pay for itself if you use it more than twice.

TOURIST NEWSPAPERS: The tourist newspaper 'Amsterdam This Week', cultural information brochures such as Uitgaan, Uitkrant and brochures for young people such as 'Use It' are also available at tourist information office.

Amsterdam is known for its boat trips around the canals in the old town section which was built at the time when the town flourished after the liberation war against Spain.

LOCAL TRANSPORT: A lot of places can be reached on foot, otherwise use the trains, buses or the two underground lines (Tickets 1/2/3/4 days for 8/10.75/13.20/15.60 gl/head). You can use the night buses for no extra charge. In spite of everything, perhaps you should take a boat trip on the canals–The 'Plas' from Damrak, 1 hour trip–cost 14 gl/head. Or take a tour round the town on the optimal transport, a bicycle (fietsen). These can be hired either at the railway station (NS), or Kronders rent-a-bike on the east side of the railway station, or Heja, Bestevaerstraat 39, Tram 13. Or take a pedal boat around the canals from Leidseplein–2 seaters 16 gl. half an hour or 4 seaters 17.50 gl. half an hour.

POINTS OF INTEREST: When you walk out of the railway station and go straight ahead along the Damrak, you will see all sorts of people. Keep going straight ahead to Dam Square with its memorial to those who fell in World War II and the Koninglijk-Paleis, royal palace, usually included in the standard sightseeing tours (Monday-Sunday 12.30-4.00 p.m.). It was formerly the town hall and is built on 13,660 piles. Dam Platz itself is more varied and interesting as artists, freaks, ordinary people and tourists all gather here. When you manage to tear yourself away, walk down Kalverstraat to Spui Square and will pass by the Historical Museum (Tuesday-Saturday 10.00 a.m.-5.00 p.m.) and the Beguine cloister (1346 A.D.).

If you like wax figures then visit Madame Tussauds. The main attaction here is Rembrandt's studio (Monday-Sunday 9.00 a.m.-6.00 p.m.). More of Rembrandt's works are found in Rembrandt House (Jodenbreestraat 4, Monday-Saturday 10.00 a.m.-5.00 p.m., 2 gl. Tram No. 9). Keep to the left until you come to Leidsestraat, which leads to Leidseplein where the tourist information office is located . Visit 'Bruinen' Cafe, Reinders Cafe or the literary Americain Cafe. The centre of the hippy colony known as the Jordaan area (formerly the people's quarter), starts behind Leidseplein (between Prinsen, Brouwers, Lijnbaans and Looiers canals). There is a pamphlet available for a walking tour which visits places of interest. Approval has been given plans to clean up the area and put it to better use.

MUSEUM TIPS: The Dutch Masters Museum, Stadhuderskade 42 (Tuesday-Saturday 10.00 a.m.-5.00 p.m. M-Karte); Maritime Museum, Kattenburgerplein 1 (Tuesday-Saturday 10.00 a.m.-5.00 p.m. M-Karte, transport Bus 22 or 28); the Van Gogh Museum, Paulus Potterstraat 7 (Tuesday-Saturday 10.30 a.m.-5.00 p.m., 4.50 gl. M-Karte, transport Trams 2, 5 or 16). Something out of the ordinary is the Kromhout Museum and Steam Ship Building Yard, Hoogte Kadijk 147, (Monday-Friday 10.00 a.m.-5.00 p.m., 1.75 gl. M-Karte, transport by the Metro); the Jewish Museum, Nieumarkt 4 (Tuesday-Saturday 10.00 a.m.-5.00 p.m., 1.75 gl. M-Karte, transport by Metro) and Anna Franks House (Prinsengracht 263, Tuesday-Saturday 10.00 a.m.-5.00 p.m., Tram 13, 17.4 gl.).

The Piggy Bank Museum is something out of the ordinary,

Raadhuisstr. 20, with 12,000 Money Boxes (Monday-Friday 1.00 p.m.-6.00 p.m.). The Neiderl Technical Museum is full of action, Tolstr. 129, (Monday-Friday 10.00 a.m.-4.00 p.m).

The Tropical Museum, Linnaeustraat 2 (Monday-Saturday 10.00 a.m.-5.00 p.m. Tram No. 9) and the Zoological Museum, Plantage Middenlaan 53 (Tuesday-Sunday 9.00 a.m.-5.00 p.m. Tram No. 9, 1 gl.) go together with the botanical gardens which is also on Pl. Middenlaan, as well as some other parks .

The Vondelpark–a little further behind the Leidesplein was once the mecca of the freaks who slept in the streets. Today it is strictly controlled–the easy life is over. Rembrandt Park is at the other end across Suriname Plein. Interesting street markets are held in Oudemunhuispoort (Books–Monday-Friday 11.00 a.m.-4.00 p.m.) in the Elandsgracht 109 'De Looier' (Antiques–Thursday-Saturday 10.00 a.m.-6.00 p.m.) as well as the international foodstuffs market in Albert Cuypstraat (Monday-Saturday) the typical dutch flower market in Amstelveld (only on Monday mornings) and a flea market at Waterlooplein (Valkenburgerstraat). The Moses and Aaron church, today an alternative museum and the Memorial to the Dockworkers Strike of 1941 against the jewish transportation are also found there. Some art is also offered for sale there.

Almost forgotten: Amsterdam is the Diamond Capital of the World. Many of the cuttings rooms have tours. Actual information on them can be obtained from the tourist information bureaux.

An indoor and outdoor swimming pool is found at Mirandabad, De Mirandalaan 9, Tram No. 25.

FOOD/PUBS: If you want to have a large meal then you had better eat in one of the chinese or indonesian restaurants which are found on every corner. A few other tips: Coffee Shop Het Ballonnetje, Roeterst 12; Sassafrass, Leidsegracht 68, Keuken van 1870, Spuist 4; t'Groene Venster, Uitrechtst 135; English fish & chips shop, Utrechtsestraat 63; Orient fast food (vegeterian), Utrechtsestraat 89; and the Broodje van Kootje, sandwich shop (e.g. Spui, Leidseeplein, Rembrandtssplein etc.) You also can eat in Melkweg, in Yoyo's, Govert Flinck/Albert Cuyp Markt or in Cok Budget Hotel, Keizersgracht 15.

ENTERTAINMENT: As far as evening entertainment is concerned, the Leidseplein and nearby streets are your best bets as there are discos, bars etc. Rock scene: Paradisco, Weteringschans 6, Oktopus, Keizersgracht 138. Salsa: De Kroeg, Lijnbaansgracht 163; Jazz. De Engelbewaarder, Kloveniersburegwal 59, Culture centre: DeIjsbreker, Weesperzijde 23; Taverns: De Huyschkaemer, Utrechtstr. 137; Cafe Hesp, Wesperzijde 130; Cafe Schiller, Rembrandtplein 16; Weltschmerz, Lindengracht 26; De Koophandel, Bloemgracht 49; De Admiraal, Herengracht 319 where you sample the drinks. Discos: De Loer, Nieuwezijds Voorburgwal 165; DansenBij Jansen, Handboogstraat.

Roller disco t'Nijpaardenhuis, Warmoestr. 170; Mazzo, Rosengracht 114; Stip, Lijnbaansgracht 161.

TYPICALLY DUTCH: A Polder Trip. Polders are areas of reclaimed land. Buses from Amstel (VAD-Line 154); Strip bus tickets are valid.

ACCOMMODATION: Youth hostel: Kloveniersburgwal 97 (metro Nieuwmarkt) Tel. 020/136 821; Zandpad 5, Vondelpark, Tel. 831 744 (Tram 1 or 2). Youth hotels: Cok Budget Hotel, Keizersgracht 15, Tel. 251 364; Adam & Eve, Sarphatiestr. 105, Tel. 246 206; Cok Budget, Koninginnenweg 34, Tel. 646 111. Camping–Youth Vliangenbos, Meenwenkaan 138, Tel. 368 855; Amsterdamse Box, Kleine Noorddijk 1, Aalsmeet, Tel. 416 868. There are a lot of inexpensive hotels (30 to 70 gl. for a double room)–Book at the tourist information.

THE HAGUE (DEN HAAG)– ROTTERDAM

Amsterdam, The Hague, Scheveningen and Rotterdam are practically one continuous city. They have some beautiful buildings, a particularly distinctive flair, the international flavour of a capital, a coastal town and an industrial harbour all rolled into one.

BY CAR: The following roads will bring you to The Hague/Rotterdam: the E36 from the Ruhr via Emmerlich; from the north the E72 from Oldenburg to Enschede and Arnheim, then the E36; from the south the E9/E10 autobahn (motorway) from Cologne, Aachen, Maastricht, Tilburg.

Parking Stations: in The Hague are to be found in the city and the green areas of Malieveld/Koekamp; in Scheveningen large parking areas are to be found along the seafront.

BY RAIL: From The Hague railway station H.S. there are numerous trains to various towns in Holland. This modern station on the south-eastern edge of the city has all the usual services. International trains e.g. from Germany also stop at central station in Kon. Julianaplein. Information Tel. 824 141. The even newer Rotterdam railway station built in the 1950s (have a look at the ceiling of the halls) also has first class train connections and services and is very near to the city centre. Tel. 117 100.

BY AIR: The Rotterdam Airport is located between the two towns. Tel. 371 144.

THE HAGUE

The Hague and its suburbs, together with the summer holday resort of Scheveningen, is Holland's second largest town (Pop. 674,000). It is the seat of the Netherlands parliament and interestingly the International Court of Justice is found in Carnegie Plein. Shell also has its head office here.

TOURIST INFORMATION: Kon. Juliana Plein 30 at Central station and in Scheveningen, Zwolse straat, next to the Europa Hotel, Tel. 070/546200. Local tourist newspaper: Info Deze Week (in three languages). Local transport: buses and trams (see Introduction to The Netherlands).

POINTS OF INTEREST: The city of The Hague begins at the Markethof in Spui str. where a market is really held. There are quite a few attractions which are very close together: The Binnenhof which was an earl's castle and has a knights' hall and now houses the Parliament and Parliamentary Exhibition (Monday-Saturday 10.00 a.m.-4.00 p.m.). Each year on the third Tuesday in September, the Queen opens Parliament. Right next to it is the Mauritsjuis built in 1644 which houses a superb dutch art collection (Tuesday-Sunday 10.00 a.m.-5.00 p.m.), Kneuterdijk 6. On the left over Buitenhof is the town hall, and the more impressive Folter Museum is in Gevangenpoort (Weekdays 10.00 a.m.-5.00 p.m., Saturday & Sunday 1.00-5.00 p.m.). In the opposite direction towards Spui str. is an arcade with small shops. Go through and keep to the right and you'll come to the Grote Kerk (church) in Groenmarkt. Go a bit further along Prinsen str. and you will come to Queen Beatrix's Palace. A bit further along past the Palace Park is Freedom Palace which is the seat of the International High Court.

In the east are extensive parklands (near central station) which act as a buffer zone between The Hague and Scheveningen. Popular: Madurodam, Holland in miniature. It is prettiest in the evenings when the lights are turned on–Haringkade 175–open daily from April to October.

There is nothing much left to see of old Scheveingen which was formerly a fishing village (the catch was mainly herrings). It is now a professionally planned holiday resort with endless beaches stretching to Kijkduin and a pier built in the english style which you can visit for 3.50 gl. It contains shell and coral displays, video games, children's playground, a casino, a health spa, and the ultra modern 'Palace Promenade' and 'De Parasol' pub.

The 'Golfbad', a wave and surfing swimming pool, which is open all year round (even in summer, the weather here is often very changeable) is rather an expensive experience, Strandweg 13 (daily 10.00 a.m.-10.00 p.m.–15 gl. for 3.5 Hours).

MUSEUMS: Museum of Sea Life, Dr. Lelykade 39 (daily 10.00 a.m.-5.00 p.m.); Education Museum, Hemsterhuis str. 2e and 154 (daily 10.00 a.m.-5.00p.m.); The Hague Council Museum, Stadthourderslaan 41 (Tuesday-Sunday 10.00 a.m.-5.00 p.m.); Museum Bredius, Prinsengracht 6, dutch masters (Tuesday-Thursday 2.00-5.00 p.m.); Museum of Puppet Theatre, Nassau Dillenberg str. 8 (Sunday 12 noon-2.00 p.m.); National Museum HW. Mesdag, Laan van Meerdervoort 7gl (Tuesday-Sunday 10.00 a.m.-5.00 p.m.); and for a look at the past 'Oud Scheveningen', Neptuns str. 92 (Monday-Saturday 10.00 a.m.-5.00 p.m.).

The Panorama Mesdag, Zee str. 65b, has an enormous round painting with an area of 1680 m² which depicts the fishing village of Scheveningen as it once was (daily 10.00 a.m.-5.00 p.m.). For relaxation: Rose and flower gardens in Westerbroekpark (park), gratis, all day.

RELAXATION with action is offered at Drievliet Park, (amusement park) April-September–all inclusive price–Jan Thijssenweg 16, Rijswijk. Something similar with water attractions and camping is offered by Duinrell, Buurtweg 135 at Wassenaar. Out this way are The Hague Woods (Haagse Bosjes) and the Huis ten Bosch (Castle).

Loved by everyone: Cycle tours through the woods and the sand dunes. Bicycles can be hired at the railway stations (deposit required). Town Tours from VVV-Office at Central Railway Station, April-October, Monday-Saturday 21 gl.

INEXPENSIVE FOOD: At Hema cafeteria style restaurant in the Kaufhaus (department store) Mark str.; Buffeterie Palace, Palce Promenade; Mr. Cocker Tearoom, Gevers Deynootweg 900-331; Pieter Brueghel, Deltaplein 631; Sherry's, Buitenhof 39.

EVENINGS: Billard Cafe: Anna's Place, Gevers Deynootweg 822; Bowling: Nederland, Gevers Deynoodt Weg 990; Roller Skating Disco: Gevers Deynootweg 822; Queens Pub, Anna str. 3; Pompernikkel, Denneweg 27.

ACCOMMODATION: Youth hostel, Monsterseweg 4, Tel. 070/250 600, Bus 123; Youth Hostels: Marion, Havenkade 31, Tel. 542 509; t'Seehuys, Zeekant 45, Tel. 559 585.
Camping: Ockenburgh, Kijduin, Wijndealerweg 25 and Duinrell.

ROTTERDAM

Rotterdam was rebuilt after the second world war in a functional style. It is the biggest harbour in the world and naturally it is dominated by the 50km wide dock and ancillary buildings area. It is a worthwhile stopover for those who are interested in that sort of thing. (Pop. 558,000.)

TOURIST INFORMATION: Head Office, Stadjuisplein 19, Tel. 136 000; and at the Railway Station.

LOCAL TRANSPORT: There are not only trams, buses and trains, but also a metro (underground) (See Introduction to the Netherlands).

POINTS OF INTEREST: Interesting for town planners: Bouwcentrum-Wonen, exhibition of homes and architecture (on the right hand side opposite the railway square). But to get to the city centre you have to turn left. Straight away you will see the 'Lijnbaan' shopping centre with the 'L'Homme qui marche' by August Rodin. Opposite Coolsingel str. is the Town Hall, further along is the Chamber of Commerce, the Stock Exchange-with small and large shops in Beursplein-and the Schielandshuis with its historical museum. Cross over Churchill Plein and you are already at the start of the harbour area. Left of the memorial erected in remembrance of the destruction of the town during the 2nd world war is the museum ship 'Buffel'. The pile driver ship has been renovated and is open for inspection.

The Schiedamsedijk (Dyke), parallel to Leuvenhaven, leads to Willemsplein, the heads, from where the Spido Harbour tours start (the big ships are all much the same-prettier in the evenings) March to October inclusive. Depending on what you can afford, you could also take a longer harbour trip or a trip to the Europoort or to the Deltawerken, only July and August. It is a town dominated by the sea, and you learn about it best from the rocking deck of a ship. . .

If you want to get a complete picture of the town then you should go to the 'Euromast Space Tower'. (Viewing Platform 100m, daily 9.00 a.m.-10.00 p.m., metro Leuvehaven, Tram 7).

A little bit of the past is found at Delfshaven (with museum, 'De dubbeide Plamboom', Tram 6,9). The Pilgrim Fathers left from here in 1620 to settle in America.

SOME MUSEUMS: Boymans van Beuningen, Paintings and Ceramics, Mathenesserlaan 18 (Monday to Saturday 10.00 a.m.-12 noon and 2.00-5.00 p.m.); Zakkendragershuisje, Zinngiesserei, Voor str. 13; Atlas von Stolk, pictures which show the history of the Netherlands, Aelbrechtskolk 12 (any questions Tel. 767 433); Museum for Land and Folklore, Willemskade 25, which also deals with cultural minorities in Holland.

The animals live in a natural environment at the Diergaarde Blijsoep, van Aerssenlaan 49. A collection of rare trees is found at the Arboretum Trompenburg, Honingerdijk–free tickets available at VVV (tourist office). The Dralingse Bos is a large park with an enormous area of water. A snuff, tobacco and herb Winbdmill 'De Ster' is found in PlasZoom str. (Monday-Friday 10.00 a.m.-12 noon and 1.00-4.00 p.m.). Catch a bus from Rotterdam CS (strip tickets are valid) for a trip through the beautiful Polder Area.

PUB TIPS: t'Fust, Lijnbaan; Le Vagabund, Nieuwe Binnenweg; Melief Bender, OudeBinnenweg; Deltsche Leeuw, opposite the G.P.O., terrific breakfast.

ACCOMMODATION: Youth hostel, Richussen Str. 107, Tel. 365 763, Tram 4,8; Camping, Kanaalweg 84; no youth Hotels; Inexpensive hotels (approx. 65 gl. for a double room): Bavri, 's Gravendijwall 70, Tel. 366 921; Metropole, NieuweBennenweg 13a, Tel. 770877.

NORWAY

The Kingdom of Norway has a population of 4.1 million and an area of 323 895 sq. km. It is a member of NATO but after a referendum decided against joining the EEC. Norwegians tend to be cool in their social relations, but in commerce they have a very open policy.

Geographically, Norway is a land of mountains, high plateaux and deep fjords. (Warm clothing is essential even in summer.) The area along the whole west coast where the fjords branch out is absolutely unique as is the midnight sun (24hour) in the far north (from Bodo).

ENTRY/CURRENCY/CUSTOMS REGULATIONS: A valid passport is required. The importation of Norwegian currency is not controlled, but one is only permitted to take out 5000 NKr.

Duty Free Allowance:
    Per person (over 20 years) up to 1 litre brandy, 1 litre wine and 2 litre beer, 200 cigarettes or 250g tobacco.

Currency/Exchange Rate: The currency of the land is the Norwegian Krone.

1A$	=	4.90 kr
1C$	=	5.40 kr
1NZ$	=	6.10 kr
£1	=	10.80 kr
1US$	=	7.40 kr

Goods in general are more expensive than the rest of Europe.

TELEPHONE:
To phone overseas dial the local Area Code without the 0.

Emergency Telephone Numbers: Doctor 20 1090; Police 11 00 11.

EMBASSIES:
Australia: Jernbanstorget 2, Oslo, Tel. 41 44 33.
Canada: Oscar's Gate 20, Oslo, Tel. 46 69 55/59
N.Z.   No Resident Representative–see The Netherlands
U.K.:   Thomas Heftyesgate 8, Oslo, Tel. 56 38 90.
U.S.A.   Drammensveien 18, Oslo, Tel. 56 68 80.

ACCOMMODATION:
Hotels, camping grounds, youth hostels, cabins: Landslaget for Reiselivet i Norge, H.Heyerdalsgate 1, Oslo 1, Te. 02/427044.
There is a bonus pass available for hotels (otherwise they are too

expensive). The Landslaget gives out a good brochure with many timetables (Rutehefter for Turister).

SPEED LIMIT:

In built up areas 50 km/h;
outside built up areas; motorways 90 km/h.

RAILWAYS:

'Nordturist'-Karte, compared to Denmark very cheap sleepers.

AIRPORTS:

International airports at Oslo and Bergen.

SHIP:

Direct service to Oslo from Kiel, Frederikshavn (Denmark) and Copenhagen (Denmark).

BERGEN

The trip by rail from Oslo to Bergen is unique. It goes across Europe's highest plateau, Hardangervidda, and along the fjords. You can't take the same trip by car. Another trip which even surpasses this one, is a side trip by train from Myrdal, Batnahalsen, Flam to Aurlansfjord. Bergen is the capital of the Fjordland (Pop. 207,000).

It is the central harbour for the offshore oil platforms. Go past the Park Lille Lungegard (where cultural performances are held under the stars) and you will come to the tourist information office (1 Slottgt, Tel. 32 14 80.)

TOURIST INFORMATION: Cabin/Hut bookings: 10 Kaigatan, Tel. 31 66 300 and the bus terminal where trips into the walking area around Fana and Og. Information: C. 3 Sundsgate, Tel. 32 46 40).

POINTS OF INTEREST: Turn right into the Vestre Torget gatan and go along to Torget where not only the excursion boats leave (very beautiful: Hardangerfjord), but also a fish and vegetable market is held at Althergebrachter Meadow (Summer and Winter). On the right of the railway station is the Hanse Museum (5NKr.) and a bit further on is the suburb of Bryggen where there are wooden houses dating back to the Middle Ages, also a museum (10.00 a.m.-4.00 p.m., 4 NKr.).

After leaving here one shouldn't wonder about the bare plateau-all the timber came from there. Everyone has made use of it, the Vikings, Hanseatic League, and to-day (thanks to the airport) all sorts of tourists. Afterwards a trip to Ulriken is nice (combination ticket only 25 NKr., city bus ticket 25 NKr./48 hours). The open air museum, Gamie Bergen, is a bit further away (11.00 a.m.-6.00p.m. Students 4 NKr., Bus 1/8) and King Gamlehaugen's residence (1.00-3.00 p.m., 3 NKr.) which has a beautiful park.

OSLO

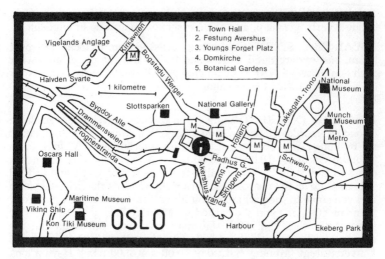

Oslo is the Viking capital. The Danes and Swedes had a say in the development of Norway for a long time and the city combines the cool flair of the north with parks and open air museums. (Pop. 450,000.)

BY RAIL: If you come from the north or from Sweden you will arrive at the terminal railway, Sentralstasjon. All services and the information office are found in the new hall. An administration tower has been built over the platform hall.

A tour to Stavanger in the south begins at the Vestbanestasjon, terminal station on the left of the town hall. Train information: Tel. 42 19 19.

BY CAR: You come to Oslo via Helsingborg-Goteborg (Sweden) along the E6, Sarpsborg-Moss. There are a few parking areas around the main railway station which is right at the entry into the town.

BY AIR: You can get to Oslo from two airports. The Oslo airport at Fornebu which is where the regular flights land Tel. 02/596 716 Bus

31, and the charter flights land at Gardermoen which is 50km from the city centre (buses leave from the main railway station).

BY FERRY: from Frederikshafen, Hirtshals or Copenhagen or from the danish mainland in the north, or just to Larvik (shorter) cost from approx. US$200 with car for up to 5 people. Oslo Harbour Tel. 02/568 150.

TOURIST INFORMATION: Town hall, Tel. 02/42 71 70; Youth information: USEIT, 2 Grubbegata, Tel. 110409. They also sell the Oslo Kortet for 50/75/100 NKr. for 1, 2 or 3 days and entitles you to free museum entry and local transport as well as many discounts.

TOURIST NEWSPAPERS: Oslo This Week (monthly in english), Oslo Guide (yearly, german), and the Norseman (magazine in english).

LOCAL TRANSPORT: Oslo has a varied system of local transport (tram, bus, underground, ferries and trains) but the prices are rather high (single trip 9 NKr. with no changes allowed). Tourist Tickets for 30 NKr/24 hours are better value for money (Route Map 'Sporveier' 10 NKr).

POINTS OF INTEREST: Tours of the gigantic town hall are available (Monday-Saturday 10.00 a.m.-2.00 p.m., gratis). More information about the building can be obtained at the Kunstlerforbundet, 3 Kjeld Stubsgt (Monday-Saturday 10.00-a.m.-5.00 p.m.). A few steps further on you come to Eidsvolls Park. Go half left across it and you come to Karl Johans Gate on the main street. Turn right, towards the railway station and you come to the parliament building, Stortine (Monday-Saturday 12 noon-2.00 p.m.) and the cathedral (Monday-Friday 10.00 a.m.-1.00 p.m.). After that you reach the main university buildings and the national gallery, a highlight for anyone interested in art, 13 Universitatsgt (Monday-Saturday 10.00 a.m.-4.00 p.m.). Have a look through the Edward Munch museum (TJ– underground Toyen from central) entry, gratis, 53 Toyengata (Tuesday-Sunday 10.00 a.m.-8.00 p.m.). The botanical gardens are also in this street and you can have a rest there and at the Natural History Museum (daily 7.00 a.m.-8.00 p.m.). The Historical Museum is part of the University collection, 2 Frederiksgate (Tuesday-Sunday 12 noon-3.00 p.m.) near the university. Don't miss out on the Kunstindustriemuseet, 1 St. Olavsgate (Tuesday-Sunday 11.00 a.m.-3.00 p.m., gratis).

You can really relax at the Toyen baths and sauna. Walk around the old suburb of Kampen (Toyen Sentrum, Kjolbergate, Kampen Steps, water reservoir) for a view of the city and then walk through the suburban streets of Bogate, Sonsgate, Normansgate (Bus 29 to the city centre). South of Toyen (Tram 9 from the city centre) is Ekeberg Park at the Sjomannsskolen tram stop. In the entry hall you can see frescoes by Per Krohg, between the school and the Kongsveien are 5,000 year old rock paintings. From here the view of the city and the fjords is really beautiful and the middle ages ruins of Oslo lie at your feet (Bus 72 to the city centre).

The state run ferries leave from Quay No. 3 in front of the town hall for the peninsular, Bygdoy which is worth seeing–you can use your tourist ticket (or Bus 30). If you have ever dreamed of sea voyages, far continents and dark ages, you will really enjoy this day trip: right at the start is the maritime museum and the polar ship FRAM which took Nansen to near the north pole and Amundsen to the south pole. Across from there is Thor Heyerdahl's balsa raft 'Kon Tiki' (proof of the early discovery of Easter Island) and the reed boat RA II which crossed the Atlantic. While we are thinking about the ships from earlier times, take a 20 minute walk to the museum of Viking Ships. Only 5 minute's walk from there is the open air folk museum containing 170 houses which have been brought from the provinces to the capital. Among them is a stave church from Gol (cira 1200). All Bygdoy museums are open from the 15th May-August daily from 10.00 a.m.-6.00 p.m.–otherwise from 11.00 a.m.-4.00 p.m. or sometimes 3.00 p.m.

Another trip is to Holmenkollen the famous ski jump and the Ski museum (daily 10.00 a.m.-6.00 p.m.). A little further to the west is the camping ground, Bogstad in Bogstad Weiher (underground national theatre 'Holmenkoll' train to the terminus). Then a 15 minute walk will bring you to Tryvannstarn where, on a clear day, you get the best view in Scandinavia. Further away: Voksenkoll, Drag stotten (memorial), but also with a good view, Voksenkollveinen, Holmenkollveien (Holmenkoll railway station).

In summer, people spend a lot of time in the parks: around the castle in the city centre or more often around the Vigeland complex in Frogner Park, founded by Gustav Vigeland (museum, 22 Nobelgate, Monday-Saturday 1.00-7.00 p.m., gratis) stone sculptures; there is a Speaker's Corner at Hambras Place near the town hall.

FOOD can be brought everywhere in cafeterias, in the street, in the pedestrian zones (K. Johans Gate and Store Torvet, Youngstorvet) or you can buy something at the fruit and vegetable market, Youngstorvet (behind the cathedral). In comparison, chinese food is inexpensive (Chinatown, 139 Trondheimsvn, Ming Wah Kro, 13 Parkvn). The Hot House, 15b Pilestredet and Jeppe's Kro (underground Vinderen) are good for a snack as well as jazz/disco, and the Hot House Pub is for food and music. For evening entertainment we recommend: Glenn's Wall, 64 Vogtsgt (music groups); Riddarhallen Disco, 5 Torgetgt; Jeggerhallen, 30 Akersgt, as well as Club 7, 15 Munkedamsveien; Last Train, 45 Karl Johansgatan 45; Jazz Alive, 2b Obersvatoriegate.

THE LATEST FOR REAL ADVENTURERS: A conducted four wheel drive tour through Oslomarka, approx. 300 NKr from the town hall.

ACCOMMODATION: Youth hostel: Haraldsheimvn. (Grefsen railway station, Bus 31) Tel. 02/155 043 Bjerke, 271 Trondheimsvn, Tel. 64 87

87. Camping: Bogstad, 7 Oslo Bus 41); Ekeberg (Bus 24 from railway station; Stubljan (Bus 75). Huts in Bogstad. Pensions: KFUK, 38 Neuberggate, Tel. 441 787; St. Katarina-hjemmet, 21b Majorstuveien, Tel. 60 13 70 or try the accommodation reservation desk at the railway station–private rooms approx. 120 NKr for a double.

PORTUGAL

Although the Republic of Portugal, in particular the northern interior, is noted for its lush vegitation, it is primarily a land of the sea and coast; without a doubt, a paradise for bathers and sunbakers. (Area 92,080 sq. km.-Pop. 10 million).

Portugal has something for every one-the Costa Verde, Costa de Prata, Costa de Lisboa, the Estoriler Coast, Costa de Dourade and the Algrave. It also has the islands in the Atlantic, Maderia, Puorto Santo and the Azores, as well as the sparsely populated interior areas of Montanaha and Planicies which are a challenge for the adventurous traveller. Because of the comparitvely low prices for Europe, and the uniquely hospitable nature of the Portuguese, how can anyone not want to go there?

ENTRY/FOREIGN EXCHANGE/CUSTOMS REGULATIONS: A valid passport is required. One is only permitted to bring in and take out 5,000 Escudos.

Duty Free Allowance:
1 litre of brandy and 2 litres of wine, 200 cigarettes or 250gm tobacco. It is likely that Portugal will join the common market in the near future. Furthermore, alcohol is extremely cheap in Portugal.

Currency/Exchange Rate: The currency of the land is the Escudo (esc.).

```
1A$   =    97 esc.
1C$   =   108 esc
1NZ$  =    78 esc
£1    =   215 esc
1US$  =   147 esc
```

Your buying power is very high. Food, alcohol, cigarettes, accommodation and fabrics/textiles are very cheap.

TELEPHONE:
Telephone calls to other countries from public telephone booths are possible but not always without difficulty. Apart from that, they are very expensive. To phone overseas dial your local area code then the number without the 0.

Emergency Telephone Number: 115

CLIMATE:
In summer on the Atlantic coast, the heat is tempered by the ever present sea breeze, whereas the south coast of Algrave has a mediterranean climate (sometimes depending on the weather, you can

even bathe in the sea in December/January).

Temperatures in July and August are extremely high. The holiday maker can expect oppressive heat in the interior. It's swimming season the whole year round on Madeiria but it cools off quickly in the evenings, so always take some warmer clothing.

EMBASSIES:

Australia: Avenida da Liberdade 244, Lisbon, Tel. 539 108.
Canada: Rua Rosa Araujo 2, Lisbon, Tel 563 821
N.Z.:   Ambassador in Rome is accredited to Portugal
U.K.:   Rua S. Domingos a Lapa 35-39, Lisbon, Tel. 661 691.
U.S.A.:   Avenida Dos Forcas Armadas, Lisbon, Tel. 725 600.

FOOD

Very tasty (it is cooked with less oil than in other south european countries) and extremely cheap. On portuguese menus the word 'aperitif' means entree and not a before dinner drink; e.g. spicy, salty fish, olives etc. For a before dinner drink you should try the dry white portuguese wine at least once. It tastes fantastic.

ACCOMMODATION:

Hotels, pensions, camping grounds: Lisbon: P. Restauradores, Tel. 363314;
Youth hostel: APPJ, Rua Andrade Corvo 46, Lisbon. Only a few youth hostels.
Camping grounds are cheap and camping in the countryside is not encouraged but is tolerated. There are plenty of cheap pensions.

SPEED LIMITS:

In built up areas 60 km/h;
outside built up areas 90 km/h; motorways 120 km/h (inexpensive toll charges). A green insurance card is mandatory.

AIRPORTS:

International airports at Lisbon and Porto.

LISBON–LISBOA

An ancient city built on seven small hills, which reached the rank of a roman town in 1 B.C. Its golden age was the 15th century after the sea route to India was discovered. Because it was a sea power which had extensive trade connections to distant lands, Lisbon became

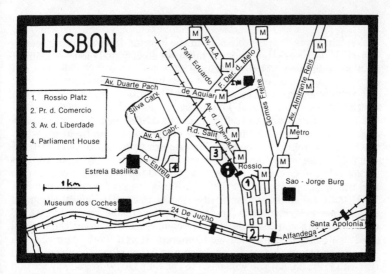

wealthy as well as becoming one of the cosmopolitan centres of Europe. Even to-day you can see its former glory when you look at the Misericordia Church, the Hieronymite Monastery or the Belem Tower.

BY CAR: The shortest route along very good roads is via Barcelona, Zargoza, Madrid, Talavera de la Reina, Trujillo, Merida, Badajoz (Border) Elvas, and Estremoz. Or you can take the long way, along bad roads, but through unusual countryside–Barcelona, Zaragoza, Valladolid, Zamora (Border)–Braganca (from here there are hairpin bends), Porto and Leira. There are motorways only around Lisbon on which you have to pay a minimal toll but are recommended because of the poor quality of the main roads. Keep in mind the motto 'blow your horn and drive on quickly' as you aren't supposed to blow your horn. In Lisbon, park in the suburbs and catch the bus or the tram into the city centre as there is too much traffic to drive right in. Comparitively speaking, there are few car thefts.

BY RAIL: Lisbon's central station is Apolonia where trains arrive from and depart for Paris and Madrid. The smaller, cleaner, Terminus station has restaurants, money exchanges, waiting room, luggage lockers and left luggage room, Tel. 876 025. Jewellery salesmen try to sell you fake jewellery. Most people don't feel very comfortable here.

BY AIR: You can get to Lisbon from many cities. There is an airport bus to the city. Information from the national airline, TAP, Tel. 802 060.

TOURIST INFORMATION: Praca dos Restauradores, Rossio Platz, Tel. 363 624.

TOURIST NEWSPAPERS: 'What's on in Lisbon' and 'se73'

(portuguese). City Tours: Rn Toiurs, av. Fontes Pereira de Melo 33, Tel. 563 451.

LOCAL TRANSPORT: There is an old but effective underground network and also ancient trams which have only one car and are extremely slow. Getting on and off is an unforgettable experience but it is an inexpensive way to see the city. The only thing that is missing are the horses out in front! The buses are generally very overcrowded but if you go upstairs to the front of the double deckers you will get a good view of the city, but the axle noises which can be heard when the buses go round the corners are enough to raise the pulse rate of every upstairs passenger. One way tickets from 15-40 Esc. 10 Trip Tickets for 240 Esc. The Tourist Ticket (good for the underground, tram and bus cost approx. $7 for 1 week.) Taxis are also very inexpensive, for US$4 you can drive practically all over town (Flagfall 30 Esc. plus 16 Esc. per km). From the Apolonia railway station buses 9 or 91, 46 or 38 will take you towards the city centre. 1.5 km along the coastal road you come to the Praca Do Comercio. If you go to the right you will come to the city centre and if you go further along the coastal road (Buses 17, 28, 35, 83) you will come to the Cais Do Sodre railway station from where trains leave for Casciais and Estoril (Lisbon's beaches). On the Praca Do Comercio is the terminal for ferries to Barreiro (orange flags in the harbour and blue to the railway station), for those who want to travel further south e.g. to Algrave. There are crossings every half an hour, approx. 70 cents; the Barreiro railway station right on the harbour is where you get into bone shaking carriages on the formerly electrified line to the south.

POINTS OF INTEREST: You can learn a little about Lisbon before 1755 in Alfama which is south-east of the Apolonia railway station. In the small lanes and backyards you get the impression that Portugal is the second poorest land in Europe. There are some beautiful churches here such as the Cathedral Se, the Santa Luzia (with a viewing terrace) and Santo Estevao.

Go down to Rio Tejo (Tagus river) and the Praca Do Comercio again where a large flea market is held (leather and woollen goods). Another market is the Market of the Thieves, which is located in the upper half of Alfama in Freira da Landra (only Saturday and Tuesday). The small streets of Beixia which lead off the P.D. Comercio are a delight for those who like window shopping, and for those with dirty shoes! Above is the Praca de Rossio with pleasant side walk cafes around the two fountains. From here you can go along the avenida da Liberdade, which is tree lined and has mosaic footpaths. Parallel to it is the R. Portas St. Antao, which has many restaurants. On the left are the botanical gardens, and above the Eduardo VII Park, further along is the Praca Marques de Prombal, which is called Rotunda and has a memorial. In the park there are diverse sporting possibilities, and another even more exotic garden is the Estuva Fria.

On this tour the Castello S. Jorge has been left out. Start walking from Rossio Square where behind the tin covered walls is a small, elevated, romantic park with exotic animals and plants which affords a fascinating all round view of the endless sea of houses, the blue band of the Tagus River and the gigantic suspension bridge, 'The 25th April'.

Bullfights, Tourada, are held in the Praca de Touros do Campo Pequeno (Sunday afternoon and Thursday evening); bigger and better ones are held further out at Sintra, where the bull is not killed, but only brought to its knees. Sintra tourist information: Praca da Republica, Tel. 923 1157.

Another part of town with a unique character is the university quarter, Bairro Alto, on the left before you come to the Praca de Rossio. There are several unusual shops and cafes and a curiosity: the Eiffel Lift, a cathedral tower from the iron age, in the ruins of the Carmo church.

PUBS: The pubs are where it's happening–a few tips: Adega Popular 33, rua da Concicao 33; Cervejaria Trindade, rua Nova da Trindade 20 (seafood, and good beer); Londres, av. de Roma 7 (snack bar, pub, and cinema); Sagitario, rua de Belem 10 (fondue); Sir Self Service, rua de Belem 10. In the evenings: Carrousel, rua Castilho 77; Night & Day, av. Duque de Laule 49.

More cheap pubs are found in the parallel streets west of av. da Liberdade. Disco: Archote, rua D., Filipa de Vilhena 6; Jazz: Hot Club, Praca da Alegria 39 (Thursday-Saturday). Fado Pubs: the best pubs in which the melodramatic, portuguese folk music is sung are: A Cesaria, rua Gilberto Rola 20 and Senhor Vinho, rua deo Meio a Lapa 18. A Severa, rua das Gaveas 55, Painel do Fado, RS Pedro de Alcantara 65-69, it is even better when a portuguese starts to sing Fado from his heart in a local pub.

MUSEUMS: the Palast Nitra, rua deo Acucar 64, next to another attraction, with the National Museum (all museums are open Tuesday-Sunday 11.00 a.m.-5.00 p.m., 5 Esc.) Erlesene with international works of art: Museum Fundacao Gulbenkian, metro ao Sebastio. Museum of Ancient Art, rua das Janelas Verdes 95; Museum of Modern Art, rua Serpa Pinto 6; Coach Museum, Praca Alfonso de Albuquerque; Marine Museum, Praca deo Imperio, Belem; Miliary Museum, Largo do Museu de Artiharia.

THEATRE: Nacional de S. Carlos, Lg. S. Carlos, Tel. 368 664; and some in Parque Mayer. A permanent circus is found at Coliseu dos Recreios; the zoo also has a lot of beautiful plants (metro Sete Rios) and you get a good view from Miradouro dos Moinhos, from where you can see among other things, the Aguas Livres aqueduct built in the 18th century and still standing to-day.

INTERESTING: If you follow the street along the Rio Tejo bank you will come to the Mosterio dos Jeronimos, the Hieronymite monastery

(16th century) built in a unique portuguese style. Here in the suburb of Belem, is also the famous Belem Tower (1515) from where many voyages of discovery started.

BEACHES: Costa do Estoril, to the west and nearer, Carcavelos, and to the south across the bridge is Trafaria where you can camp.

ACCOMMODATION: Camping in the outskirts. Take the No. 14 or 43 bus from Praca Do Comercio; rua Andrade Corvo 46, Tel. 53 26 96 (Metro Picoas). Hotels: Residencial Aleluia, rua Luciano Cordeior 32, Tel. 57 37 02 and Pensao Nova Castanheirense, rua Gomes Freire 130, Tel. 55 86 17 (both relatively central and cheap, Bus 12). Streets with cheap accommodation: rua Castilho and avenida Duque de Avila.

ROMANIA

The Communist Republic of Romania (Area 237,500 sq. km.–Pop. 22.7 M.) is bordered in the east and north by the Soviet Union, in the west by Hungary and Yugoslavia, in the south by Bulgaria and has at the Danube delta, a Black Sea coastline. The local people are genuinely friendly.

The geographical features of Romania are the Carpathian mountain range which runs from the south-west to north-west and the Danube which forms the border in the south-west and south and which, when it nears the coast, bends to the north and then to the east to form a wide delta. The high land of the north-west, around the seven hills, was the goal of many waves of german speaking immigrants and has been under Austrian/Hungarian administration since 1918.

ENTRY/FOREIGN EXCHANGE/CUSTOMS REGULATIONS: A valid passport and visa is required for entry which is obtainable at the border (also on the train) or from a Romanian Embassy for $12 US. You must change $10.00 US (or the equivalent in other western currency or traveller's cheques) per day at the border for every day you are in the country (minimum of 3 days). It is possible to exchange more than this, but if you decide to leave earlier you can only change back your left over Lei into foreign currency for any whole days. It is better to exchange money only at banks and you must keep the dockets. If you book and pay for your trip beforehand this doesn't apply. The trip doesn't have to be part of a package deal, camping ground or hotel vouchers from the Romanian tourist office are sufficient and are usually cheaper.

Romanian currency may not be brought into or taken out of the country. Any left over Lei are worthless, sometimes you can keep them.

Duty Free Allowance:

2 litres of spirits, 4 litres of wine, 200 cigarettes or 250g tobacco and food. Everything else is restricted to your personal needs. Customs check very thoroughly for any pornographic material, drugs, and newspapers or magazines which are not allowed.

Currency/Exchange Rate: The currency of the land is the Lei (LL.)

Check the exchange rate with your local bank near the time of your departure. We are unable to give you a decent approximation at present.

Changing money on the black market is forbidden but you may be offered 4 or 5 times as much, but be extremely careful!! The official exchange rates for individual travellers are not in keeping with the prices. So, it is recommended that you book your holiday either through Rotours, the Romanian Travel Agency or a Western travel agency.

Much sort after items are silk stockings, cosmetics, writing pens/ material, cigarette lighters, coffee, and western cigarettes. Don't forget that you are only allowed to bring in these items in quantities for your own needs!

TELEPHONE:

You have to go to a post office for calls to places outside Romania.

Emergency Telephone Number: 055

EMBASSIES:

Australia:	No Resident Representative-see Yugoslavia
Canada:	36 Nicolae Iorga, 71118 Bucharest, Tel. 506 290
N.Z.:	No Resident Representative-see Austria
U.K.:	Str. Jules Michelet 24, Bucharest, Tel. 111 635.
U.S.A.:	Tudor Arghezi 7-9, Bucharest, Tel. 506 140.

SHOPPING TIPS:

At Comturist shops you can buy (with western currency) international and Romanian goods e.g. objects of art and embroidered blouses (very expensive) and drinks.

READING MATERIAL:

Newspapers, magazines and books from other countries should not be taken into Romania.

ACCOMMODATION:

Hotel, camping grounds: ONT Carpati-Bucuresti, Magheru Bd 7, Bucharest. Tel 145 160;
There are no international youth hostels.
Accommodation in private homes is not permitted (only relatives up to third generation are allowed).
Camping in the countryside is not permitted.

SPEED LIMITS:

60 km/h in built up areas;
outside built up areas 80 km/h.
Petrol can only be purchased with coupons and should be done at ONT Carpati-Bucuresti at the border-cost for super approx. US$1.30 (expensive).

Hotel/camping ground coupons (with or without bookings) are cheap-US$25/15 per person including 5 litres of petrol. A green insurance card is mandatory.

RAILWAYS:

Inexpensive tariffs-sometimes romantic steam trains-extensive network.

AIRPORTS:

The main airport is Bukarest-Oposti, Bucharest, 17 airports in the country.

BUCHAREST

The capital of Romania is known for its distinctive building style and the boulevards of its city centre but it loses its glamour in its neighbouring suburbs and in the new zones (e.g. around the main railway station, Gara di Nord). (Pop. 1.92 Million).

BY CAR: You can reach Bucharest by taking either: the E94 via Yugoslavia (Munich-Salzburg-Zagrave-Belgrade) then Temeswar-Craiova-Bukarest (the disadvantage of this route is the heavy traffic on the Balkan route and the petrol coupons in Yugoslavia); or the E5/E15 (Munich-Linz-Vienna-Bucharest) Oradea-Cluj-Brasov-Ploesti-Bukarest which necessitates the procurement of a visa for Hungary. If you intend going through Romania then you would naturally choose the second route.

BY RAIL: The railways follow much the same routes, only for the first one you have an awkward change of trains in Belgrade (only one train daily to Bucharest). By train, the second route is better. The Gara di Nord (main railway station) in Bucharest doen't live up to expectations. It has bad food, no information, and no international ticket sales office. For international railway information, tickets and seat reservation you must go to the head office, Agentia CFR, Brezoianu Str. 10 (Tram 12, 32 from Gara di Nord 3 stops).

BY AIR: Bucharest is 2100 km from the centre of western Europe and therefore it makes sense to fly. The airport is in the north of the city–bus connection, Tel. 33 3137. Tourist Information: Main Office Magheru Boulevardul 7, Tel. 14 5160. Youth Information: BTT, Strada Onesti 4, Tel. 140 566.

LOCAL TRANSPORT: Underground 1 Lei, Bus 1.75 Lei, Trolley bus 1.50 Lei, Trams 1 Lei; There are more buses and trams. City Tours: 6.50-16 U.S. Dollars.

POINTS OF INTEREST: The central square of the northern city centre is the Piata Victorieri with its impressive historical museum (all museums May-September, Tuesday to Sunday 9.00 a.m.-7.00 p.m., October-April 10.00 a.m.-6.00 p.m.). To get there from the railway station go along the Calea Grivitei on the left. Between Calea Grivitei and the

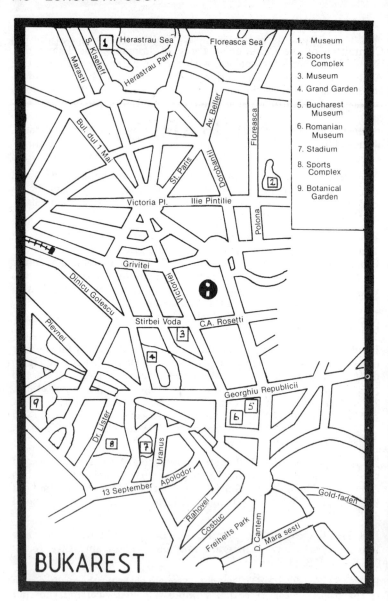

1. Museum
2. Sports Complex
3. Museum
4. Grand Garden
5. Bucharest Museum
6. Romanian Museum
7. Stadium
8. Sports Complex
9. Botanical Garden

BUKAREST

parallel streets of blvd. Ipatescu, blvd. General Magheru, blvd. N. Balecescu, blvd. 1848 lie the most imposing buildings: e.g. the Central Committee of the Communist Party of Romania, the Palast der Republik, former king's palace, with the romanian art museum, the Athenaum. Near the intersection of the majestical blvd. Gheorghiu Dej/blvd. Republicij is the university and the National Theatre. Just to the south is Curtea Veche, the oldest church of the city and the remains of an earlier castle (with museum), also the Manuc Hostel, which was formerly a business house. Now we come to the remodelling of the old town. Let's begin with the removal of the Hihai Voda Church to a site 227m to the south. The church was moved on rails. You then come to the Art Museum.

South of the railway station are the extensive botanical gardens. South of the National Versammulung is Freedom Park where centuries old grape vines once grew. In the park is a war memorial and a new roman arena for 5000 people. Adjacent to it, in the south is a youth park, with sport and culture stadiums. The Herastrau Park is in the north and is very large and includes the Herastrau, Floreasca and Tej lakes. You can swim in the Tej lake. The Village Museum is also there and it is full of peasant style houses from all over the country.

MUSEUM TIPS: The Museum of the Communist Party of Romania is housed in a very beautiful building, Calea Victoriei 15 (Open the same times as above); the National Museum, blvd. 1848; the central Military Museum, Isvor str. 137; the Art Museum of the SRR, Stirbei Vodas str. 1; and last but not least the Railway Museum, C. Grivitei 193.

FOOD: The former much loved romanian food is, because of the problems of the land, the thing that is most hard to accept. The food in self-service restaurants is only able to be taken in small doses. Local tips: Bucur, 2 Porenadu Bordea str.; Hanul Manuc, 62, 30th Dec. str.; La Doi Cocosi, Seseaua Straulesti, Bus 177, Mogosoaia; Carul cu Bere, Stavrepoleos 5, affordable only if you change money on the black market.

ACCOMMODATION: Hotel rooms can be booked at the tourist information office. They cost roughly the same as anywhere else in Europe at the official exchange rate, even though the hotels are not of the same standard. Camping: Baneasa, on a lake, Bukarest-ploiesti Chaussee.

CONSTANTA

The most loved town on the Romanian Black Sea Coast (Pop. 293,000). It lies on a plateau above the sea, and is not only famous for its endless hotels.

TOURIST INFORMATION: In Hotel Continental, blvd. Tomis 69, Central accommodation reservations, Camping: Perla in Mamaia (Bus 30, 40) north of Constanta.

POINTS OF INTEREST: This town which has seen the Greeks, Persians and Romans come and go, is to-day very proud of its archaeological inheritance. At Parcul Arheologie, an open air archaeological museum, finds are displayed as well as the places where they were dug up. A walled roman settlement (Zidul roman de incinta) and the Turnul Macclarilor tower are nearby. Another public building from antiquity (Edificiul roman cu mozais) with remnants of a beautiful mosaic floor, is being dug up next to the town hall, Piata Ovidiu 1. You can steep yourself in the past at the Archaeological Museum, Muzeelor str. 213. In this street which leads off the main square, Piata Independenei, you can see a reminder of the turkish occupation with a 50m high minaret. Also in the same street as the museum is the Orthodox Church built around 1884 which reminds one that numerous cultural and ideological influences are found together here in a very small area. There is also a Catholic Cathedral in the N. Titulescu street, and the building of the Local Area Communist Party with a bust of the archaeologist, Vasile Parvan, who worked in this area. Independence Square is not only the centre of the old town and the place where you can see the world famous statue of the Roman storywriter, Ovidius Naso, who was exiled, but it is where the tourists gather in summer. The luxurious casino building and the Aquarium with its display of black sea fauna are found on the beach promenade. Of importance to shipping: The small lighthouse (Farul genovez) was only replaced in recent times by the new 90m high one (Noul far).

SWIMMING: To swim you must travel to the north to Mamaia or south to the so-called Romanian riviera coast. From Eforie Nord in the south there are row upon row of concrete towers which have been stamped into the sand like letters and given such illustrious names as Neptune, Jupiter, Venus and Saturn. No question that the Olympic hotel group's Neptune is the ultimate in comfort and also in price.

SPAIN

Spain is a constitutional monarchy, with an area of 504,782 sq. km and a population of 37.9 million.

The Spanish Peninsular has always drawn lots of visitors: Celts, Carthaginians, Romans, Goths, Byzantinians and Arabs all left their mark on Spain.

This is a land of many facets with its atlantic and mediterranean coasts, its mountains, wide plains and mediterranean climate and its varied population-73 % Castillian, 24% Catalonian and 2.4% Basques. As well as High Spanish, other dialects are spoken namely Castillian (mainly in Salamanca), Catalonian and Basque.

Spain is developing more and more into a goal for youthful travellers, however, be careful of car thieves.

ENTRY/FOREIGN EXCHANGE/CUSTOMS REGULATIONS: A valid passport is required and Australians also require a visa which is best obtained beforehand. There are no restrictions on the amount of currency which may be brought into the land but only 100,000 Pesatas may be taken out.

Duty Free Allowance:
Up to 1 litre Brandy or 2 litres wine, 200 cigarettes or 25gm. tobacco.

Currency/Exchange Rate: The currency of the land is the Spanish Pesata (ptas).

1 A$	=	88 Ptas.
1C$	=	95 Ptas.
1NZ$	=	75 Ptas.
£1	=	200 Ptas.
1US$	=	125 Ptas.

Alcohol, cigarettes, leather goods are good value for money and accommodation in pensions is very reasonable.

TELEPHONE:
To dial overseas after dialling the 07 wait for the special tone-then dial the area code without the 0.

Emergency Telephone Number: Police 091.

EMBASSIES:

Australia:	Paseo de la Castellana 143, Madrid, Tel. 27 98 501.
Canada:	Edificio Goya, Calle Nunez de Balboa 35, Madrid, Tel. 431 4300.
N.Z.:	No Resident Representative-see Italy.

U.K.:   Fernando el Catolico 16, Madrid, Tel. 41 91 528.
U.S.A.:   Serrano 75, Madrid, Tel. 27 63 400.

FOOD:

In restaurants usually around 400 Pesatas for set menu.
A good tip–the individual faculties of universities. If you wish to buy
your own food and cook it yourself then it is best to buy in the local
supermarkets, Mercados, which are found in all the larger towns.

BULLFIGHTS:

In reality, if you wish to see a genuine bullfight, there are two
possibilites: firstly, take part in one of the fiestas which take place in
practically all the small spanish towns during the summer months;
or else, visit one of the bullrings in Madrid, Pamplona, Ronda, Seville,
Barcelona or Valencia where the absolutely first class bullfights take
place. The bullring is called 'Plaza de Toros' and the bullfights are
usually held on Saturdays or Sundays at approximately 6 p.m.–cost
around 1000 Pesatas.

ACCOMMODATION:

Hotels, camping grounds and apartments: Secretaria General de
Turismo, Catello 115, Madrid 6, Telephone. 411 6011.
Youth hostel: REAJ, Jose Ortaga y Gaset 71, Madrid 6, badly organised.
Inexpensive rooms are available in hostels (HS) and Casa de Huespedes
(CH).

SPEED LIMITS:

In built up areas 60 km/h; outside built up areas 100 km/h; motorways
120 km/h–tollways.
   Green card insurance is compulsory.

RAILWAYS:

Cheque-tren up to 20,000 or 25,000 ptas brings between 15 and 25 %
reduction;
not a very good network–it's slow and has an extremely bureaucratic
system of extra charges. You must always have your tickets stamped
before you board the train.

AIRPORTS:

There are 38 large airports in Spain.

Stockholm: Palace

Sweden: Ice Skating

Rome: Trevi Fountain

Rome: Piazza de Popolo

BARCELONA

1. Picasso Museum
2. La Lonja
3. Colombus Memorial
4. Park d.L. Clubadela

BARCELONA

The inhabitants of the 4 million metropolis are catalans through and through. Even Franco couldn't really change that, and now that Spain has become a democracy, this catalanic core has become more evident. Barcelona is the industrial heart of Spain but it is, for the traveller, a crazy, pulsating and fascinating large town on the gentle Mediterranean Sea. Bathing is impossible on the beaches close to Barcelona.

All possible forms of transport, with the exception of space transport, go to Barcelona.

BY RAIL: If you come by train from central Europe then you will arrive at the Terminus station, which is located in the middle of the transport terminals and right next to the metro station: Barceloneta. Bus No. 39 runs to the City Centre/Plaza Cataluna. The big new railway station Santa-Central for inland trains is found approximately 5km from the centre of the old town; Train Information Tel. 310 7200. Everything travellers need is found here: money exchange, luggage lockers, good information on towns. Take metro 3 to the city centre.

BY ROAD: You need to take note of the main streets Diagonal and Gran Via de les Cotas Catalanes. Parking stations are found on the Pl. Cataluna (Cortes Ingles Department store) and on the Pl. Urquinaca, both are very central. Cost approx 75 ptas per hour.

BY AIR: The airport El Prat is on the outskirts 14 km from the centre in the direction of Castelledefels (relatively good beaches which are close to town). Trains leave Estacion Central-Sants every 15 minutes.

TOURIST NEWSPAPERS: 'Dia a Dia' and Guia del Ocio'.

LOCAL TRANSPORT: Before we get to sightseeing, first a word about transport. The most important transport is the metro. For approx. 30 Ptas you can go to all the important parts of the town. Metro maps are available everywhere e.g. at the Tourist Info, Gran Via 658, Tel. 301 7443 behind the Uni. If we were to explain the town bus system we would fill the book. One thing to remember: All buses with red destination signs will get you sooner or later to the Pl. Cataluna or the old Uni. i.e. right in the city centre. Bus route maps are obtainable from the Bus Info on the Pl. Cataluna.

POINTS OF INTEREST: So now we are ready to see and admire: Barrio Gotico, the gothic quarter around the cathedral Santa Cruz. You can also look at the inside of the church, its treasures and the sarcophagus of St. Eulalia after whom the cathedral is named. The building was finished in 1448. It took 150 years to build. The Town Archives with its beautiful courtyard and the Bishop's palace are in the gothic quarter. Take a map from the tourist office with you. It is between Las Ramblas and Via Layetana (metro station).

The town park, Cuidadela, is right next to the youth hostel. It is 30 hectares in area with a zoo, the Museum of Natural Science and the particularly impressive, museum of modern art, Palacio Real. In front of the park, near c/Princesa, is the Picasso Memorial Fountain designed by Miro. A nonsensical work. Can you work it out?

The Parque Giuell, calle Larrad, was laid out by the strong willed Architect Gaudi. It was once the summer retreat of the Countess of Guell but is now practically surrounded by the ever growing town. It is laid out in the romantic style and has a terrific view of the whole town. In the park is the Casa Museum Gaudi which is open only in the afternoons after 4.00 p.m.

While we are talking of Gaudi and his many buildings, the landmark of Barcelona is undoubtedly the 'Sangrada Familia', which because of

Gaudi's death in 1923 was delayed because he didn't leave any plans. It is an almost utopic masterpiece. The 'Holy Family' (the english translation of the name) can be reached by the metro and is open during the day except for the siesta time from (2.00-3.30 p.m.).

More of Gaudi e.g. the Palacio Guell, Nous de la Rambia, 13. A great modern style building, to-day a theatre museum. Private houses built by Gaudi are found at Paseo de Gracia 92 and at 43 in v/Carolina 24 and 48 v/Caspa. As the visitor will soon find out, Antonio Gaudi is the Don Quixiote of spanish architecture.

Now we come to Columbus. Built in memory of him is a 60m high column at the end of Las Ramblas. You can go up by lift and enjoy an extensive view of the harbour area. Directly under the column is a copy of the orignal 'Santa Maria' in which Columbus brought back some american indians. You can visit the Cairn of the discoverer for 125 Ptas from 9.00 a.m.

THE HARBOUR: Still the most important harbour in Spain. From here ferries leave for the Mediterranean Islands of Palma and Ibiza as well as freighters to all parts of the world. The Maritime Museum which is housed in a 14th century ship building yard is on the Plaze Puerto de la Pax and is open in the mornings until 1.30 p.m. and in the afternoons from 4.00-6.30 p.m. It is worth a visit.

MUSEUMS: Already we are in the middle of the Museum world of Barcelona. Here is our priority list: Definitely visit: The Palacio Nacional with the Museum of Catalanic Art (Bus 1 or 101 from Montjuich)–sculpture, wall paintings etc. Entry approx. 75 Ptas. The Picasso Museum, Montcada 15, is more modern and has fine works by the spanish genius. The Wax Museum in the Pasaje de la Banca is not so interesting, although it is well known. Pueblo Espanol is more interesting with its copies of characteristic houses from all over Spain. It is also full of pubs, restaurants and tourists.

ENTERTAINMENT: The Amusement Park at Tibidabo, is high above the town and is best visited at weekends when a lot of people go there–merry-go-rounds, ferris wheels and the big dipper. A funicular leaves from the end of the Avenida del Doctor Andreu (Cost: 100 Ptas up and back).

We only mention the cable car which goes over the harbour from Miramar out to the Towers of James I (near the ferry terminal) and San Sebastian. Cost 125 Ptas for the one way trip. There is another fun park at the foot of the Montjuich Mountain and from there a funicular goes up the mountain to the castle at the top. Now to the central meeting places: Las Ramblas naturally, which runs from the harbour to Plaza Cataluna. During the day and in the evenings the chirping of the birds for sale and the perfume of the flowers from the florist shops in the middle of the popular street add to the atmosphere. The prostitutes hang around the harbour end each in their own particular place. A day at a cafe on Las Ramblas is compulsory in Barcelona.

Also compulsory, a visit to Cafe Zurich, right on Plaza Cataluna (at the Las Ramblas end). Cafe Zurich is the day meeting place, the 'scene', partly because it's near the university which is on the Plaza of the same name. About the university: The new one is right near the soccer stadium (F.C. Barcellona) but it's rather lifeless, whereas the old university is definitely worth a visit. Go through the big Portal on the Gran Via and you step into the world of the student. By the way there are several inexpensive cellar bars in the individual faculties. There are also spontaneous cultural shows in and around the Uni.

Another few popular tips: Cafe de las Opera, Rambla 74, it is a run down youth style house with original guests. London Bar, 34 Nous de la Rambla, is rather like a pub, but very homely. Discos: New York, c/Escudellers 5,for a long time the No. 1; King's Club, c/Buscarons, 24.

FOOD: A lot of inexpensive and original restaurants can be found in the Calle des Escudeliers, one of the side streets off Las Ramblas. Two names: Caporal at the start of the lane, with its speciality barbecued chicken, and Los Alamos at No. 12. Now a culinary feast: Los Caracoles (watch out for the snails) a truly unique restaurant where the chickens are barbequed outside and quite often cooked inside in full view. The favourite is the paella and all that goes with the famous dish. It is frequented by famous people as well as the working class and is so popular that usually you have to sit in the small bar for a few minutes and drink a vino tinto while you wait for a table. But it pays to wait.

Because it is a harbour town, Barcelona offers all sorts of culinary delights. Chinese: Gran Chino, Carrer des Banys Nous, 8, quite close to the cathedral. Another place for tasty paella: Set Portes, Paseig Isabell II. A good restaurant chain is XAICA: Jovellanos 5, Fontanella 14 and Conde de Borrell 308.

ACCOMMODATION: The Hostal de Joven, 29 Passeig Pujades, is international, central, clean but the doors are locked at midnight. A tip for night owls: one of the inexpensive hostels around Las Ramblas (list obtainable from the information office). A tip: Hostal Victoria, Condal 9, Tel. 317 45 97. Room 700 Ptas.

The town camping ground is called 'Barcino' and is found at 50 Laureano Miro. metro Pubilla Cases, Line 5. It is clean with a well looked after swimming pool. A meeting place for young people from all lands.

DISTRICT: A tip: If you want to visit a beach resort try Sitges, 30 kms south and in the leisure park Isla Fantasia you can practise your bull fighting either on the water or with a cow. (Premia de Mar, Train or the A 19).

MADRID

MADRID

Norte

Gran — Via

Centro

Paseo de le Castellana

C.D. Alcalb

Jeronimo

Paseo del Prado

Parque Del Retiro

C.D. Atocha

Rastro Market

Atocha

1 kilometre

1. Pl. Colon
2. Pl. Espana
3. Pl. Mayor
4. Pl. Del Sol
5. Pl. Cibeles
6. Pl. INDEP
7. Prado
8. Castle

The spanish capital, Madrid lies in the centre of Spain and is the cultural, political and spiritual focal point. It is a beautiful town which became the capital in 1561 by order of Phillipp II and very quickly grͦ (Pop. 3.35 million).

BY CAR: It is best if you drive straight to one of the large parking stations because most hotels don't have garages. You will find such parking stations at the Plaza de la Carmen or the Plaza Zarragoza. You will know them by the large blue P signs. They are not cheap (approx. 75 Ptas per hour), but it's probably better to park there instead of in the street because of the many car thieves, and if you park in the wrong place the police will have your car towed away as quick as lightning. All the national main roads branch out in a star-like pattern from the city centre around the Puerta del Sol and the Gran Via.

BY RAIL: The city has three railway stations. The newly renovated Charmatin railway station (information desk, luggage office, and underground) which is situated away from the city centre at the end of Passeo de la Castellana; the Atocha railway station is located at the end of the park El Retiro (luggage office, metro station) and services the south of the land; and the smaller Del Norte, services the local traffic and Galizien. To get to the different railway stations and the city centre, it is best to use the metro, but there is also a direct train every quarter of an hour between Charmatin and Atocha Stations (Information, Tel. 733 30 00).

BY AIR: Madrid's airport, Barajas, is approx. 15 minutes by bus from the Plaza de Colon from where the airport buses, the metro and your luggage (if you don't watch out) leave. The airport has all the necessary facilities such as a city information office (but its miniscule) and hotel reservations.

TOURIST INFORMATION: 3 Plaza Mayor, Tel. 241 2325; a terrific office. You should certainly get their city map and the local transport route map.

TOURIST NEWSPAPERS: 'En Madrid' a free information sheet; Guia de ocio, although in spanish, has a lot of addresses and helpful advertisements, even if you don't understand spanish. If you are staying a little longer in Madrid and want to learn a little of the language, then you should get 'Guia Informal' by Juan Manuel Munox.

LOCAL TRANSPORT: The best form of transport undoubtedly is the metro, the price rose to 40 Ptas in 1985 and was the cause of many protests, but it is comparitively cheap and goes to all the important parts of the town. There are 10 lines which are marked on a handy pocket map, which you can obtain at the information office or at a metro station. While the thick red lines of the city bus routes are almost impossible to work out (the Madrilenos know the routes, so ask for help), the 11 yellow lines showing the micro-bus routes are much easier to see and to follow. They join together above ground, all the marked points of the city. On every stop there is a board which shows the routes of the different lines. You put out your hand to stop the micro-buses at the marked stops. The central meeting place is the Plaza Sol and Gran Via/Galerias Preciados. Cost: approx. 50 ptas which you pay to the driver.

POINTS OF INTEREST: The central points of Madrid life are at the same time, the attractions. Let us firstly take in the famous Puerta del Sol, to which the main roads come in a star shape. It has lots of traffic, gypsy beggars dressed in a theatrical manner, pick-pockets, a busy metro station, advertisements for the specials in the shops which are to be found in the direction of Gran Via, and expensive cafeterias next to cheap ice cream parlours. You could spend hours here just watching. From there go 400m to the Gran Via the most splendid street in Madrid, with its huge cinemas with their colourful programme signs, and numerous hamburger shops competing with old time cafes. In the summer, half of Madrid sits along the wide footpaths. Then you can walk along the just as busy Plaza Mayor which perhaps, caters more for the tourists, but offers some culture with the open air festivals and the open air theatre. The unique thing about the Plaza Mayor are the authors who try to sell their poems for a few hundred pesetas. They are beautifully written and if you like, they will read them for you. At night a lot of people go to the large bingo halls. The central point of the Plaza Mayor is a statue of Philip III mounted on horseback, which points the way to the hundreds of pubs, mesones and restaurants in the nearby old town.

Perhaps you would like to go a bit further in the direction of Rastro, an area full of crummy shops which turns into a huge flea market every Sunday morning. A lively place, but watch out for thieves.

There are numerous parks all around the town. The most elegant is the Retiro in the middle of the city which competes with the polular Casa de Campo. In the latter is the famous zoo and a large amusement park. As well there are the city woods and a lake. At the Retiro Park you can row on the lake as well as look at the Memorial to Alfons XII, the prominent building Cason del Buen Retiro and the army museum (Tuesday-Friday 10.00 a.m.-5.00 p.m.). Both parks are meeting places for travellers but it's better not to go there at night. A chic place to swim is in the first tall building Torre de Esplana which has a swimming pool and there is music at the Baby Q (Motorway Escoril) until 5.00 a.m.

The squares of Madrid deseve high praise. They mostly have superb memorials and fountains: Plaza de Espana has Don Quixote and his servant Cervantes; Plaza de Colon is built in modern style with imposing fountains. It has a culture centre, a metro station, the terminal for the airport bus, luggage room, and parking station. Diagonally opposite is the Wax Museum, a lot of fun for about 400 Ptas.(open daily 10.30a.m.-2.00 p.m. & 4.00-9.00 p.m.). A few hundred metres further on is the most famous square of Madrid, Cibeles. The pompous building on its eastern side is the central post office. Its main attraction is that for a few pesatas you can have letters and packets elegantly packed and wax sealed. Something unusual to send to someone at home. From Cibeles Square go down the Passeo del Prado and you come to the Plaza Canovas del Castillo (with an 18th century Neptune fountain) and then to the part of Madrid that is best known throughout the world, the Prado Museum.

The Museo del Prado is housed in a long classical building (parking in front) and contains in great numbers works of the most famous old Masters. The Museum is open from 10.00 a.m.-5.00 p.m. Museums are the Cason de Buen Retiro,–upperhalf, east of Prado, and the Museo del Arte Contemporaneo, 2 av. Juan de Herrera, at the Ciudad Universitaria (10.00 a.m.-6.00 p.m.) which specialises in modern spanish art. The

Archeological Museum is found in a large classical building at the National Library along the Paseo de Recoletos (cnr. Colon and Cibeles). It's really worthwhile to see as it provides an insight into iberian history. (9.30 a.m.-1.30 p.m.).

Because Spain is a monarchy, the Palacio Real is the king's residence and not really a museum. It is on the southern edge of the old town near the Plaza del Oriente on Calle de Bailen. The exact location is unnecessary because you really can't miss seeing this impressive building with its large courtyard. If there isn't a State Visit taking place (and then the gates are shut) you can see over it between 10.00 a.m.-1.30 p.m. & from 3.30-6.30 p.m.

BULL FIGHTS: If you want to see one go to the Plaza de Toros Monumental, Alcala 237 (metro Station: Ventas). Usually on Sundays about 6.00 p.m. Entry is very expensive (not under 1000 Ptas). For first-class bull fights buy your tickets before hand at Calle Victoria (city centre).

THEATRES: The daily programmes appear in all the Madrid daily newspapers, e.g. El Pais. There are 15 regular theatres, but three really stand out: Teatro Espanol, 25 Principe, Tel. 429 6297 with old and modern pieces. The National Theatre, Maria Guerrero, 4 Tamayo y Baus (metro Station: Banco). The Ensemble of the Centro Dramatico Nacional presents a wide range from classical to modern. The Calderon Theatre, Plaza Benavente presents lighter plays such as Evita or Hair more suitable for foreigners. In comparison to bull fights, theatre is reasonably priced, for about 350 Ptas. you can get a good seat. You can buy your tickets before hand at the individual theatres during normal trading hours.

MUSIC: Information about live rock & pop shows at Guia de Ocio obtainable from Mala Sana, c/San Vincente Ferrer. If you want to hear spanish pop music you can try the Sala Windsor, 65 Raimundo Fernandex Villaverde (metro Station: Nuevos Ministerios). It's dripping with sentimentality.

LIBRARIES are a R & R (rest & recreation) place in the noisy city. In Madrid, the Biblioteca Nacional, 20 Paseo de Recoletos (a large, old building next to the Prado) is also worth seeing because of its architecture and atmosphere as well as its contents. It's open to the public (except on Sundays)-exhibitions, photocopier, cafe, restaurant and friendly people.

ENTERTAINMENT: The entertainment area and pub scene are the same-around Calle Ballesta, c/Dr. Flemming and c/Orense. The locals gather in these streets whereas the tourists mostly gather around the Mayor, which has, in the meantime, become very expensive. Visit some mesones, Jeunesse ole at the Cafe Gijon, boulevard Castellana; Two jazz pubs: Dallas, 34 Orense and Ragtime, 20 Ruiz (metro Bibao). The main place for intellectuals is the same as it always was the Cafe Gijon, between Colon and Cibeles Squares (No. 21). They gather there until late at night. And while it's just nearby: Museo del Jamon, 44 Paseo del Prado, which has thick bocadillos which are good value for money.

FOOD: You can buy your own food at one of the supermarkets if you wish e.g. Mercado de San Miguel, Plaza Mayor or even better Mercado Municipal Maravillas, Plaza Mayor cnr. Bravo Murillo, or try the cocido (casserole) at the Gran Tasca, 1 Ballesta.

ACCOMMODATION: Youth hostel, Richard Schirrmann, Casa de Campo, Tel. 463 56 99, 120 beds. There are plenty of inexpensive hostels and casas de huespedes (guest houses) around the Puerta del Sol. List available from the tourist information office: Hostal Santo Domingo, 6 Luna, Tel. 231 3290; Hostal Milano, 20 Huertas, Tel. 227 2510, metro Sol, very cheap, simple.
Camping: Madrid, Cerro del Aguila, on Main Road No. 1 at the 7km post, also bungalows.

PALMA DE MALLORCA

Palma de Mallorca is called La Ciudad (the city) by the locals; and Palma is also the heart and soul of the island group. Palma could be the synonym for 'Tourist Industry' in all middle Europe. No where else is the tourist industry as concentrated as it is here in Mallorca. In spite of this, the town of Palma has retained it's southern spanish charm, which by any stretch of the imagination, is absent from the large holiday towns of El Arenal and Palma Nova. Pop. 283,100.

BY AIR: How do you get there? The quickest and cheapest way is by charter flight from any of the large middle european airports. Ask about the Hit or Camping Flights which are offered by the larger travel agencies who sell the unbooked seats on the charter machines. You can generally get a return flight to Palma for approx. US$250.
The airport is approximately 6km from the city centre; a bus runs every 30 minutes to the airport from Plaza Espana from where all buses, including the city buses, depart.

BY SHIP: The second way you can get to Mallorca is by sea from Barcelona or Valencia and in summer also from Sete in France. The ships of the Transmediterranea Line sail direct to Palma. From Barcelona and Valencia the cheapest fare is approx. 3300 ptas. If you take your car with you then it will cost approx. 8,000 ptas one way!
The boats depart from the ferry harbour in Barcelona near the

Columbus Memorial daily at 11.45 p.m. and in summer often in the afternoons as well. You disembark at the Paseo Maritimo in central Palma.

TOURIST INFORMATION OFFICE: On arrival in Palma obtain a map of the city from the information office at Plaza Espana (Bus station), 11 Santo Domingo near the Town Hall (a bit hidden) or at the Public Transport office, 10 Avenida Jaime III, Tel. 212 216. Regional information can be obtained at the Mallorca Tourist Office, 1 Calle Constitucio. There is another tourist office at the airport.

POINTS OF INTEREST: Straightaway you will see the fantastic cathedral, the pride of the city. When you see the inside you will understand why it is called 'The Light'. The constant sun shines throught the colourful windows and rosettes. Its surroundings are delightful; a park and old winding lanes, in one of them, calle San Roque, the venerable, small university of Balearen is hidden. It offers very interesting language courses in the summer. For further information contact:

Sr. Secretario de los Cursos de Verano,
Estudio General Luliano,
4 calle San Roque, Palma.

As far as tourists are concerned the centre of Palma is a street, Passeig d'es Born which runs from the harbour up to the Avenida Jaime II which is the shopping centre of Palma. But let's get back to Passeig d'es Born. Along the footpaths are unusual and old world sidewalk cafes. On the green strip which runs along the street, buskers busk, hopeful Van Goghs draw, beggers beg, singers sing and sailors spend time with their sweethearts. One of the top places to enjoy yourself during the daytime. It is only spoilt by the large numbers of pick-pockets and other thieves.

After the Passeig d'es Born you should perhaps go to the quieter, nearby Plaza Mayor which isn't very lively by any stretch of the imagination but it is surrounded by the lanes of the old town in which you will find original shops. Around the plaza there are sidewalk cafes and bars in which traditional snacks (e.g. tapas) can be selected from trays. The plaza is more lively on Saturdays when a handicraft market is held from 10.00 a.m. to 2.00 p.m. to which all the artists come. Quite frankly, you won't find anything really exciting there.

On the other hand, there is nothing dull about the Plaza Gomila which is the centre of the nightlife and at 6.00 p.m. is already rather crowded and full of international visitors. It is a crazy mixture of seamen, chic tourists, snobby natives and tatty tramps. The bars around the Plaza Gomila are in comparision, rather expensive but sometimes you only need to buy a beer and you can sit for hours and 'watch the world go by'. From May to October every day there is an open air theatre performance but if that isn't enough for you, and you have enough money, go to the biggest nightclub in Europe, Titos, and see a real show.

Cost: approx. 1500 ptas per person and you have to be 'correctly' attired.

Because there can never be enough shows, a new tourist mecca has opened, the Pueblo Espanol. It contains copies of houses from all parts of Spain and in them are speciality shops and restaurants. It's not too bad. It's worth a day trip. Catch the bus from Plaza Espana to the village. The last bus leaves the village at 8.15 p.m. for the return trip.

Palma de Mallorca has grown so much that sightseeing here is more like a pub crawl. During the day if you are part of the 'In' crowd, you get to the Bar Bosch near Plaza Pius XII about 11.30 a.m. for breakfast, or else around 5.00 p.m. to catch the latest developments and see who's new and if you want to speak to him/her or buy them a drink. The drinks are reasonably priced. Don't ever let on that you booked your flight through a large travel agency, always have a good story on hand of how you came to Palma and in the bar you should order Bosch!

Something quite different, the Cafe Miami diagonally opposite. Time has stood still here, you could be back in the 1920s. They have ancient waiters, freshly squeezed orange juice (approx. 200 ptas) and crowds of well dressed ladies eating cakes and drinking coffee. The Miami has completely forgotten that we are living in the eighties.

El Arenal, even though it belongs to a different council area, is a popular tourist resort which has only a small sandy beach but an unending collection of tourist infrastructure–discos, take-away shops and pubs spread over 20km. You can't miss it. From Palma catch the bus from Plaza Espana.

The most beautiful beach in Mallorca is Es Trenc, which is approximately 35km from the capital. Catch the bus going to Sant Jordi or La Rapita. Part of Es Trenc is unofficially for nudists.

Back to our theme: Palma. Lastly there are still a few small things: a terrific small railway which goes to Soller. The Ferrocarril de Soller is one of the most unusual railways in Europe. It connects the capital, Palma, with the village of Soller, with its orange orchards; a bit much for the old electric/wood locomotive which makes five return trips daily. The best trip is the one which leaves around 10.40 a.m. and stops for 15 mins. on the way so that you can take pictures. Cost: approx. 500 ptas return. Don't sit on the hard wooden seats but travel on the platform.

Next to the Soller railway station on Plaza Espana is the more lively railway station from where the trains to Inca and La Puebla leave. This trip, even though it has been set up for tourists, is still of interest to railway buffs. The cost of the long trip to La Peubla is only approx. 200 ptas.

SPORTS: The Palma Soccer team plays in the 2nd Spanish Division. There is regularly a lot happening in Estadio Lluis Sitjar. For more specific information, look in the local newspapers: Dia de Balares, Diario de Mallorca or the evening newspaper, Ultima Hora or The Mallorca Daily Bulletin.

Back to sport: For squash–43 Romon Servera Moya. Riding and golf–the best place is at Club Son Vida, take the No. 7 bus. Horse Racing–on the road to Soller at Son Pardo. Greyhound Racing–go to the Calle Miguel de los Santos Oliver Racetrack where for 100 ptas. you can have a few interesting side bets. It can be fun even if you know nothing about greyhound racing.

FOOD: Distingo, Calle San Felio, 7 Pizza, spaghetti and other italian dishes around 300 ptas.

In the Bar San Felio, 5 Calle Felio, a whole meu is offered for 200 ptas; Not so cheap but fantastic for seafood, La Cueva in Calle Apuntadores; If you are a fish lover then go to Caballito de Mar, 5 Paseo Sagrera close to the old harbour but if you are a steak lover then go to Olas, 4 Calle Schembri.

ACCOMMODATION: (If you get there early enough you can get the actual list from the Tourist Information Office). Hostal Ferrando, 52 Calle Juan Alcocever, Tel. 21 48 71, 38 rooms for about 500 ptas; Hostal Cuba, 1 San Magin, Tel. 238 159–clean rooms around 1000 ptas; Hostal Tirol, 19 Apuntadores, Tel. 21 18 08–61 rooms for approx. 500 ptas. Leave plenty of time to look for a room if you have not booked.

SAN SEBASTIAN

The 'capital' of the Basques region, San Sebastian lies on the spanish-french border and because of its beauty, its attitude to life and its size and political importance it shouldn't be overlooked. In summer a large number of lively travellers come to this town with the Basque name of Donostia, and return each year. Perhaps San Sebastian is popular because it retains its youthful character; similar to its french sister town of Biarritz. (Pop. 174,800).

BY RAIL: Some claim San Sebastian became important because Spain has a different gauge railway system to the rest of europe and train travellers must change trains on the borders. Train travellers who come from France already change at Irun but because it is such a dreadful place nobody stays there and San Sebastian's del Norte railway station has become a favourite stopping off place for rail travellers. It cost 40 ptas on the bus from the station to the city centre. The centre of San Sebastian is the old town which is behind the Puerto (port). Tel. 272 771.

BY CAR: At Cervantes and Cataluna Squares, car drivers will find comfortable parking stations. The Quendo parking station is recommended by the tourist information office. Parking stations are not cheap here either (approx. 75 ptas per hour) but are recommended because of the numerous break-ins and thefts of cars with foreign number plates.

LOCAL TRANSPORT: Buses play an important role in Spain and are the cheapest form of transport. Buses come from all over the country to San Sebastian's bus terminal on the Plaza Pius XII. There is a good service from here to Pamplona and it is heavily used during the festival and the running of the bulls, from the 7th to 14th July each year. You have to have been in Pamplona during the Festival to really appreciate it. (Read the description of it by Hemingway in 'Fiesta'.)

TOURIST INFORMATION: Reina Regente, Tel. 421 002.

POINTS OF INTEREST: Back to San Sebastian and its three beaches. The Playa de Gros is the most popular amongst young people. They hang around the pubs along the av. de Zurriol and there are also hire stands and juice bars, Pukas.

The Playa de la Concha is where the very rich gather. It is the longest and cleanest of the beaches with all the usual resort infrastructure (chaise lounges, sun umbrellas and sunscreens) which people seem to want nowadays. Elegant taverns are found along the Paseo de la Concha.

The Playa de Ondaretta is through the tunnel in the direction of Monte Igueldo. At the tunnel entrance there is an enormous anti-nuclear poster on the wall. (Typical of the state of the movement?) The Ondaretta is a family beach full of excited children.

San Sebastian owes its charm partly to its architecture which is demonstrated by the hotel buildings along the beach promenade. The names of two of them, 'London' and 'Nice' say it all–english snobbery combined with southern french flair (Double room prices at the London 7,500 ptas).

There are a few SPECIAL SIGHTS as well as the town as a whole:

Firstly, the old town at the foot of Monte Urgell. In the narrow lanes which are in part, closed to traffic, (a sensation in Spain), things really swing day and night. The market in Calbeton Street is where the main action is in the mornings, and in the evenings it is mainly in the lanes. There are hundreds of terrific taverns in the old town.

The fishing harbour (Puerto de Pescadores) owes part of its charm to the local fishermen but the fishing industry has lost its importance with the rise of the tourist industry in San Sebastian. For travellers the harbour is an interesting place and one where they can try tasty basque cooking in one of the many fish restaurants. Local speciality: sardines, fresh from the grill–very tasty and cheap.

The castle on top of Monte Igueldo on the western side of the town overlooks the three beaches and the whole of the province of Guizuzcoa. A funicular goes up to the castle and costs approx. 75 ptas. for the return trip. At the top there is an expensive hotel and an amusement park. Even if you drive up the hill you have to pay the entrance fee.

Monte Urgel which towers over the old town is of more interest to those who are interested in history as the fortress of Santa Cruz de la Mota stands on top. It was built in case of attack by France. It is now an army museum (Tuesday-Sunday 10.00 a.m.-3.00 p.m. & 4.00-6.00 p.m.). It takes about 30 mins. to walk to the top but the view is worth it.

Because San Sebastian is a spanish-basque town, it has to have a large cathedral. It is built in gothic style with a 75m. high bell tower. In the old town is the monastery of San Telmo which is now a museum; as well as the beautiful architecture, there is also a painting by Sert. A light & sound show is also held in the former monastery. The two towers of the elegant town hall which is at the beginning of the Playa de la Concha, are very impressive.

San Sebastian is a coastal resort and caters for all tastes. The av. Embeltran at the edge of the old town is the centre of things. It has very nice sidewalk taverns along its wide footpath. Another lively area is around the Calle Fermin Calbetron. In Jose Marieta Bar you can get small beers (Canas) and tasty ham for a reasonable price. The rucksack travellers seem to congregate in the back room of the Izkina which has a cheap menu around 300 ptas.

FOOD in San Sebastian is a real pleasure. You can easily get an inexpensive and very tasty meal at one of the numerous restaurants or you can buy something at the market in Calle San Juan. The Gayarra in Calle Mayor is a self-service restaurant which offers inexpensive filling meals cooked while you wait in pretty surroundings. Visit one of the harbourside fish taverns in the early morning if you like good coffee and fresh croissants e.g. Halzea, calle San Juan.

WHO MEETS WHERE IN SAN SEBASTIAN? The freaks usually hang around the long promenade in front of the Playa de Gros. It's more civilized around the Plaza Cervantes. Now that the early evening hours have been spent, it's Disco time: three favourites are: La Perla del Cantabrico, with neon lighting, Zorongo, 66 Cale Martin, for the young, and KU, Igeoldo an off shoot of the famous Ibiza nightclub.

FESTIVALS: There is the famous Jazz Festival which is always held in July; the film people meet in September and the drummers play in January. The most interesting, at least for the locals, is the Town Festival in August, which features all the basque sporting events. If you can't be in San Sebastian at this time then you still can see some of the basque games, e.g. Pelota, at the Anoeta which has a licensed public restaurant for spectators, Paseo de los Podavines.

ACCOMMODATION: You can get very inexpensive private accommodation. Go to the information office and ask for the list with all the names and address. Rooms for approx. 600 ptas. for two are easy to find. You can expect to pay approx. 1500 ptas per night at hotels and hostels, sometimes with private facilities. Three names: Hostal Gran

Bahia, 16 Embeltran, Tel. 42 38 38, very centrally situated and a nice host. Hostal Garate II, 24 San Bartolome, Tel. 46 68 92 which is also central and has cheap rooms without private facilities, more expensive with bath. Hotel Isla, 17 Miraconcha. Youth hostel: Ciudad Depostiva Anoeta, Tel. 452 970.

The CAMPING GROUND behind Monte Igueldo is well signposted and is a good one, but rather expensive–300 ptas. In spite of this, most travellers seem to patronise it.

DISTRICT ATTRACTIONS: There are many. We recommend the romantic fishing village of Pasajes de San Juan approx. 10km north. In the opposite direction, is Lequeito also a beautiful fishing village with a small beach and a colourful harbour. The basque town of Guernica is famous because it was flattened by bombing during the civil war by fascist planes on the 16th April 1936. On the other hand, the town of Guernica offers a lot of unimpressive architecture and has practically no charm. The only thing worth visiting is a tavern nearby, the Lezika in Santimamine, which has a large dining area under shady trees.

SWEDEN

The 449,964 sq. km. kingdom of Sweden is inhabited by 8.32 million people. It has a democratic parliament whose beginnings can be traced back to 1866.

Geographically, Sweden encompasses the flat area in the south, the lake basin, the Scharen Cost along the Baltic Sea and the mountain country of central and northern Sweden. Its large iron ore and timber exports, as well as its industry have helped it to enjoy a high per capita income.

ENTRY/FOREIGN EXCHANGE/CUSTOMS REGULATION: A valid passport is required. There are no restrictions on the importation of currency but only up to 6,000 Skr. may be taken out.

Duty Free Allowance:
1 litre spirits, l litre wine and 2 litres beer as well as 200 cigarettes or 250 gm tobacco. Important: under 20 years no alcohol allowance and under 15 years no tobacco allowance.

Currency/Exchange Rate: The currency of the land is the Swedish Krone (SKr.).

1A$	=	4.50 kr
1C$	=	4.90 kr
1NZ$	=	3.60 kr
£1	=	10.00 kr
1US$	=	6.80 kr

Food, even meals in restaurants, fast food chains and take-aways is rather expensive. Alcohol is extremely expensive.

TELEPHONE:
After you dial the international code wait for the beeps before dialling the local area code without the 0.

Emergency Telephone Number: 90 00 00

EMBASSIES:
Australia: Sergels Torg 12, Stockholm, Tel. 14 46 60.
Canada: Tegelbacken 4, Stockholm, Tel. 23 79 20
N.Z.   No Resident Representative–see Netherlands
U.K.:   Skarpogatan 6, Stocklholm, Tel. 67 0240.
U.S.A.:   Strandvagen 101, Stockholm, Tel. 63 05 20.

ACCOMMODATION:

Hotels, youth hostels and general information: STF, Vasagatan 48, 10
120 Stockholm, hotel vouchers up to 130/180 SKr. per person per night.
Cheap special: Biltur Logi;
Camping grounds; SCR Kungsgatan 19, 45 117 Uddevalla.
Camping in the Countryside:
Everyone is permitted to make use of the general right to camp in the
countryside for one night only on unfenced land. It is forbidden though
to pollute or destroy the countryside. (Heavy fines can be imposed for
non-compliance).
Central information office: Statens Naturvardsverk, box 1302, 17 125
Solna.

SPEED LIMIT:

In built up areas 50 km/h;
outside built up areas 70-100 km/h; motorways 110 km/h.
Whilst driving you must switch on your headlights even in the daytime.

RAILWAYS:

Lagpriskortet, yearly ticket up to 110 SKr.; 45% reduction and
'Nordturist' see Denmark.

AIRPORTS:

International airport at Stockholm; airtaxis to 22 airports.

FALUN

Falun has been chosen not because of it's size but because of its
industrial history. It is a small town in the middle of Sweden's romantic
lakeland district, Dalarna. Falun acquired its town charter in 1641, long
after the mining companies had made inroads into this area. According
to the sagas, there have been mines in this area for over a 1000 years.
It is one of the earliest planned towns and has been laid out in chess-
board style with small wooden houses. (Pop. 50,000).

BY RAIL: Falun is north-west of Stockholm and you travel via Uppsala,
Avesta, Borlange. You might need to change trains in Uppsala. The
railway station is small but has a few luggage lockers. Tel. 023/1 00 58.

BY CAR:: If you don't want to travel via Uppsala, (E4, Road 72 to Sala)
you can take the direct road to Falun which is the E18 direction
Enkoping, from there take Road 70 to Sala, Avesta, Borlange, from there

the 60 to Falun. Right next to the first main street crossing on the left is the copper mine and parking area. The city is on the right and it's not far to walk. There are some short term parking areas in the city.

BY AIR: There is a small airport south of Borlange (Dala Airport) with a direct bus connection to the city. From the airport there are connections to Stockholm, Tel. 0243/39090.

TOURIST INFORMATION: Stora Torget, Tel. 023/83637.

POINTS OF INTEREST: Because of the importance of copper, which is the mainstay of Swedish development, Falun has reached a position out of all proportion. People talk of turning it into a large town with monumental buildings. No doubt, progress will catch up with it one day and the town which is now the seat of the local and provincial governments, will become more commercialised.

With this in mind, behind the Stora Torget where the town hall (Stadshus), the St. Kristine's church built in 1660 and the head office of the mining company are located, workers' suburbs have been opened up–Elsborg (left of the street leading to the Museum), Gamla Herrgarden and Ostanfors (in the north-west). At the moment the red wooden houses sitting on top of slag heaps are very traditional in design.

The Kopparsberg Bergslag Story, the mining company, which was founded in 1288 (lead, sulphur and zinc are mined to-day) can be seen in the Mining Museum, Stora Koppersberg (daily 10.00 a.m.-4.30 p.m.). The 600m Mine Tour is more gripping (May-August daily 10.00 a.m.-4.30 p.m., otherwise only Saturday & Sunday–closed from 16th November until February). Geological Museum in Borlange (June-August, daily 11.00 a.m.-5.00 p.m., otherwise Sunday). The Dalarna Museum, is a very modern ethnological museum, Stigaregatan 2 (daily 11.00 a.m.-5.00 p.m.) with cafeteria 'Kupferbar'; the open air museum, Dossberget-Bjursas (daily 11.00 a.m.-6.00 p.m., Railway Bus), in Bjursas there is also a Pottery Museum; in Svardsjo there is also a Motor Bike Collection (only Saturday & Sunday 1.00-4.00 p.m., end June–beginning August, daily 11.00 a.m.-4.00 p.m.); A similar museum in Borlange Gammelgarden, Stenhalsgaten is easier to get to (mid June-August, daily 11.00 a.m.-4.00 p.m.); Korsa Bruk is interesting from an industrial point of view, unfortunately it's a bit out of the way (east of Falun) but you can see an enormous Lancashire blacksmith shop and films with a guided tour (May-August, daily 10,00 a.m.-5.00 p.m.).

If you are a sports enthusiast, you can go to the Sport and Recreation Centre, Lugnet where there is a 90m ski-jump and also a camping ground, Bus 3, Tel. 8 33 95.

ACCOMMODATION: Youth hostel: Haraldsboskolans elevhem, Tel. 023/10560 (Bus 1,4). Camping: Lugnet, Tel. 83563, to the north-west. Hotel: Samuelsdals, Tel. 11225.

GOTEBORG

A large town versed in the ways of the world. Because of its harbour and industrial layout perhaps of more interest to those with a technical bent, but it also has more parks and open space than other industrial towns. Added to that the stiff and sometimes off putting swedish manner is not so noticeable here on the west coast. (Pop. 426,000).

BY RAIL: You travel via Copenhagen, Helingsor, Helsingborg and sometimes you have to change trains in Astorp. There are good connections from here to Oslo and Stockholm. Goteborg has a modern railway station with the usual facilities and an underground passage. Tel. 031/17 50 00.

BY CAR: See Stockholm for description of route to Sweden and then take the E6 along the west coast of Sweden. Park & ride from Molndal, Tram 4, 10.

BY AIR: Goteborg's international airport, Landvetter, is situated 30 minutes from the city centre. There is a regular airport bus service.

BY SEA: There are ferry services from Denmark as well as from Kiel and Travemunde.

TOURIST INFORMATION: Kungsportsplatsen 2, Tel. 031/100 740 and Ostra Nordstadstorget, Tel. 031/15 07 05, from the railway station go through the subway.

TOURIST NEWSPAPER: The newspaper 'Goteborg this Week', printed in many languages will let you know what's on in town.

LOCAL TRANSPORT: Travel with 'Kal and Ada' in the trams. Although the nick-names of the Goteborgers seem rather provincial, their tram and bus map/timetable is very professional. The map alleviates the need for a map of the town. Getting around is easy, just take a tram (Tickets 3.50 SKr, 16SKr for 24h, Goteburgskortet 60 SKr.).

POINTS OF INTEREST: Take Tram No. 5 to Liseberg, an even larger amusement park than the Tivoli; Tram Nos. 1, 2 or 7 to the peaceful Botanical Gardens; Tram No. 2,3,4,6, or 7 to the Antikhallarna (antique market); Tram 3 to the fish auctions, C.Johans Kyrka; Tram No. 1 to the Skansen Kronon (fortress with military museum), also the old suburb, Haga, with a 19th century worker's cottage, Bergsgatan 19; the Kronjus suburb with its arts & crafts industry, and the oldest building in Goteborg (1643) and the former Swedish Parliament building (1660), or the historical museum at Ostindiska Huset on the canal (Stora Hamnkanalenz). There are very beautiful canal trips in open boats from Kungsportplatsen, 22 SKr.). A visit to the large free port directly next to the railway station is also very interesting. Lastly, you can visit the Elfsborg Fortress by ship from Stenpiren, Lilla Torget, 20 SKr.

Back to the city centre again–the old town looks even older than its 350 years. The stock exchange is on Gustaf Adolf Square as is the town hall. The cathedral is to the south in Kungsgatan, a park with running water where the city walls once stood. In a section of it is the big theatre 'Stora Teater'. Follow the wall and you come back to the railway station again. Then go to the right along Ullevigatan a bit and there is a trade centre, a big exhibition centre and Sweden's largest undercover stadium, 'Scandinavium'. You get a good view a little further to the south west from the Sjomanstorn (sailors' tower). There is a Sailors' Memorial at the Fish Harbour (fish auctions). Don't miss out on seeing the Free Port and the newer part of the city which lies to the north of the Gotaalv River. Both bridges which span the river are very impressive, particularly the first one, Alvsborgsled, up river, which was built in 1966; on the right of the railway station is the Gotaalvbro bridge built in 1939. The highest geographical point on this side of the river is the Ramberget (Tram 2/5, Bus 31).

CULTURE AND CONCERT HALLS with varied programmes: the Konserthuset at Gotaplatsen, Bla Stallet am Angereds Torg 13 (Tram 8) and the Frolunds Kulturhus, Valthornsgatan (Tram 2,3).

PARKS: Tradgardsforening with its large hot house of palms, is near the railway station; Keillers Park is around the Ramberget; Slottskogen, Goteborgs largest park (Tram 1/2). An open air museum with simple buildings from the 18th century: Gathenhielm reservatet (Tram 3/4).

MUSEUM TIPS: Hours for all Museums Tuesday-Saturday 12 noon-4.00 p.m., Sunday 11.00 a.m.-5.00 p.m. Archaelogical Museum, Norre Hamngatan 12; the Historical Museum, built in fascist-momumental style; Art & Sculpture Gallery, Gotaplatsen; Natural History Museum, Slotsskogen; Rohsska, Arts & Crafts Museum, Vasagatan; Industrial Museum, Avagen; the Theatre History Museum, Slotsskogen; Maritime Museum with boat hall; an open air museum, Lila Bormmen; National Library, Gotsplatsen (Monday-Friday 9.00 a.m.-10.00 p.m.).

ENTERTAINMENT: Jazz: Erik Dahlbergsgatan 3; Restaurant Faust, Jarntorgsgatan 4; Piano bar cafe: pa Brautigams, Hornet Ostra Hamngatan/Kungsgatan; Pub Camle Port, ostra Larmgatan 1; Theatre: Folkteatern, Jarntorget.

ACCOMMODATION: Youth hostel Ostkupan, Mejerigatan, Tel. 031/40 10 50 (Bus 62/64); Torrekulla, Kallered, Tel. 751 495.
Camping: Karralungs, olbergsgatan; Tourist accommodation: Tellusgatan, 22 Bergsjon, Tel. 031/44 77 88.

STOCKHOLM

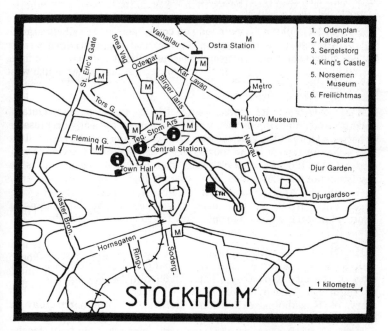

Stockholm has functional architecture, snobby department stores, underground passages, and is more modern than its german counterparts which were rebuilt after the war. It was last occupied in 1523. (Pop. 647,000.)

BY RAIL: The fastest and most comfortable railway connection is via Malmo, or Helsingborg in the south, to Stockholm. The international trains are shipped between Puttgarden and Rodby and Helsingor and Helsingborg, at additional charge to passengers. The main railway station appears to be black/grey in colour on the outside but it has a terrific entry hall, snack bars, train information, and a luggage room in the basement, Tel. 08/22 50 60.

BY CAR: If you come by car you will have to come on the same ferries as the trains and it will cost at least US$55 (A$80) on the ferry. In Sweden the E4 goes via Helsingborg, Jonkoping, and Linkoping to Stockholm. A prettier way is via Malmo, Kristanstad, Karlskrona and Norrkoping. Park in the outer suburbs at Lilijeholmen, on the left of city exit of the E4. There are numerous parking stations in the city.

Be careful if you park in the streets as they have a complicated time limit parking system.

BY AIR: The airport is 45 km from the city centre in Arlands. A bus runs from the airport to the main railway station at 14 Vasagatan. Airport: Tel. 08/780 30 30.

TOURIST INFORMATION: A special youth centre: 142 Valhallavagen, Tel. 087/634 389. City information: Svergehuset, Kungstradgaden, Tel. 08/789 20000 and you can telephone 'Miss Tourist'.

TOURIST NEWSPAPERS: 'Stockholm this Week', 'Stockholm' (small book); 'Stockholm Magazine'.

LOCAL TRANSPORT: Most people like to travel on the modern underground (Tunnelbana, technically good and artistically decorated). Otherwise there is the city railway (Jarnvagslinjer) or the buses. The best value for money is the tourist ticket 28 SKr. for 24 hours. If you want to save 120 SKr. on a city tour from Sverigehuset, buy a 1 to 4 day Stockholm ticket which also provides free entry to all museums for 60/100/150/200 SKr. and visit the historical sights yourself using buses and ferries as you need them. Even the boat trip to Drottningholm is included in the price. If you don't buy the Stockholm ticket it is really too expensive to travel by public transport.

POINTS OF INTEREST: See Stockholm first from above. Go to Kaknas Tower the highest building in Scandinavia as it offers the best view of the city and islands (Bus 68/69 May-September 9.00 a.m.-midnight otherwise only until 6.00 p.m.). In the Kultur Huset are the story of Stockholm, exhibitions, libraries etc.-no entry fee. At Stockholm castle on Gamia Stan you can see the Changing of the Guards at 12.10 p.m. and the castle museum which is built on the foundations of the earlier Vasa Castle, Tre Kronor (June-August daily 12 noon-3.00 p.m.).

The OLD TOWN is near by: From the railway station go to the right and you are on the small main island of the city, Gamla Stan. In the pubs and taverns with music you pay approx. 50 SKr. cover charge. Everyone in Stockholm, even in the communes, charges entry fees and seem determined to get your last cent. The lanes and the guesthouses are the 'In Places' in Scandinavia. Jazz: Stampen; Music & disco: Gamlingen, Engelen, 59 Kornharmstorg; Cafe Susan, 44 Skeppstron.

Naturally, its worth wandering through the old town even in the daytime. It has beautiful small lanes-Gasgrand, Skeppar olofa grand, Staffan Sasses grand-restored houses, small shops and also worth seeing is the Riddarholms church where some swedish kings are buried (daily 10.00 a.m.-3.00 p.m.), the Riddarhuset (knight's house) with knight's hall next door, the Storkyrka church near the castle which has been used for the last 700 years on State occasions. North of Gamla Stan is the new suburb of Norrmalm. In the evenings: Disco

Backahasten, Hamngatan 2, Disco Daily News, Kungstradgarden; Hard Rock Cafe, Sveavagen 75; Martini, Norrmalmstorg 4.

Futuristic city life: the Passage Galleries of the Tunnelbana (underground) Kungstradgarden to the Hamngatan/Sergelstorg. Between Kungsgatanand Gamla Brogatan is the traditional department store, PUB. In the square in front, Hotorget, there is usually a lot happening.

Gamia Brogatan is the oldest of the new suburbs and is a mixture of red light district and youthful enterprises. Under the Hotorget is an indoor market while the sales go on as usual above.

South of the old town is the suburb of Sodermalm, which has been recently built, and homes on the hill of Mariaberget have been partly renovated. Immediately on your right are steep steps, Maria Trappgrand, which lead up to Brannkyrkagatan . In the opposite direction along the harbourside street is Fafangan Hill, the former defence structure from where you get a good view of the Skansen and the town. Return via Folkungatan where you will find some rebuilt small, old wooden houses. Something better: St. Sofia's church.

On the island of Kungsholmen, behind the railway station, is the Stadshuset (town hall) and the beach promenade, Norr Malarstrand. Then behind there is the modern part of Mariaberg, but it's better to go in an easterly direction as next to Gamla Stan is the small island of Skeppsholmen on which is the Museum of Modern Art (Monday-Friday 11.00 a.m.-9.00 p.m., Saturday & Sunday 11.00 a.m.-5.00 p.m., 15 SKr). Already on the bridge leading to the island you will see modern sculptures. The adjoining island is the fortress island of Kastellholmen.

MUSEUMS: Now its time to look at the well presented museums: If you take the Tunelbana (underground) you will go past Odenplan where the Transport Museum is found (Monday-Friday 10.00 a.m.-5.00 p.m.); the Architectural Museum, if you are interested in town planning, is at Skeppsholmen (Monday-Friday 9.00 a.m.-5.00 p.m.); the Army Museum is at Riddargatan 13 (daily 11.00 a.m.-4.00 p.m., gratis); the Biological Museum is at Djurgarden (daily 10 a.m.-4 p.m., 5 SKr.); the Dance Museum is unusual, Laboratoriegatan (Tuesday-Sunday 12 noon-4,00 p.m.); the Gustav III, Paviljong, is at Haga (Tuesday-Sunday 12 noon-3.00 p.m.); the Historical Museum, where you can meet the vikings, Narvavagen 13 (Tuesday-Sunday 11.00 a.m.-4.00 p.m., 15 Skr); the Hologram Galleries are at Drottninggatan 110. You can see three dimensional works of art there (Tuesday-Sunday 11.00 a.m.-4.00 p.m., 15 SKr); the Toy Museum is at Mariatorget 1 (Tuesday-Sunday 10.00 a.m.-4.00 p.m., 10 SKr); the Natural History Museum is at Roslagsvagen (daily 11.00 a.m.-4.00 p.m., 2 SKr.); the National Maritime Museum is at Djurgardsbrunnsv. 24 (Monday-Friday 10.00 a.m.-5.00 p.m., 5 SKr.); the National Museum is on Blasieholmskajen (Tuesday-Sunday 10.00 a.m.-4.00 p.m., 10 SKr.); the Norsmen Museum, is on Djurgarden, (Tuesday-Sunday 10.00 a.m.-4.00 p.m., 10 SKr.); and the Music Museum, at Sibyllegatan 2 (Tuesday-Sunday 11.00 a.m.-4.00 p.m., 8 Skr.) and the Tobacco Museum, Skansen (daily 11.00 a.m.-3.00 p.m., gratis).

And we haven't even mentioned the viking ship, Wasa, at Wasavarvet, Skansen. 333 years after this ship sank on its maiden voyage, it was raised and carefully reconstructed. A film of how this was done is shown daily between 10.00 a.m.-5.00 p.m., in summer until 7.00 p.m., 8 SKr.

PARKS: Now before you collapse into a heap, relax in one of the parks: Humlegarden quiet, Ostermalmstorg, the islands of Skeppsholmen and Kastelholmen at the 'af Chapman' or Kunstradgarden with free entertainment on the open-air stage for those who never have enough (ask at the tourist information).

You can combine the parks and museums: the oldest open-air museum in the world is found on Skansen: everything from a stave church made of sticks, to farm houses, to town houses: Djurgarden (daily 8.00 a.m.-6.00 p.m., in summer until 11.50 p.m., 15 SKr.). The Berglanska Botanical Gardens are rather exclusive and have a Palm House. Frescati (the high school area–daily 1.00-4.00 p.m., 5 SKr). Grona Lund is a large amusement park and Djurgarden is also popular. Millesgarden on the Lidingos cliffs has works of art and an even better view (daily 10.00 a.m.-5.00 p.m.). It's also worth visiting the Drottningholm Castle gardens.

FOOD: Self service: Tumba Stinsen, T.Stationsplein; King David, Regeringsgatan 30; Cafe Eclair, Hamngatan 6; Mama Rosa, Sveavagen 55; in summer: Solliden, Skansen for every budget. It's worth a trip to Lindhagaberg's Vardshus, where you can catch your own trout.

ACCOMMODATION: The most fantastic youth hostel ever: on the sailing ship 'af Chapman', Skeppsholmen, Tel. 103 715, 205 705. You have to book beforehand. Others: Professorsslingan 13, Tel. 157 996. Pipmakargrand 2, Tel. 685 786.

Accommodation in private homes can be arranged through the tourist information office or at the railway station; youth hostels: Columbus, Tjarhovsgatan 11, Tel. 404 077;

Camping: Anby, Bromma, Tel. 370 420, hotels are very expensive.

DISTRICT: A beautiful area is the village of Vaxholm (with the railway bus). It has a fortress, the Suderhafen (harbour) where the tourist information office is located, and old wooden houses which blend in with the Scharen landscape.

MUSEUM TRAIN: To the south-west of Stocklholm is Sodertalja, from where you can take a sidetrip to Laggesta. Opposite the railway station is the Ostra Sodermanlands Jarnvag railway (600mm, 3.5km track, steam). At Mariefred is the renaissance castle, Gripsholm (1537) where Kurt Tucholsky lived and which is full of works of art (daily 10.00 a.m.-4.00 p.m., 10 SKr.).

UPPSALA

A tour of Sweden wouldn't be complete without a visit to the university town of Uppsala. (Pop. 147,000.) It not only has the oldest university in Sweden and the pub scene that goes with it, but an old town which is rich in tradition. Three former pagan kings are buried in Gamla Uppsala. According to legend, around 1000 A.D. there were gold covered temples to Thor, Odin and other germanic gods here. (Tourist information: Kungsgatan 42, Tel. 018/117 500 and at the cathedral).

POINTS OF INTEREST: the cathedral and the Gustavianum, the Carolina Rediviva library which is between the castle and the cathedral up on the hill and has a silver bible written in gothic script. You should also see the down to earth local museum Uppland, and the viking burial mounds of Valsgarde, where 15 viking chieftans undertook their last journey to Valhalla. At Vendel there is another iron age ships museum. Gamla Uppsala in the north is the birthplace of Sweden (open air museum) and at Odinsburg you can drink genuine mead! A beautiful place to see is the home of the botany professor Linne which has a small botanical garden in Linnegatan (there are also botanical walking tracks and a botanical garden at the University).

If you are a steam train buff, take a ride on the Lennakatten railway which starts from the railway station and goes through beautiful countryside.

ACCOMMODATION: Youth hostels, Sunnerstavagen 24, Tel. 018/3245 220 (very good); Norbyvagen 46, Tel. 108 060; Gammel-Granome, Tel. 13 108; Camping, Granebergs, Sunnersta; Sandvikens, Bjorklinge; Hotel: Elit, Bredgrand 10, Tel. 130 345; St. Erik, Bangard 10, Tel. 130 384.

SWITZERLAND

The Swiss Federation has a direct democratic parliamentary form. (Area 41,293 sq. km.–Pop. 6.4 million.)

It wasn't until 1848 that Switzerland officially became a Federation. Since then the Swiss are not only liberal and neutral, but they aren't keen to talk with anyone who does not have a red Swiss Passport.

ENTRY/FOREIGN EXCHANGE REGULATIONS: Germans and Austrians only need an identity card otherwise passport without visa. No currency restrictions.

Duty Free Allowance:
200 cigarettes or 250g tobacco, 2 litres wine or champagne, 1 litre spirits.

Currency/Exchange Rate: The currency of the land is the Swiss Franc (SFr.).

1A$	=	1.08 SFr.
1C$	=	1.20 SFr.
1NZ$	=	0.86 SFr.
£1	=	2.40 SFr.
1US$	=	1.64 SFr.

Other currencies have become weaker in comparison to the strong franc, so you must be rather frugal in Switzerland.

FOOD:
At all railway stations there are modern automatic vending machines selling a wide variety of food. (24Hrs.) The self service restaurants e.g. Migros, are inexpensive, have good food and can be found throughout the land.

TELEPHONE:
From coin operated telephones it is possible to dial other countries direct. Dial the area code without the 0.

Emergency Telephone Number: 117, Ambulance 114.

EMBASSIES:
Australia: Alpen Strasse 29, Berne, Tel. 43 04 43.
Canada: 88 Kirchenfeldstrasse, 3005, Berne, Tel. 44 63 81.
N.Z.:   No Resident Representative -see West Germany.
U.K.:   Thun Strasse 50, Bern, Tel. 44 50 21.
U.S.A.:   Jubilaum Strasse 93, Bern, Tel. 43 70 11.

BUYING TIPS:

Swiss chocolate is legendary and if you buy it at Migros it not only tastes good, but it is good value for money.

ACCOMMODATION:

Hotel association (Hotelier-Verein, Monbijoustr. 130, 3001 Bern, 031/507 111. Youth hostel, Wildhain Weg 19, 3012 Bern, 031/123 822:
Exchange housing: Intervac SLV, Reher Str. 6a, 9016 St. Gallen, 071/354 910.

SPEED LIMITS:

In built up areas 50 km/h;
outside built up areas 80 km/h. motorways 120 km/h–these are tollways and you require stamps (Vignette) which cost up to 30 SFr. These can be purchased at the border;
It is possible to have your car sent by train across the Simplon, Lotschberg, Albula, and Furka passes.

RAILWAYS:

Holiday tickets for 4/8/15/30 days for 145/170/205/285 SFr.
50% Elite-Abo for 15/30 for 60/75 SFr.;
50% fare for under 25s for 35 SFr.

AIRPORTS:

Geneva, Zurich, Bern have international airports.

BERN

Upstanding, patriotic, ancient swiss and easy to get along with are adjectives which describe the people of Bern although not always in a positive way. Even to-day Bern is an incomparable, closed, single minded city. (Pop. 144,0000). Bern was a popular gathering place of farmers from the various valleys which had their own dialects. Herzog Berchtold V of Zaehringen founded the city around 1190.

BY CAR: To-day for car travellers the N12 from Genf-Lausanne, and the N1 from Zuerich-Basel meet here and the N6 goes to the Bernese Oberland. City information and hotel booking offices are found in the parking places at: Grauholz on the N1 and Nuensingen-Nord on the N6. All exits from the motorways lead directly to the city centre, and to the parking areas before the old town, which is surrounded by the Aare-Schleife river. Hotels are sign posted, and the first letter denotes the area of the old town e.g. B-Bundeshaus, R-Rathaus, W-Waisenhaus.

BY AIR: There is a small airport at Bern, Belpmoos, from where flights leave to some european centres and there are a lot of connecting flights to the international airport at Zurich, Kloten.

BY RAIL: The Railway doesn't quite reach to the heart of the City. Bern has a very modern railway station which is on the western side of the old town. Shops and offices have been built over the railway station and other cities have copied this. Naturally, the capital of Switzerland is the main station for the inter-city trains Tel. 222404.

CITY TOURS: Daily at 2.00 p.m. from the main railway station by Bus Perron 3. The central tourist information office is at the station. Tel. 0311/227676, from the main hall of the railway station you go up the escalators.

TOURIST NEWSPAPERS: To find out what's on look at the 'Berner Wochenbulletin' as well as the daily newspapers. Alternative programme newspapers for the whole of Switzerland are the 'Wochenzeitung' WOZ and the 'Magma'.

LOCAL TRANSPORT: Green buses and trams (from 1.40 SFr). Day tickets 4 SFr. Touristenkarte (Tourist Tickets only 3.0 SFr. 3 Day Tickets 6.00 SFr. Umwellpass, which is valid for one month).

POINTS OF INTEREST: Some interesting houses: the May-Haus, Muenstergasse 32, the oldest surviving house built in 1515; the Erlacherhof, former town hall; the Beatrice von Wattenwyl House built around 1706 in the Junkerngasse; Einsteinhaus (Einstein's home), Kramgasse 19, (Tuesday-Saturday 10.00 a.m.-5.00 p.m. gratis); and the most famous building, the Zytglogge, the town tower which was part of the first town wall. It contains the astronomical clock built in 1530 with the figure of Hans von Thann as the hour hand, and underneath the little figures. You should get there four minutes before the hour when the figures commence moving. (In the old town north of the Town Hall (R-gasse) and south of the Munster–cathedral (M-gasse).) On the other side of the old town the Nydegg bridge which spans the Aare is the second landmark of which the people of Bern are very proud.

Since 1848, when the Federation came into being, Bern has been the Capital of Switzerland. That led to the building of the beautiful florentine style Parliament House. (From the railway station walk along Spitalgasse, Baerenplatz, Bundesplatz, tours daily from 9.00 a.m.-4.00 p.m. but not when Parliament is in session). There is a beautiful view from the terrace behind Parliament House where you can see among other things, the Kunsthalle (art gallery) and the museums on Helvetiaplatz: the Bern Historical Museum (Tuesday-Sunday 9.00 a.m.-noon and 2.00-5.00 p.m., gratis). You can look at the Burgunderchronik written by Diebold Schilling, and you will learn that the people of Bern and Switzerland were a mightly military power in the 15th Century; the Natural History Museum, Berna Strasse 15; Schweizerisches PTT

(Post Office) Museum, Helvetiaplatz 4 (Monday-Sunday 2.00-5.00 p.m., gratis); the Swiss Alpine Museum (daily 2.00-5.00 p.m., gratis); the Swiss Schuetzen Museum, Berna Str. 5 (Tuesday-Saturday 2.00-4.00 p.m. gratis); as well as the Swiss National Library, Hallwyl Strasse 15, gratis. And now to the Art Gallery, Hodler Str. 12, which apart from general works has paintings by Ferdinand Hodler and the large Klee Collection (Tuesday-Sunday 10.00 a.m.-5.00 p.m.).

THEATRES: There is a very strong 'little theatre' scene. In the old town: Katakoembli, Kramgasse 25; Kleintheater, Kramgasse 6; Theater am Kaefigturm, Spitalgasse 4; Theater 1230, Kramgasse 4; Theater am Zytglogge, Kramgasse 70 and for the young at heart: Puppet Theatre, Gerechtigkeitsgasse 31; Marionettenkeller, Gerechtigketsgasse 50, Particularly recommended: Zaehringer Refugium, Badgasse 1. Alternative Culture: Restaurant 'Bierhuebli', Neubrueck Strasse 43 and Mahagony Hall, Kloesterlistutz 18. The small theatres are mostly found in the cellars of the old town houses. The programmes are advertised at the theatres or obtainable in part at the tourist information. Although there is an Old Town Summer Programme, Bern isn't a tourist town and all theatres close for a summer break. As a result it is better to come on a long weekend in spring or autumn.

If you want to study theatre yourself in Bern, you should study at the 'Kulturmuehle Luetzelflueh' (CH 3432 Luetzelflueh, Tel. 034/613623). School for 'Total Theatre'.

FESTIVALS: The International Jazz Festival is held at the beginning of May; in June the Festival of the Small Stage; in July the Folk Festival on the Gurten.

PUBS: In old Bern prior to 1798, there were 200 wine cellars but even to-day in the pubs which are called Beizen here, there is something happening in the evenings. In summer people go to the 'Spatz' on the Barenplatz where there are always snacks offered for sale. Hot chips with curry sauce is the favourite of most young people. The Kornhauskeller is a typical swiss restaurant, Kornhausplatz, in the middle price bracket where you should try the 'Rosti'. (The official National Theatre is on this Square and also the Swiss Gutenberg Museum–Monday-Friday 2.00-5.00 p.m., gratis). Another similar tavern is the Kloetzlikeller in Gerechtigkeitsgasse, recommended after 10.00 p.m. Young people also gather at the Cafe B in Munstergasse and Rest. Teestuebli, Postgasse 49. People talk politics at the Della Casa, Schauplatzgasse 10, and because it's close to Parliament House the people who frequent it are also supposed to be in the know. The Glocke, just past the Zytglogge on the left, has folklore evenings. Also recommended: the Jugendzentrum (Youth Centre) Sandrain Strasse 25; the Dance Hall Matte and the Disco Chikito, Neuengasse 28; ZAFF, Villentemattstr. 7.

MARKETS: are held on Tuesday and Saturday in the centre of the old town streets; the meat market in the Munstergasse; the traditional market 'Ziebelemarit' is held on the 4th Monday in November, although it's not really the time for travelling.

TIPS FOR VEGETARIANS: Restaurant 'Bubenberg Vegi', Bubenbergplatz 8 and Restaurant, 'Vegetaris Fit', Neuengasse 15. Kosha Restaurant: Hotel Bellevue, Kochergasse 5.

ACCOMMODATION in Bern is expensive, if you don't take notice of the recommendations in a tourist newspaper you will sleep on a park bench (you can see that Bern isn't really a tourist centre). The youth hostels are in the lower levels of Parliament House, rather primitive accommodation, Weihergasse 4. Tel. 031/226316. Advantage: It shuts its doors at midnight. Camping, south, Tram 9.

There aren't really any inexpensive hotels. Hotel Schonbuhl, Bern Str. 11. TEl. 85 03 12 but it is 9 km from the city centre. Hotel Arca, Gerechtigkeitsgasse 18. Tel. 22 37 11; Hotel Kreuz, Zeughausgasse 41, Tel. 2237 11; Hotel Kreuz, Zeughausgasse 41, Tel. 22 11 62; Hotel Goldener Schlussel, Rathausgasse 72, Tel. 220216. Another possibility for people travelling by car or train and who have a map, look for accommodation in the smaller towns. You should check out Bern a la Cart Weekends-offered by the tourist information office.

LUCERNE

It was the first town to join the Federation in 1332 as far as the forest cantons are concerned. Lucerne has on one side the Vierwaldstattersee (lake) and on the other the foothills of the alps. Many international companies have offices in Lucerne. It has a rich heritage, if you haven't seen the wooden Kapellbrucke (chapel bridge) over the Reuss, then you have missed out on something. It remains unique. It has a beautiful dreamlike panorama of lakes and alps.

BY CAR: You won't have any problems getting to Lucerne as it is the gateway to the Gotthard Pass. The main axis for international motorists is the Expressway N2/E9 (Basel, Olten, Luzerne, Gotthard, Milan) but if you come from Zurich the roads are well signposted and there are also short stretches of expressway. Tip: Just before Lucerne take the road via Ebikon. In the city just before you get to the centre, is the parking station (24hrs) on the right hand side, or in Ebikon turn left into Scloss str. towards the Hospital, then go along Adlingenswiler str. to the corner of Dreilinden str. and you will find a parking area. Then take the No. 14 bus (St.Anna) to the city (other parking stations are found in the old town).

BY RAIL: The railway goes straight into the city centre. The railway station is opposite the harbour, on the lake in the old town on the left bank of the Reuss River–most of it was built in the 19th century. Every hour swiss inter-city trains arrive at the railway station from the main line (Zurich, Fenf, Lugano). International trains on the eastern line from Zurich travel via Arth Goldau to Gotthard (where you have to change to the city train). Lucerne railway station: Tel. 041/2321 22.

BY AIR: Direct trains run from the international airport Zurich-Kloten, to the city (you can also book your luggage through).

BY SEA: You can also come by boat. If you choose to come from the south from Altdorf or Stansstad, then you will come along the romantic and at the same time, historically oldest line. To-day there aren't any ferries, only motor boats which are designed to cater for the tourists. On Sundays, in good weather the steam ships also run.

PUBLIC TRANSPORT: Only buses and trolley buses. Single tickets 1.40 SFr. (Tourist Tickets 2 days, 5 SFr. but only in conjunction with a hotel booking). City bus from the railway station, orange & white, gratis.

TOURIST INFORMATION OFFICE: From the railway station turn left into Pilatus str. and the tourist information office, Verkehrsverein Luzern, is at No. 14, Tel. 041/517171. Ask for the official guidebook 'Luzerne' which contains some hotel stamps and also a few entertainment stamps (only in conjunction with hotel accommodation).

TOURIST NEWSPAPER: 'Magma'.

POINTS OF INTEREST: Soak up the colourful summer evening city-life. If you can tear yourself away from the picture postcard beauty of the harbour (railway station, bus terminal, all together) you will want to go across the Kapellbrucke (bridge) which lies only a few steps from where the River Reuss flows into the lake, and the modern bridge, which carries the vehicular traffic across the lake. Both sections of the old town are connected by the Kapellbrucke which, in the past, was an important vehicular crossing. It is recognised as one of the oldest intact wooden bridges in Europe (cira 1300). It is decorated with late renaissance pictures by Hans Wagmann (from 1614). The night would be over in Lucerne if you tried to decipher all the pictures. It is very peaceful in the Folterkammer of the Wasserturm (tower in the water) which is the home of the Artillerie Verein (artillery association).

Along the promenades on both sides of the river is where the action is, particularly in old town on the right bank of the Reuss River. In the evenings there are usually buskers etc. and at least, it's always international. Lucerne was one of the earliest tourist centres. One of the results of this is the high prices, particularly for accommodation. Go across the Kappelle Bridge which leads to the chapel (the old town on the right bank) and then turn left along the Rathausquai (town hall quay) until you come to the town hall with it's tower from the middle ages. There is another bridge made out of iron, for pedestrians. In the arcades under the town hall (a little taste of Bern) on Tuesday and Saturday the fruit & vegetable markets are held (flea market: in Reusssteg, Saturday 7.00 a.m.-5.00 p.m.). Here is also the 'Am Rhyn-Haus', the pride of the town which contains a collection of Picasso's paintings (May-September Tuesday-Sunday 10.00 a.m.-12 noon and 3.00-6.00 p.m. 2 SFr, Students 0.50 SFr., Entry from 21 Furren Gasse). At the town hall turn right and go up to Kornmarkt, turn right again to Kappell Gasse and the numerous other lanes of the old town where under the flags, during the day is a very busy shopping centre around Hirsh Platz, Weggis Gasse and Hertenstein Strasse, and where in the evenings people stroll along or eat in restaurants. Kepell Platz, Sternen Platz and Schwanen Platz are almost next to one another, are easy to find, and are typical of Lucerne. Kapell Platz has an historical fountain like every other swiss town.

ENTERTAINMENT: If you come here in the evenings in summer, and you haven't already had a drink at one of the many sidewalk cafes along the Rathausquai (e.g. Mr. Pickwick Pub), you should go into one of the old town pubs: a first-class tip: Restaurant Fritschi, a restaurant since 1602. All ages groups go there and you can eat well and inexpensively (for Lucerne)-cheese fondue approx. 12 SFr., 5 Sternen Platz. In the same street are also the Video Disco, Gerbern-Old Lucerne Inn and the Lucerne 'In Place' the Stadtkeller (folk music-Landler & Jodler) providing something for everyone's taste.

Other places a little further from the centre of the old town: If you really don't want to miss out on the typical local culture then go to the rather classy Landlerkeller at the Hotel Flora, 5 Seidenhof str., on the left hand side of the old town; or in the same street the Chuchichaschtli at No. 8; or a little further north of the city to the Isebahnli, 24 Basel str. If you want another drink try the 'William Tell' a ship anchored at the Schweizerhof Quai. Cultural highlights during the year: In winter: the Fritschi Umzug (carnival procession) on Maundy Thursday and the International Music Festival in August-September-Information, Tel. 235 272.

FOOD: You can also take advantage of the excellent swiss cooking. Usually restaurants are clean and well looked after. If you don't only want to go to Fritschi's you can get a quick lunch at the Cafe Gipfel, 20 Hertenstein str. or at the Golden Lowen, 22 Kappell Gasse. But we recommend the self service restaurants e.g. Migros, 44 Hertenstein str. or Coop, three buildings further along. For vegetarians, Restaurant Bristol, 3 Obergrund Gasse; Koscher food is offered at Hotel Drei Konige, 35 Bruch str. Try the Pickwick Pub if you want to serve yourself.

Now to the VERKEHRSHAUS: News techniques, shipbuilding and tourist information, plane and space, postal service, cars and especially

Rome: St. Peter's

Lucerne: Chapel Bridge and Water Tower

don't miss a trip on the Gotthard Locomotive Simulator, the Planetarium, the only one in Switzerland. Something more unusual and not to be missed: the new Swissorama, a 360 degree cinema. All special shows are included in the price 9 SFr., students 6 SFr, if you have an inter-rail ticket then its free. Daily 9.00 a.m.-6.00 p.m., bus 2 from the railway station. If it's nice weather then go one way by boat from the harbour-Lido.

Other IMPORTANT things to see in the area around Lowen Platz: the Lowen Memorial in memory of the Swiss Guards at Tuilereinsturm-in summer it's a popular meeting place; the Gletscher Garden, a natural memorial, with mirror maze, water lift and museum, 4 Denkmal str. (summer 8.00 a.m.-6.00 p.m., daily, otherwise limited, 4.50 SFr., students 3.0 SFr.) and the Grande Panorama, 18 Lowen str. (3 SFR/1.50 SFr) where you can see the french army crossing the border into Switzerland in the Prussian War of 1870/1-very impressive (daily 9.00 a.m.-6.00 p.m.). Particularly in the old town: the Musegg Tower, part of the old town wall in the north with 9 towers. It's lit up in summer and you can actually walk along it in parts, e.g. from the Nolli Tower near the Geissmatt Bridge (from Rathaus Quai straight ahead along Weinmarkt and Muhlen Platz, then along Bruggli Gasse). There are also two covered wooden bridges, the Spreuer and Heu Bridges built in 1408. The Death Dance pictures by Kaspar Meglinger (1630) from the time when death was a public theme in life are very impressive.

IMPORTANT MUSEUMS: Art Museum, 1 Robert Zund str., near the railway station, (Tuesday-Sunday 10.00 a.m.-12 noon & 2.00-5.00 p.m., 4 SFr/3.50 SFR) with typical swiss works of art; Natural History Museum, 6 Kasernen Platz,(Tuesday-Sunday 10.00 a.m.-12 noon & 2.00-5.00p.m., 3 SFr/2SFr) with a lot of live animals, modern displays; Richard Wagner Museum which has beautiful grounds (Tuesday-Sunday 9.00 a.m.-12 noon & 2.00-5.00 p.m. 3 SFr/2SFr), 27 Wagner Weg, Bus 6 or 7 to Wartegg, then towards Tribschen. Now to the outskirts: Schweizerisches Trachten Museum (traditional clothing), (Easter until 1st November daily 9.00 a.m.-5.30 p.m., 2.50SFr/1.50SFr.) at Utenberg, Dreilinden str. At the mountain station of the Dietschibergbahn (model railway).

ACCOMMODATION. With luck you might find something available at the Youth hostel (YHF membership card necessary), Rotsee, 12 Sedel str. (Bus 1 to Maihof, then along the Friedentaler str. about 15 mins walk.) Tel. 041/36 88 00. There is a Camping Ground at Lido (Bus 2 or by boat) Verkehrshaus (Tel. 312146). Pensions and Hotels are both very expensive. Value for money: Garni Hotels, Krone, near Muhle Platz Tel. 516251, Pickwick, Rathaus 6 Quai (very central), Tel. 515927 and Spatz, 103 Obergrund str., Tel. 41 1075. Private pensions are handled by the tourist information office, Lucerne Weekend Special.

SIDE TRIPS: A great many are offered and therefore we have only selected a few: by ship across the Vierwaldsee (lake) (return trips between 17 & 30 SFr. depending to which town you go). You can go to Landungsstelle Kehrsiten and from there by train to the modern Burgerstock or to Vitznau, then take the oldest alpine funicular in Europe (1871) up to Rigi Kulm. You can go down to the valley on the other side to Goldau where there is a nature reserve and animal park (Bergsturzgebiet) Tel. 041/821510) and return by train to Lucerne–cheap round trips are offered at the railway station. Or you can take a long trip to Rutli or Tellskapelle (on the Axen str. It's also beautiful by car). The locals also like to go there. Lucerne has it's own mountain, the Pilatus. From Kriens (Bus 1/15) by Gondella or from Alpnachstad with the steepest funicular in the world (48 degrees) or you could make it a round trip.

ZURICH

Zurich is swiss, prosperous and reserved. (Pop. 354,200).

In the 19th century when other cities of this region e.g. Constance and St. Gallen, suffered a decline, Alfred Escher reigned in Zurich. He had a seat on the parliament, was the founder of the railways and banks, and with his forward looking policies managed to turn Zurich into Switzerland's richest centre .

BY RAIL: One of Escher's memorials is the terminal railway station building built in 1871 and still highly regarded to-day. In the sixties an underground shopping centre was built under it and another centre is to be built over the platforms. All the services you need are to be found here although take-away food is expensive. There are showers in the shopping centre underneath. The left luggage room is in the central hall (1SFr per piece every 2 days!) and also the railway information office. Follow the yellow line to the well run Swiss Information Office. On the right of the main platform is a hotel bookings service which is manned day and night but you won't get anything under 50 SFr. Railway information Tel. 01/211 50 10.

BY CAR: The northern bypass has been opened. The motorways are the N1 from Munich, Lindau, St. Gallen, Winterthur, or in the opposite direction from Stuttgart, Singen, Schaffhausen, Winterthur or N2/N1 from Frankfurt, Basel, Olten. Both of which join the new underground city road. If you want to park in the city in business hours then expect an hour wait. A cheap and relatively close parking station: Feldegg at Seefeld. Drive to Heim Platz (Kunsthaus/Scauspielhaus) and then turn right at Schauspielhaus into Zelt Weg. Drive along Zelt Weg to Kreuz

Platz and it is signposted from there. From the parking station go down to Seefeld Str. and catch Tram 4 to the city centre.

BY AIR: The largest airport in Switzerland is at Zurich, Kloten. Terminal A is for charter flights and flights to Germany, Austria, Israel and Eastern Bloc Countries and Terminal B caters for domestic flights and those to western Europe and countries which don't have charter flights. If you aren't being picked up (e.g. by a hotel bus) then take the train from the airport to the city. It is the cheapest, easiest and fastest way. On your way home you can send your luggage to Kloten from over 100 railway stations (9 SFr per piece; FLY RAIL. Airport Tel. 81 27 11 11.)

TOURIST INFORMATION: Central railway hall, Tel. 211 40 00.

TOURIST NEWSPAPERS: none really. The Zuri Tip in Friday's 'Tagesanzeiger' (Tagi) gives you some information; the WoZ which comes out each week and the Wiener Verschnitt MAGMA. Cinema etc. Programmes: Zurich im Blickpunkt and the Zurich News.

POINTS OF INTEREST: The railway station is right in the city centre and you have three choices:
You can go right to Bahnhof Str., the main shopping street, where in the small park in front of the Globus department store you'll probably meet a lot of young people–the street at the back of it leads to the lake; OR go straight ahead across all the tram lines and traffic lanes and Limmat Quay to Central, then keep to the right and you'll come to Niederdorf Str. (first parallel street to Limmat Quay) where the Zurich Scene is;
OR turn left to some culture: the first class Swiss Museum (Tuesday-Sunday 10.00 a.m.-12 noon & 2.00-5.00 p.m., gratis).

LOCAL TRANSPORT: You can see a lot on foot. The white and blue trams are very fast and go all over the city (the same tickets may be used on buses, the mountain railway and trams-tickets from 1SFr-15 SFr-Day Tickets are better value). The people of Zurich voted against a fast train in 1973 because they thought the trams fitted in better with Zurich's charm. A city railway is being built and should be opened in 1990 and will serve the 'Gold Coast' and the right bank of Zuri Lake.

CITY TOURS: From tourist information office, open 10.00 a.m.. Night tours at 8.00 p.m.–terrific. By tram from May-October Wednesday, Friday, Sunday from 10.30 a.m. in front of the Globus department store.

BICYCLE HIRE: At the railway station, Tel. 2 45 34 77, from 6 SFr.

SHOPPING: Naturally you will want to buy something in or around the Bahnhof Str. But that's not all Zurich has to offer.

HISTORICAL CENTRE: Along Limmat Quay are the Town Hall and the Wasser Church and the small lanes on both sides of Limmat Quay.

A bit more uplifting: the Gross Munster (cathedral) (daily 10.00 a.m.-6.00 p.m., gratis).

The pride of Old Zurich: the Guild Houses are found at 40, 42 & 54 Limmat Quay and 8 & 20 Munsterhof. Changing exhibitions are held in the Stadthaus across the Munster bridge (Monday-Friday 8.00 a.m.-6.00 p.m., gratis). Nearby is the Art Gallery, Heim Platz (Tram 3, Tuesday-Friday 10.00 a.m.-9.00 p.m., Saturday, Sunday 10.00 a.m.-5.00 p.m., 1-7 SFr.) and the Schauspielhaus (theatre). Kunstgewerbe Museum, Austellungs Str. 60 (Tuesday-Friday 10.00 a.m.-6.00 p.m., Saturday & Sunday 10.00 a.m.-12 noon & 2.00-4.00 p.m. to the left of the railway station) which has changing exhibitions. There are changing exhibitions too at the Heimhaus, Limmat Quay 31, the Indian Museum, Schulhaus Feld Str. 89 (Saturday 2.00-5.00 p.m., Sunday 10.00 a.m.-12 noon, Tram 8, gratis). The collection at the university, Kunstler Gasse 16 (Tuesday-Friday, take the Polybahn from Central). At the Toy Museum, Fortuna Gasse 15, lectures about toys are given by Franz Carl Weber (shop in Bahnhof Str. Monday-Friday 2.00-5.00 p.m., gratis) and the Kulturama at the Roten Fabrik, See Str. 409 (Monday-Friday 10.00 a.m.-5.00 p.m., Bus 65).

IMPORTANT: Museum Rietberg, with permanent exhibitions of european art and the pride of the city is in two buildings: Villa Wesendonck, Gabel Str. 15 (Tuesday-Sunday 10.00 a.m.-5.00 p.m.) and Hirshen graben 20, (Tuesday-Friday 2.00-7.00 p.m., Saturday & Sunday 2.00-5.00 p.m.).

Housing Museum, Baren Gasse 22 (Tuesday-Sunday 10.00 a.m.-12 noon 4.00-5.00 p.m., gratis). At the Zum Rech building there is a model of the city in 1800, Neumarkt 4 (Monday-Friday 8.00 a.m.-6.00 p.m., gratis). The Centre Le Corbusier, his last work, finished after his death 1967, is at the northern end of the Zurihorns (Tram 2 or 4). Nolder Zoo, Zurichberg Str. 221 (daily 8.00 a.m.-6.00 p.m.–Tram 5 or 6, 6.60 SFr. students 3.30 SFr). The Paradies der Alpenbahnen with the longest O size model railway track in the world (April-October daily 11.00 a.m.-6.00 p.m.) is also there.

MODERN ARCHITECTURE: The Rote Schloss (red castle), Gl Guisan Quay 20, the Werkbund settlement, Neubuhl, Wollishofen Nidelbad Str. and post modern: PTT Fernmelde Zentrum, Autobahn No. 1.

ENTERTAINMENT: If you don't want to go to one of the suburban pubs and mix with a wide range of people in Aussersihl, then the place for you is the Roten Fabrik in spite of its cheap appearance. Niederdorf Str. is the street where it all usually happens–buskers, boutiques, toy shops, comfortable pubs and sometimes street markets against a background of beautiful old houses.

Good pubs around here: Schlauch, Obere Zaune or Munster Gasse; mad: Gloria, Schoffel Str. 7; Malatesta (Niederdorf 15), the Rheinfelder Bierhalle (Niederdorf in direction of the railway station), Splendid bar,

Rosen Gasse 5 (very full but very Zurich), Kon Tiki (Niederdorf) New wave, Gantasio Bar, Schoffel Gasse 2.
A bit further: Limmat Quay 82 (jazz club also there); Cafe Plaunsch, Lang Str. 62 (music) also Bazillus, Niederdorf Str. 13; very traditional, the Weisse Wind, Oberdorf Str. 20; cheap snacks: Bar Bellevue, Tor Gasse and also very traditional: Wirtschaft Eckstein, Schifflande 10.

Worker's pubs: Popolo, Lang Str. 209; Gotthard, See Str. 19; Down to earth: Seeburg, Dufour Str. 175; Cheerful, Tiefenbrunnen; not only for railway workers: Rangier Bahnhof, Neufranken Gasse 29, Aussersihl.

FOOD: Traditional: Zahringer (Bio, Zahringer Platz 11) or also there Schwanli, Weisses Kreuz, Falken Str. 27; Bierhalle Kropf in Gassen 16; Blutige Tume, off Rheinfelder Bierhalle, or the alcohol-free restaurant of the Frauen Verein or any of the inexpensive Stadtkuchen which can be found in the telephone book. Drania Laube, Urania Str. 9; Vegetarian: Gleich, Seefel Str. 7;Kocher: Restaurant Shalom, Lavater Str. 33. More Exclusive: Bodega Espanola, Munster Gasse 15; Open until 2 a.m.: Odeon, Limmat Quay 2.

People sit around on the Lake Promenade from Bellevue Square, at Zuri Horn (Bellerive Str. young people), on the Spitz Square, on Burkli Square (end of Bahnhof Str), in the parks and at the lake beaches at Mythen Quay and a bit further along. A flea market is also held on Burkli Square on Saturday mornings.

ACCOMMODATION: Youth hostel, Mutschellen Str. 114, Tel. 01/482 35 44, Tram 7; Camping on the lake at Wollishofen, Bus 61/65.
Pensions: Ascona, Meinrad Lienert Str. 17, Tel. 46 32 723; Olympia, Badener St4. 324, Tel. 491 77 66; Bristol, Stampfenbacher Str. 34, Tel. 47 07 00; Limmathof, Limmat Quay 142, Tel. 47 42 20. Bahnpost, Reiter Gasse 6, Tel. 241 32 11.

DISTRICT ATTRACTIONS: Go up Util Berg with the Sihital/Zurich/Utli Mountain Railway. There is always a crowd up there, particularly in summer when the steam train runs (usually Wednesday, Sunday afternoons: SZU), Inter-rail 50% discount. The Planeten Weg is an easy walking track to Felsenegg, chairlift to Adliswil and return with the SZU, or go a station further to the Langenberg Nature Park. Or take a boat trip on Zuri Lake. The best one is from the railway station Landes Museum at 9.00 p.m. on summer evenings.

WEST GERMANY

The Federal Republic of West Germany consists of ten states and West Berlin which has special status. (Area: 248,553 sq. km.–Pop. 61.5million).

The Republic of West Germany was established in 1949 after the second world war. The capital is Bonn on the Rhine but three cities, Frankfurt, Hamburg and Munich, compete for the position of most important city in West Germany. The old capital, Berlin, should be happy to have a secure 4 Power status. The borders of West Germany are the Baltic and North Seas, the Rhine River and the Alps as well as the barbed wire along its border with East Germany.

Particularly beautiful countryside is found in the north in Friesland and the Lunebureger Heide and in the south around the Black Forest, Lake Constance (Bodensee) and at the foot of the Alps in Bavaria. In between are low hills and the rather bright city life of many of the german towns even though Germany lacks a centre like Paris or London.

ENTRY/FOREIGN EXCHANGE/CUSTOMS REGULATIONS: A valid passport is required. There are no restrictions placed on the amount of money brought into or taken out of the country.

Duty Free Allowance:
200 cigarettes or 250 grms tobacco, 2 litres of wine and 1 litre of spirits. There are strict border controls as much for illegal immigrants as for drugs.

Currency/Exchange Rate: The currency of the land is the Deutsche Mark (DM).

1A$	=	1.28 DM
1C$	=	1.42 DM
1NZ$	=	1.02 DM
£1	=	2.84 DM
1US$	=	1.94 DM

The cost of living is lower than in Switzerland but higher than in Austria.

TELEPHONE:

It is possible to dial other countries direct from telephone boxes with a green quadrant on the door.

Emergency Telephone Number: 110 112.

EMBASSIES:

Australia: Godesberger Allee 107, Bonn, Tel 81 030
Canada: Europa Centre, W. Berlin, Tel. 261 1161

N.Z.   Bundeskanzlerplatz 5300, Bonn, Tel. 214 021
U.K.:   Uhland Str. 7, W. Berlin; Amalien Str. 62, Munich.
U.S.A.:   Clay Allee 170, W. Berlin; Koningin Str. 5, Munich.

ACCOMMODATION:

Numerous tourist information offices offering information about hotels, pensions and camping grounds.
Youth hostel Juhe, DJH, Bulow Str. 26, Post Fach 220, 4930 Detmold.

SPEED LIMITS:

50 km/h in built up areas;
100 km/h outside built up areas.
There are no speed limits on the motorways in West Germany but the recommended speed is 130 km/h. There is a dense motorway network and a lot of dying forests.

RAILWAYS:

For foreigners DB tourist card for 9/16 days for 220/285 DM. A lot of special offers such as Netzkarten, tramper monthly tickets for under 26s for 238 DM, junior pass for 1 year 50% for under 23s or students under 27 for 110 DM or the roserote Wochen special from 99 DM per person.

AIRPORTS:

Large airports are found at Frankfurt, Colonge, Bonn, W.Berlin, Hamburg, Munich, Stuttgart, and Hanover and there are numerous small ones.

COLOGNE-KOLN

Cologne is famous for its Carnival, and has the most important urban building in Germany-the Kolner Dom (Cologne cathedral)-it has a wealth of architecture from all centuries, which is usually only found in large metropolises of Europe. But the town remains just as it always has been: firstly a workers' town, simple and straight, not only since 1933 when Konrad Adenaur the then Lord Mayor, had the bridge over the Rhine tiled brown. And to-day the town offers everything you could wish as far as the cultural scene is concerned (Pop. 995,0000).

BY CAR: Cologne is surrounded by a wide Autobahn Ring, to which come the A3 from Frankfurt, the A61 from Ludwigshafen/southern Germany, the A4 from Aachen/Belguim, the A1 from Hamburg/Bremen, and the A4 from Olpe/Frankfurt/Wurzburg.

Parking areas: From the east along Zubringer strasse (Bundes Autobahn Kreuz Gremberg) to the Messe in Koln-Deutz, and then Tram 1/2/7 to the City or the S Bahn; from the west take the Koln-Lovenich exit along the Aachener str. to Mungersdorfer Stadion (Stadium)–an interesting stop, with swimming pool, sports school and from the south, the woods (Animal Park)–from here you can take Tram 1 to the City. For those who are really in a hurry there is also a parking station near the main railway station (Breslauer Platz).

BY RAIL: The railway goes right to the middle of the city. The main through railway station is right next to the Hohenzollern railway bridge–a technical work of art which stands in the shadow of the cathedral. Over a very short distance 4 tracks branch out to become 12 tracks. The steps from the railway platforms widen out to form a wide passage along which are found the usual services. Railway information is at the front on the left. You can see the cathedral through the glass at the front (Tel. 2761).

BY AIR: An avant gard airport, Cologne-Bonn was built in 1970 and bus 170 leaves from the main railway station (Tel. 02203/40 22 22).

BY SHIP: The Rhine ships of the Koln-Dusseldorfer Line dock just after the Deutzer Bridge (Tel. 20881).

TOURIST INFORMATION opposite the cathedral, Unter Fettenhennen 19 (Tel. 0221/221 33 40).

TOURIST NEWSPAPERS: 'Schauplatz' and 'Stadtrevue'.

LOCAL TRANSPORT: The widely spread network of U-Bahn (underground), trams and buses which connect with the S-Bahn (City Train) traffic of the Ruhr network, give you optimal public transport coverage. The last train leaves the city centre at approx. 1.00 a.m. Information Tel. 547 33 33. The cheaper 24 hour tourist ticket is recommended for tourists.
  Organised city tours leave from the Verkehrsamt, usual tour approx. 2 hours & 16 DM, in July/August, also evening tours on Friday, Saturday at 8.00 p.m. which visit some lively pubs. You can also take a joy flight over the city. From Easter to October the Rhine Ship Cruises leave from between the Hohenzollern and Deutzer Bridges.

POINTS OF INTEREST: But now to the important sights, naturally the cathedral surrounded by a small square–an international meeting place–it was under construction from 1248 to 1560 and in the 19th century until 1880. Even over such a long period of time the gothic style has been adhered to, and the interior in particular, is very peaceful even though it is situated in the middle of the hustle and bustle of the city. You may climb the 509 steps to the viewing platform 97m above the city in the south tower which is 157m high, for a good view over the city. Many works of art are to be found inside, among them the

Munich: Marienplatz

West Germany: Cologne's Hohe Strasse

Switzerland: PTT Bus near Himmelrank Tunnel

wooden crucifix carved in 969, the Bible window in the choir, the Shrine of the Magi which is said to hold relics of the Three Kings, an expensive mosaic floor in the Choir. Not to be forgotten: the Treasury of the cathedral (daily 9.00 a.m.-4.00 p.m., Saturday and Sunday from 12.30 p.m.). Also: the Archbishop's Diocesan Museum (Tuesday-Saturday 10.00a.m.-5.00 p.m.).

MORE MUSEUMS: On the south side of the cathedral there isn't only the Kolsch-Brauhaus Fruh (Brewery) which has a large city atmosphere, but also the Germanisch-Romische Museum (germanic-roman), located in a functional new building with fantastic mosaics, frescoes, a roman glass collection, coins, the Tomb of Poblicius–the museum and the historical site are the same–the 40 x 65m remains of a roman villa; In 50 A.D. Cologne was a roman city, built on the site of the germanic settlement of Ubier 38 B.C., which was conquered by the Romans (Tuesday-Sunday 10.00 a.m.-10.00 p.m./2 DM.).

HISTORICAL PLACES: Along Unter Goldschmied str. on the next corner under the 'Wickuler im Romer' restaurant is a 100m long roman drainage channel which you can walk along (the new city hall is also here) and the remains of the roman town wall around the corner of Komodien & Tunis strs. and the corner Zeughaus & Auf dem Berlich strs. From the new city hall you can get to two other interesting places which are in opposite directions: On the left is the centre of the old town which is now a pedestrian zone. St. Martin's church is surrounded by new buildings which blend in with the old town–an early example of present day interest in preserving the past; and along Rhine Ufer strasse which is the direct access route to the Rhine bank. This part of the old town offers Kings Cross style entertainment: the old market, Salz Gasse, fish market, Mauth Gasse, An der Brand; Also beautiful: Sion Brewery, Unter Taschenmacher, Papa Joe's Bier Salon, old juke boxes, Alter Markt 50; the Altstadt Paffgen, Am Heumarkt 62; a beer hall, like Zur Malzmuhle, Heumarkt 6; in the Keule opposite you can eat until 3.00 a.m.; at Haus Heumarkt/Augustiner str. lives OTTO (Motor); Ancient: Bier Esel, the oldest place serving muscels, Briete str. 114.

Back to the new City Hall, on the right is Hohe str. with streetlife, pedestrian zones and shopping centre, which leads to Gurzenische strasse and to the right the Schilder Gasse, Neumarkt, Mittel strasse, have a look at the Bazar de Cologne, a modern shopping arcade built mainly of glass and steel. In the meantime you have reached the ring road, which was the edge of the city in the middle ages.

Now to shopping on the Ring (road): Saturn am Hansarr Ring (U-Bahn), the world's largest hi-fi and record shop. It is in a high-rise building which, when it was built in 1925, was the highest in Europe and which like the Cologne Messe is an interesting example of 1920s architecture. On Hansar Ring parallel to Gereon's Wall and Klingelputz strasse is where the famous gaol stood (now parkland).

A few buildings from various eras: the three large archways on Ebert Platz, Rudolf Platz and Chlodwig Platz, as well as the Ulreforte, seat of the 'Roten Funken'; the Overstolzhaus from the 13th century, Rhein Gasse 8; the Gurzenich in Martin str., a gothic reception centre; the Zeughaus in the same street, which houses the City Museum (U Appelhof Platz, Tuesday-Thursday 10.00 a.m.-5.00 p.m.); the original 4711 building in Glocken Gasse, next to the new opera house on Offenbach Platz; the highest apartment building of Europe, Colonia, on the Rhine which has 46 floors, a concrete mountain. And: Antoniter church, built in the 14th century, with memorials to those who fell in the two world wars and the 'Death Angel' by the Expressionist, Ernst Barlach.

MUSEUM TIPS: The Wallraff Richartz Museum, and Museum Ludiwg and Cinemathek (paintings from the middle ages until the present, An der Rechtschule, Tuesday-Sunday 10.00 a.m.-5.00 p.m.); the Schnutgen Museum, museum of art from the middle ages, Cacillien str. 29 (Tuesday-Sunday 10.00 a.m.-5.00 p.m.); Rautenstrauch-Joest, ethnological museum, Ubier Ring 45 (Tuesday-Sunday 10.00 a.m.-5.00 p.m.) and the Museum for Ostasiatische Kunst (East-Asian Art), Universitats str. 100 (Tuesday-Sunday 10.00 a.m.-5.00 p.m.). Modern: Motor Museum, Deutz-Mulheimer str. 111 (Monday-Friday 9.00 a.m.-4.00 p.m.).

AND: The university quarter is found around the open space south of Aachener Weihers.

PARKLANDS: Officially in 1st place is the Rhine Park (north of the Messe) with thermal baths and Tanzbrunnen (summer programme), with a Gondel lift over to the zoo/botanical gardens in Riehl; popular among young people: the Volksgarten with beer garden in the southern workers' suburb; Konigsforst (king's forest–end stop of the U9) has beautiful walking tracks; Theodor Heuss Park on the banks of the Rhine; the T.V. tower in Kanal str. (horse-drawn coaches 6DM). The Romer Park on Agrippina Ufer (U Ubier Ring).

ENTERTAINMENT: Is here in the south of the city. For inexpensive food: 1A Kartoffeltopfe in the Grauen Grans, Barbarossa Platz; Korinth, Martin Luther Platz, Klasse Gyros until 4 a.m. or the whole night through at Wurst Willy's Stand (Cologne's answer to Harry's Cafe de Wheels), cnr. Klapperhof/Ring. Pubs: Live music at Luxor, Luxemburger str. 40; next to it the Blue Shell; Video games arcade, Ubier ring 58; Stollwerck, Anno str. 24, the Culture Centre where the top group, BAP, got their start; Eckstein's pub with dancing, Ubierring 24 until 3.00 a.m.; Peppermint Lounge, Hansa Ring/Zulpicher Platz, next to there, the Savoy Ballroom.

In the other areas: The teachers' scene at Feez, Holbein 35, Cafe Fleur, Linden str. 10; Fabrik, Merheimer str. 202, breakfast until 2.00 p.m.; Super disco: New York, Luthansa Building; In Place: Saturday disco after 9.00 p.m. in the old waiting room, main railway station until 4.00

a.m., 15 DM; for eating; the Platik Grieche, Kaspar Str; homely: Goldener Kappes, Neusser str.; Schreckenkammer, Ursulagarten str. 11.

CONCERTS: Large Concerts are held in the Sports Hall or in the Satory Halls (Salen), Friesen str. 44.

THEATRE: Absolute leader: Comedia Colonia, Lowen Gasse 7; Theatre, Der Keller, Kleingedank str. 6; Millowitsch, Aachener str. 5; Theatre Kefka, Albertus/Magnus str.; Cinema: Broadway, Ehren str. 11;

MARKETS: Flea market at Nippes, Wilhelms Platz, as well as a weekend market; in the south, Vorgebirgstor.

FESTIVALS: The carnival, Gaukler Fest in September.

ACCOMMODATION: Hotels and pensions through the tourist information; Youth hostel: Sieges str. 52, Tel. 81 47 11; Konrad Adenauer Ufer 11, Tel. 731720; Guest House Riehl, An der Schanz 14, Tel. 76 7081; Camping: Berger in Rodenkirchen, Ufer str. 43.

FRANKFURT

Where formerly the franken army crossed the lower Main–in 794 their Pfalz was called Franconfurd from which the name Frankfurt is derived. Frankfurt is situated very centrally at the cross roads of Germany. It is a city with Pop. 618,000, smaller than Essen, a little bigger than Dortmund. It is an important european town. On one side of Borsen Platz you have the important banks–Mainhattan (a corruption of Manhattan) and at the other end, The Zeil, a shopping street which has the highest turnover in West Germany.

BY CAR: Frankfurt hasn't a motorway circle around it but has instead, the famous Frankfurter Kreuz (Frankfurt crossroads) where the A5 from Basel, the A3 from Munich-Wurzburg or from Cologne (depending which direction you come from) and the A7/A48 from Hamburg-Kassel all meet. There are a great number of parking stations in the city centre e.g. near the central railway station (Wilhelm-Leuschner str.) or near the motorway exit from the A5/A648 Theodore Heuss Allee, and also in front of the Frankfurter Messe in the Am Romerhof str.

BY RAIL: The Frankfurt central railway station is, since electrification, the central point of the inter-city-network of the West German railways with underground inter-city parking. Even though it is not the biggest railway station in West Germany, it has 25 platforms and all sorts of services from fast food shops to tourist information and public showers. From the outside it is one of the most beautiful railway stations. You can leave it by a subway which leads to Kaiser str. It also has a computerised timetable. Information–Tel. 23 03 33.

BY AIR: Frankfurt airport is the largest airport of W. Germany because of its location and the third runway (Startbahn West). It has motorway access, a shopping town, and an inter-city and S. Bahn railway station in the airport building, and it takes only 11 minutes to get to the city by train. Because of this, quick trips to the city are possible (even between flights). Information–Tel. 069/690 3051.

TOURIST INFORMATION: Head office at the railway station near platform 23. Tel. 069/212 88 49: City office: Hauptwache, Tel. 212 8708.

NEWSPAPERS: For tourists: the 'Frankfurt Aktuell' and the 'Frankfurter Woche' also the 'Gastefuhrer' which is full of ads; newer are the 'Frankfurt Lebendige Stadt' (exclusive), Standgut (alternative) and 'Skyline' (new wave, gratis); a magazine for young people is 'Live'; good illustrated magazines are the 'Pflasterstrand' (the oldest), the 'AZ' (both very critical) and the 'Auftritt' (new wave); From AZ-Verlag there is also the Rhein-Main Book. An inheritance left by the now defunct 'ID's fur unterbliebene Nachrichten' is found at 45 Hamburger Allee (Monday-Friday 1.00-4.00 p.m.), the first archive for alternative media.

POINTS OF INTEREST: There are some beautiful corners in Kaiser strasse and even more in the parallel Taunus Strasse, but you may be confronted more by the new flowers of the oldest profession in the world. Lord Mayor Wallmann (CDU) wanted to clean up this area and move them to the outer suburbs. But you can usually walk unmolested along Kaiser strasse to Graven strasse the border of the old town. Here, on the left is a statue of Goethe, the BfG (Union) building, to the far right the theatre and opera house and the Marchenbrunnen (fairystory fountain). Go half left along Frieden strasse and Ross Market and you are in the centre of the city–or you can take a side trip along Am Salzhaus str. to Hirschgraben where Goethe's House is found (reconstructed in the 1756 form). A very readable description of the way in which it was built is found in 'Aus meinem Leben–Dichtung und Wahrheit'. Goethe museum (Monday-Saturday 9.00 a.m.-6.00 p.m., Sunday 10.00 a.m.-1.00 p.m.).

In the pedestrian zone at the end of Schiller strasse, left of the Borse, is the richly decorated and neo-classical, Eschersheimer Turm, which stands right in the middle of the hustle and bustle. (The Warten and Turm–lookout posts and towers–in Sachsenhausen, Bokkenheim and Friedberg are also beautiful.) Turn left into Tauben strasse–the city baths are on the right–and go along Borsen strasse to Grosse Bockenheimer strasse which is called 'Fressgass' (street where you can stuff yourself) by the locals. Some popular places: The Schwille Coffee Shop which has a viennese atmosphere; and the young & chic Bistro Tomate (around Bockenheimer str.): Dominique, and Bodega Barcelona in the Klein Bockenheimer str.; Strawberry Shop, Zwinger Gasse; Jazz

Keller, Kleine Bockenheimer str.

The old opera house is the exclusive bad taste place–simply go in once, Operncafe. On the square in front is an ostentatious fountain, an example of every architectural species which attempts to redeem the town's image.

Go back to the Hauptwache and St. Katharine's church. It's easier with the U-Bahn–(underground), tram or bus, even though it costs money: One way l.80 DM, Day Ticket 7.00 DM/24h–automatic ticket vending machines at the bus/tram/train stops. Go along Liebfrauen strasse and the small lanes and you're come to the best part of town. St. Paul's church, on the corner of Berliner strasse (daily 10.00 a.m.-4.00 p.m.) was the seat of the German National Parliament during the 1848/49 Revolution. A bit further along is the Romer which has been rebuilt after the 1944 bombing. It is a town square around which are the five gabled town hall (Kaisersaal open daily 9.00 a.m.-5.00 p.m.), Stienernen Haus, and the recently finished Romerberg Ostzeile (made out of six buildings). In the middle is the Freedom Fountain. If you are so inclined, you can purchase a HO model railway building of the square.

A little behind is the rather unspectactular Dom (cathedral), near the tower is the archaelogical garden of Urzelle (a Carolingian queen). Towards the Main River is St. Nikolai's church and the site of the former castle of the Staufisches (Burg des Saalhofes), today a modern building with an historical museum (Tuesday-Sunday 10.00 a.m.-5.00 p.m.) including children's museum.

At last you come to the Mainkai (quay on the Main River) and in front of you is the Eisernen Steg (iron foot bridge) which was built by the people in the 19th century, and in those times the bridge toll was 3 Pfennigs. The Riverbank railway which goes along the river is run by railway clubs on the 1st weekend in every month–rides 5.00 DM, day ticket 20.00 DM. If you wish to ride in the driver's cab then it costs 15.00 DM. Steam locomotives 001 & 050. You also can take a boat trip on the Main from here. On the Sachsenhausen side is the Schaumainkai (quay) where the traditional flea market used to be held on Saturdays. Now it is held 800m to the east at the old Schlachthof (abattoir). To the east is the east harbour and in front, Uhland str. 21, the Roman Fabrik, a new culture centre financed by a business tycoon.

MUSEUMS ON THE RIVERBANK: the most important one which should not to be left out is the art gallery Stadel (Tuesday-Sunday 10.00 a.m.-5.00 p.m.); the Ethnological Museum (Tuesday-Sunday 10.00 a.m.-5.00 p.m.) and the new Film Museum and Communal Cinema (Tuesday-Sunday 11.00a.m.-7.00 p.m.) as well as the Architectural Museum which has examples of Frankfurt architecture (Tuesday-Sunday 10.00 a.m.-5.00 p.m.).

OTHER MUSEUMS: The Frankfurter Brauerei (brewery) Museum at Henninger Turm, Hainer Weg 60 (Tuesday-Sunday 10.00 a.m.-7.00 p.m.)

with views of Sachsenhausen, the town woods (bus from Hainer Weg) and the Goether Turm (keep fit track); the Stolzentrum and the Stoltzemuseum in the courtyard of the Stadtsparkasse (bank) Tonges Gasse 34 (Monday-Friday 10.00 a.m.-5.00 p.m.); the Struwwelpeter (Shock Haired Peter–children's story) museum, Hoch St. 47 (Tuesday-Sunday 11.00 a.m.-5.00 p.m.); the Museum fur Vor and Fruhgeschichte (museum of pre and early history) in picturesque wooden houses and small castles, Justinian str. 5 (Tuesday-Sunday 10.00 a.m.-5.00 p.m.). Whatever you do, don't miss out on the Naturkunde (natural history) museum, Senckenberg, Senckenberg Anlage 25 (daily 9.00 a.m.-5.00 p.m.) dinosaur skeletons.

The large Messe buildings to the north-west of the railway station have less soul than actual worth; new architecture: the Galeria, a glass gallery by Ungers, and a multi-story building 'Gleisdreieck'.

See everything once again from above: from the Gernmeldeturn (Tower) Rosa Luxemburg strasse. Nearby is also the Deutsche Bundesbank (German National Bank).

PARKS: The Palmengarten (palm garden) with wonderful hot houses in Siesmayer str., Tram 19; also the open air concert stage, and next to it the Gruneburg Park (the gigantic building on the right there was formerly the head office of IG-Garben). The zoo which was founded in 1858, Am Tiergarten, Tram 13. A good swimming pool: Rebstock, August Euler str. 7.

ENTERTAINMENT: In the districts of Bockenheim and Sachsenhausen. Tips: Mackie-Messer Club, Mainzer Land str. 17 (rock pub with 68ern (beer)); Sinkkasten, Bronner str. 5, with entertainment; Funkadelic, also No. 11, black Disco; Dominicus, wine cellar, Bruckenhof str/Main str; Grossenwahn, Lenau str. 97; Uno, Bieber Gasse 9, new wave; Dr. Flotte, on the Bockenheimer Warte, rock pub; Club Voltaire, Kleine Hoch str. 5, Intellectual meeting place: Batschkapp, Maybach str. the absolute culture centre; Cafe Albatros, Kies str. 27, alternative and new wave, breakfast until 3 p.m.; Statt Cafe, Gremp str. 21; Bistrot, Stift str. 6, until 2 a.m.; Cafe Bohne, Senlos str. 24 with parking; Palm Cafe, Schiffer str. 36; Disco Roxane, Zeil/Gr. Friedberger; Cafe Zippo, Textor str. 71; Tasteless: SACHS, Pub centre on the Darmstadter Land Str; Good sound: Cooky's Am Salzhaus 4 and Morrison Hotel, Weissadler Gasse 5; Zocker-Treff: Galerie Pub, Jordan str. 10; Hippy meeting place: Brotfabrik, Bachmann str. 2; Homely: Bistro Jean Bastos, Graf str. 45; Bockenheimer Weinkontor, Schloss str. 9; Cabaret/Theatre: Die Maininger, Neue Rothof str. 26a, Tel. 28 02 27; the Schmiere, Beckbacher Gasse, Tel. 28 10 66; Cafe Theatre, Hamburger Allee 45; Theater Am Turn, TAT, Eschersheimer Land str. 2 Tel. 154 5100.

Two good cinemas–Berger 177, Berger str. and Harmonie, Dreieich str. 54.

Sachsenhausen: The Abbelwoi Zentrum (apple wine centre–get off at Affentor Platz); Dauth Schneider, Klaane Sachsenhauser; A painted house, Schweizer str./Textor Str; Kannonensteppel, Textor str. (try the Schneegestober); Spritzenhaus, Grosse Ritter Gasse (musical groups); in the Klappergass: Klapper 33, Goriel Schwenker. Further out in Sachsenhausen: Abtskeller, Abtsgasse, meeting place of lawyers; Fichte-Kranzi. Beer Garden Pubs: Gerbermuhle, 300m from the Schlachthof. For the lastest disco cults: Flughafen-Disco, Dorian Gray.

For Gourmets: Get 'Rawulps' handbook or go to the small market hall on Liebfrauenberg. Tips: Zur Stallburg, Glauburg str. 80; Pie Shop, Jordan str. 3; Pizza: Dick & Doof, Berger str. 238; Dionysos, Rodelheimer str. 34; Vegetarian: Eden, Palmhof str. 4; Pizza Wolkchen, Textor str. 26; Real Country: Binding Nr. 19, Rohrbach str. 19,; Kafenion, Gluck str. 21; Solzer Karl, Berg str. 260; Tav. Sparta, Friedberger Land str. 140; Very sporty: Zum Adler, Schmidtborn St. 12.

ACCOMMODATION: Youth hotel: Am Deutschherren Ufer 12,Tel. 069/61 90 58; Camping: Niederrader Ufer, Tram 15; Pensions through the tourist information office.

HAMBURG

The number of towns in Europe, which possess more than one face, more than one facet, and can satisfy more than one requirement, is small–Paris, London, Berlin and very definitely–Hamburg. One shouldn't reduce it to St. Pauli, the area between the harbour and St. Michael's Cathedral, the exclusive shops in Jungfernstieg, the Alte area, the high class suburbs, the music scene, which gave us Udo Lindenberg and the Fabrik Culture Centre, the run-down main railway station, the razzle dazzle of Poseldorf and Willkommhoft or to Sachsenwald, where the forest is dying; Hamburg is more–you have to breathe its air yourself, even the pollution hasn't been able to spoil it. (Pop. 1.62 Million).

BY RAIL: Hamburg has two important railway stations: the main through railway station, in the east of the city, and Altona, a terminal station from which you can only travel further on the S-Bahn. Long distance trains and inter-city trains usually stop at both, as well as at the through railway station, Dammtor, where you change for the U Stephansplatz and for the exclusive northern suburbs. The Altona railway station has already been renovated inside. At the main railway station on both of the high standing, transverse platforms, old splendour and building works dominate–a feature since 77–but it has all the services you need, even a post office. Information Tel. 33 99 11.

BY CAR: Five important autobahns (motorways) go to Hamburg, one goes around the town in the east; the A7 goes through a six lane tunnel under the Elbe River (from Hannover, southern Germany and also from Denmark-Flensburg); the newest is the A24 from Berlin; the oldest is the A1 from Bremen-Ruhr Area, which goes on to Lubeck-Fehmarn in a straight line. You can park & ride from near the Berliner Tor or from Wandsbekker Chaussee (from all directions).

BY AIR: In an old exclusive suburb in the north is the Hamburg airport, Fuhlsbuttel. It connects to all european major cities. Airport express bus to U/S railway station, Ohlsdorf, at Hamburg transport company prices. The airport bus which goes to the railway station is more exclusive; Information Tel . 508 25 57. At the airport, you can see a model of it as well as look at the actual thing (10.00 a.m.-4.00 p.m.).

BY SHIP: If you come by ship–from either England or overseas, you will land in the centre; usually at the St. Pauli Terminal or east from there at the overseas terminal. Nearby are the old Elb tunnel, taverns which serve fish, the youth hostel, the underground and city railway stations, and the Landungsbrucken (boat terminals), DFDS Prinzenlines. Tel. 38 90 30.

TOURIST INFORMATION: Main office is at Hachmann Platz in Bieberhaus, Tel. 040/248700, which is north east of the railway station and rather out of the way. The city office is better, Gerhart Hauptmann Platz (from Monckeberg Str.) Tel. 32 47 58. As well there are information offices at the main railway station, at the airport, at the terminals on the harbour and at the petrol station/restaurant/parking place on the Autobahn at Stillhorn. Good information is contained in 'Hamburg-fur wenig Geld viel loss–there's a lot happening which doen't cost much'.

TOURIST NEWSPAPERS: Musikszene (programme); Tango (culture, new wave), Oxmox (already older, alternative) Szene (new wave); Tip (culture and politics, overlap); Blickpunkt (youth); HH Termine (dates); new, the C.D.U. Postille; Ciao.

LOCAL TRANSPORT: Buses, fast/night buses, the underground and city railway, all under the control of the city transport department. For real action filled days there is the Tageskarte (day ticket) for 7.50 DM with which you can travel not only on the city railway 1st class, but also on the night buses which leave from Rathausmarkt and travel in all directions. Watch out: It is valid only after 9.00 a.m. Single tickets from 1.60 DM.

TOURS: Small, large and night city tours leave from Kirchen Allee railway station (2.00 p.m., 10.00 a.m. and 8.00 p.m.); highly recommended are: Harbour trips with the small launches from the Landungsbrucken (from the inner side), they cater for the tourists, but they really are the best; Alster boat trips which leave from Jungfernstieg (daily 10.00 a.m.-6.00 p.m.); Tip: A boat trip around the Fleets, leaving from

Dammertorn; the City Health & Building Department run tours which leave from Moorweide/Mittelweg at 2.00 p.m. on Saturday, for those interested in architecture etc.–tickets available from the information office at Gehart Hauptmann Platz; an alternative city tour is to the concentration camp Neuengamme in the marshland of the Elbe (Vierlande) which is part of the Hansa City of Hamburg. This area is also good for long romantic walks (Information: Tel. 250 30 95; Buses from S Bergedorf); also the the Heimat Museum, Rieck Haus, Curslacker Deich 284, (Tuesday-Sunday 10.00 a.m.-5.00 p.m.)

POINTS OF INTEREST: The town is too spread out to take a walking tour, you should use the underground or the city train. Firstly to the harbour (U Landungsbrucken) that is if you won't get itchy feet and head off overseas. . . As well as the usual boat trip on the harbour (there is an alternive one run by the DGB- Jugend. Tel. 185 82 43), you can take a bus trip over the Kohlbrand Bridge (Bus 150/151, reminiscent of the Elbe Bridge plans of the Third Reich) to the old town wall (now open space). Further east are firstly, the Fleets and the old Speicherstadt, tall brick warehouses (east of U Baumwall), then either cross over the Niederbaum Bridge, which leads to the duty free harbour, Speicherstadt, or look at the historical merchant buildings on Nikolai Fleet.

Near the Landungsbrucken are the legendary taverns which sell fish dishes. They have become rather expensive. The combined old town/shopping tour starts either from here or from the railway station at the other end: south of the railway station is the Museum of Arts & Craft (Tuesday-Saturday 10.00 a.m.-5.00 p.m.), a little further south is the antique centre and the culture centre, Markthalle. Go west along Monckeberg strasse where the big department stores and St. Jacobi's church are, and you come to the pedestrian square in front of the town hall (Tours Monday-Friday 10.00 a.m.-3.00 p.m., Saturday & Sunday 10.00 a.m.-1.00 p.m.). Take a small side trip to the right to Jungfernstieg. The Binnen-Alster is here and modern shopping arcades, Hamburger Hof, Galleria, Hanse Quarter, all in Grosse Bleichen str. and the Burgerhof Arcade in Gansemarkt.

Go past the stock exchange behind the town hall and you come to a row of small lanes where there are all sorts of pubs. A bit further along are the ruins of Nikolai Tower and the Nikolai Fleet.

A tour to the west begins near U St. Pauli (station) at the Bismarck Memorial. Behind you is Hamburg's main church St. Michaelis, called Michel for short. In the old town wall area is the Museum for Hamburgische Geschichte (Hamburg's history) an absolute must (also the Kramer Amts Wohnungen, Krayenkamp 10, Tuesday-Sunday 10.00 a.m.-5.00 p.m., with model railway); now go along Reeperbahn and you will come to the Panoptikum (Germany's only wax works), Davidswache (the most famous police station in the Republic), and to-day a place where tourists are ripped off (Zillertal). Be careful of the pubs with the

'Bier 4 DM–Beer 4 DM' signs in the window, as they are rather suspect.

Grosse Freiheit str. is a ghetto of legalised sex shops and shows. Only those who can look after themselves should go south of the Reeperbahn in the evenings as the real harbour/street scenes and the legendary Herbert strasse are found here. The fish market near the water is held on the right on Sunday mornings from 6.00 a.m.–unique scenery–dealers and market ballyhoo, now very much for the tourists.

The centre of Altona is west of the railway station. There are not only attractions such as the Norddeut. Landes Museum (North German), Museum str. 23 (Tuesday-Sunday 10.00 a.m.-5.00 p.m.), the town hall, St. Christian's church, and the Patrizier Houses on Palm Aille but left and right of the railway station are the streets and squares, where, during the Weimarer Republic, the street fighting between the Nazis and the Left took place. Arnold Zweig in his novel, 'Das Beil von Wandsbek' describes it so well.

The first culture centre, Fabrik, in Barner str. to the north-west, was rebuilt after a fire. It always has concerts. As you come out of the S Dammtor railway station/U Stephans Platz, you will see a lot of open space. On the right along Renommier str. is the Planten un Blomen (park) with its Congress Centre, left of it is the Messe, exhibition halls, and the Ernst Merck hall where large concerts are held, south of the old town wall is the music hall, roller skating rink, the court building, and the T.V. tower (with viewing at 128m). North east of Dammtor railway station is the main building of the university, left of it is the Von Melle Park University and adjoining it is the lively university quarter with good pubs and street life; Music: Logo, Grindel Allee 5. If you go left you come to the Poseldorf area (Milch strasse) which was cleaned up at a cost of millions, and finally to Alster Park.

IMPORTANT: The Islamic Mosque, beautiful view, the town park (U Borgweg) and the parklike Ohlsdorfer Friedhof (cemetery) (U Ohisdorf); the Alster indoor swimming baths, Iffland str. 21 (U Lubecker Str); Volk Park Stadium, HSV home games (soccer) (S Stellingen); Hagenbecks Animal Park (underground station of the same name); Isemarkt, typical suburban market in Hoheluft (U H'Brucke), directly under the town railway; Hamburger Kunsthalle, (art gallery), Glockengiesserwall (Tuesday-Sunday 10.00 a.m.-5.00p.m.). Hamburgisches Museum fur Volkerkunde, Rothenbaumchaussee 64 (Tuesday-Sunday 10.00 a.m.-5.00 p.m.); Ernst Barlach Haus, Baron Voght St. 50a (Tuesday-Sunday 11.00 a.m.-5.00 p.m.); open air museum Kiekeberg, Ebestorf/Harburg (Tuesday-Sunday 10.00 a.m.-5.00 p.m.); and trips to Blankenese, to the exclusive suburbs, to Willkommhoft, Fahrhaus Schulau (S Wedel) where the ships are berthed; Eating Tip: Greek Thasos, Spitzerdorf str. 3, Wedel; the windmills at Osdorf (Bus 267 from Blankenese); the Alten Land in the south west (with Bus 150/157/157) or the ferry to Cranz from Blankenese, very idyllic and almost not Hamburg. . .

THEATRE: Ohnsorg Theatre, Grosse Bleichen 23, Tel. 35 28 28; Das Schiff, Nikolaifleet, Tel. 36 47 65; St. Pauli Theatre, Spielbunden Platz 29, Tel. 31 43 44. Or only listen by phoning the Literaturtelefon 11510. Pubs with Music: Cotton Club, Alter Steinweg 29 (Jazz); Art, Brandstwiete 24. Nachwuchsforum: Onkel Po, Lehmweg 44; Top Ten, Reeperbahn 136.

PUBS: Bazille, Sievekingsdamm 56; Fricke, Fricke str. 46; Mader, Beim Schlump 33; down to earth: Bodega Nagel, Kirchen Allee 57; Neon: Champinsky, Faber str. 7; ha Chga, Dragonerstall 15; Max & Consorten, Spadenteich 7, in the suburb of St. Georg; Zum Hirschen, Gartner str. 45.; for lukewarm evenings the Alte Muhle, Eppendorfer Land str. 176; New Wild in Cafe Vienna, Fett tr. 1. Students: Niewohner, Gertig str. 14; Poppenspeeler, Grasweg 9; young & chic–Sugar, Moorhof 2a; classical music at Sperl, Wex str. 30; and Schwenders, Grossneumarkt, another area with a lot of pubs; Cafe & Buch; Libresso, Binde str. 24; Culture scene: Subito, Stesemann str. 71. Discos: late psychodelic: Grunspan, Grosse Freiheit 58; Madhouse, Valentinskamp 46a; Kir, Poppenbutteler Weg 236; schwartz: Bendula Club, Feld str. 48; also Shakatak, Eimsbutteler str. 13; Disco City, Spielbunden Platz 4; Dance Hall, Trinity, Eimsbutteler Chaussee 5; Sounds, Wandsbeker Zoll str. 87.

FESTIVAL: Twice yearly: 'Nom', Folk Festival at Heiligengeistfeld (U St.Pauli).

ACCOMMODATION: Youth hostel at Stintfang, A-Wegener Weg 5, Tel. 040/313488; Horner racetrack (Rennbahn), Tel. 615 1671; Youth park, Langenhorn, Tel. 59 7350; Pensions through the tourist information office.

MUNICH

Munich, in the prosperous south, the centre of the hi-tech industry, is growing in every way-population, culture and recreational facilities. (Pop. 1.29 million).

BY CAR: You can drive along the motorways quite easily unless it's Friday afternoon. Around the railway station there are parking areas but its better to park & ride: in the east at Pasing; in the north around the Olympic Centre; and in the south at Ramersdorf/Karl Preis Platz.

BY RAIL: The largest railway station of the german railways is west of Munich city. It is really three separate railway stations under one roof: Starnberger railway station (Platforms 1-7); Hauptbahnhof (Platforms 8-26) and the Holzkirchner railway station (Platforms 27-36).

The inside is futuristic: It's a railway station with a shopping centre, a shopping arcade, a communication centre, a pub section, and an underground passage with connections to the city railway. The tourist information office is on the right of the terminal platform. Good inter-city connections, Tel. 50 29 91.

BY AIR: The international airport is Munchen-Riem, the new one is not yet built. Bus No. 91 goes to the city. If you don't have much luggage, you can walk to the city railway station, Munchen-Riem, as it's just under a kilometre. Flight Information: Tel. 921 12127.

LOCAL TRANSPORT: In Munich itself you can get around well by train, either the city train, which is being extended or the underground. There are also trams and buses. The Munich network is set out in complicated zones. For the city centre it is recommended that you buy a 24hr. Ticket for 6.50 DM. For further out it costs 12DM for 24hrs but for short stretches it's best to buy the strip card for 4.50 or 9DM.

TOURIST INFORMATION: Head office is at the railway station (south exit, Bayer Str.), Tel. 089/23911. In the city: Rindermarkt 5; Community information: Stachus Ladengeschoss, Tel. 55 44 59: Youth information: Paul Heyse Str. 22, Tel. 53 15 55 (Monday-Friday 11.00 a.m.-7.00 p.m., Saturday until 5.00 p.m.). Accommodation and tips and social welfare help.

TOURIST NEWSPAPERS: Official the monthly programme 'Munchen'. Entertainment information in the Munchner Stadt Zeitung.

POINTS OF INTEREST: A trip around the town can start on foot from the railway station. Go along the extension of the platforms to the pedestrian zone, Schutzen str. to Karls Platz which the locals call Stachus. Through this square passes the largest volume of traffic in the Republic. Luckily, it has an underground pedestrian tunnel. A great place for young talent, winoes and street theatre. Behind the high court is the old botanical gardens. Go further along Neuhauser str. through Karlstor, past the Burgersaal church, the old Academy, St. Michael's church and St. Augustine's church–all on the left (St. Michael's is built in renaissance style and is the vault of the Wittelsbacher Royal Family) and you have reached the city centre. You'll know when you get there because of the shop windows, hoardings, buskers and international conversation. Go half left across Augustiner strasse to the Frauen church (recommended that you climb the tower!) or go straight ahead to Marien Platz with its neo-gothic town hall which has been the centre of the city since its foundation in 1158. It has a tower and Glockenspiel at 11.00 a.m. daily and in summer also at 5.00 p.m. and 9.00 p.m. On the right in Rindermarkt is the 'Old Peter' church. It is the oldest and the most loved church of Munich. You can climb the stairs and look at the view. If you now wish to go down into the valley to Isartor Platz, you should keep left and you will come to the Viktualien markets, the largest markets.

From here you can go two ways: Either keep going along Rosental str. to the Stadt museum (Tuesday-Sunday 9.00 a.m.-4.30 p.m.) on St. Jackobs Platz and then the Asam Kirche in Sendinger str. with bavarian rococo creations, then along the Ring to Sendingertor Platz; OR go in the opposite direction along Sparkassen str. and on the right is the square with the Hofbrauhaus. On the left is the old court of the bavarian Kaiser, Ludwig IV. Further along is Max Joseph Platz with the National Theatre (opera) and the Residenz, which is open for inspection (Tuesday-Sunday 10.00 a.m.-4.30 p.m.). Inside are the coin museum (Tuesday-Sunday 10.00 a.m.-4.30 p.m.), the Egyptian art collection (Tuesday-Sunday 9.30 a.m.-4.00 p.m.) and don't miss out on the Schatzkammer, on the left hand side is the Army Hall which was copied from the Loggia dei Lanzi in Florence. Behind there is the Theatiner Church with its impressive dome and towers on Odeons Platz.

Once again there are many choices–and not only for shopping: You can turn left into Brienner str. and go along to the Platz der Opfez des Nationalsozialismus–so aptly named, and you come to the area of the former Fuhrer and nazi party buildings: past the obelisk covered in granite tiles, to the Konigs Platz which dates back to the 19th century and was turned into the National Socialist Party's Cult Square. On the northern side is the old Gyptothek (greek and roman sculptures, Tuesday-Sunday 10.00 a.m.-4.30 p.m.), on the western side is the Propylaen and on the right hand side is Lenbach House, the city gallery–highly recommended (Tuesday-Sunday 10.00 a.m.-5.00 p.m., free on Sunday). At the end of Brienner str. is Stiglmaier Platz with the Lowenbrau Keller and beergarden–genial Munich.

OR you can go straight ahead along Ludwig Strasse which has the national library and St. Ludwig's church on the right and the university on the left. At Geschwister Scholl Platz, turn into Leopold str. which is also known locally as rue de Gallop, to the Siegestor where Schwabing starts. It is partly a residential area and has its own charm. Cafe Stephanie is the place where the great names of literature once came (e.g. Thomas Mann and Erich Muhsam) and also the postcard painter, Adolf Hitler, began his career here. It has lost its bohemian charm to the field of commerce. Go along Hohenzollern Strasse past the department stores and down Leopold Strasse to the Siegestor (victory arch).

OR if you turn right at Odeonsplatz and go across the Hofgarten, you will pass the art gallery which was built during the Third Reich and is an example of the architecture of that era. To-day it is just the opposite as exhibitions of modern art are held in the annex of the gallery of modern art. Continue past there and you will come to the Englischen Garten (english garden), the centre of the urban idleness with a beer garden, the Chinese Tower, the Kleinhesseloer See (lake) and Monopteros where the young people congregate. You may find nude sunbathers in the meadow circled by a horse riding track or along the Eisbach, a tributary of the Isar.

There are plenty of other interesting sights: Firstly, the Olympic centre which, nowadays, is partly used for student accommodation. The Olympic Tower is 290m high and has a viewing platform which is open from 9.00 a.m.-midnight. Exhibitions are held in the Olympic halls and soccer matches etc. are held in the stadium, Tel. 30623577. Bavarian rock groups also hold concerts every second Sunday at the Theatron, the open air stage at Olympic Lake. In the west of the city is Schloss Nymphenburg which has beautiful grounds and a large lake (Tram 27) and the botanical gardens. The schloss was the baroque summer palace of the bavarian royal family. In the schloss is the Schonheitsgalerie (gallery) of Ludwig I (Tuesday-Sunday 10.00 a.m.-12.30 p.m. and 1.00-4.00 p.m.).

In the south west (U5) is the Teresienwiese, in short die Wies'n, where the annual Oktoberfest has been held since 1811. West of it is the Messegelande, and south-west of the Ruhmeshall is the bavarian freedom statue with five viewing slits along the 130 steps, approx. 30m high. Munich has become the town of T.V. productions and film makers: The T.V. studios of the ZDF are in the Unterfohring; the Bavarian T.V. studios are at 418 Schleissheimer str. (Tram 12/13 Sudetendt Strasse) where on Monday from 7.00 p.m. a youth programme with discussion 'Formel Eins' and a youth concert is held and for DM10 you can be on T.V. But the Bavarian Film studios, Bavariafilm Platz, Geiselgasteig, are the best, Tel. 64 90 67. This is where the most is happening and you can see some of it.

ANOTHER IMPORTANT CORNER: South of Isar Platz (S-Bahn) across Ludwig Bridge and opposite the German Patent's Office (cheaper) is the Deutsche Museum on an island in the middle of the Isar (daily 9.00 a.m.-5.00 p.m.). The name 'German' Museum is rather misleading, it really should be called the 'Technical Museum'. It is the largest museum of its type in the world. Special: Its underground mining section and the locomotive and automobile collections. Tops for railway buffs: the Bundesbahn Ausbesserungs Werk (German railway research & development factory) is at Munich-Freimann, and sometimes it has exhibitions (U6).

FURTHER MUSEUMS: The Alte and Neue Pinakothek are what art gallerys are supposed to be, both are very important (27 & 29 Barer str., Tuesday-Sunday 9.00 a.m.-4.30 p.m.); Bavarian National Museum, paintings and crafts, 3 Prinzregenten str. (Tuesday-Sunday 9.00 a.m.-4.30 p.m.); adjoining that is the Meissner Fine China Museum in the Schloss Lustheim, Schloss Schleissheim Park (take the city railway (S-Bahn) to Freising, Oberschleissheim, Bus 292 Tuesday-Sunday 10.00 a.m.-12.30 p.m. and 1.30-4.00 p.m.); You can also see through the Schloss Schleissheim with its baroque rooms and art gallery (daily 10.00 a.m.-12.30 p.m. & 1.30-4.00 p.m.); the German Jagd und Fischerei (hunting & fishing) Museum, 53 Neuhauser str. (Tuesday-Sunday 9.30a.m.-4.00 p.m.); the Valentin Museum, at Isartor Tower has a lively cafe (Monday, Tuesday, Saturday, Sunday 11.01 a.m.- 5.29 p.m.). Technical: the BMW Museum, 130 Petuerl Ring (daily 10.00 a.m.-4.00 p.m.); and a sad museum; the Dachau Concentration Camp, take the S2 and Bus 722 (Tuesday-Sunday 9.00 a.m.-5.00 p.m.).

The Zoo Hellabrun is open daily 9.00 a.m.-5.00 p.m., Bus 31, 52, 57. The DGB run other city tours to see the past, 64 Schwanthaler str., Information Tel. 53 0821 or visit the Theater 44, 20 Hohenzollern str. 20, Tel. 328 748.

ENTERTAINMENT: Near the university: Cafe Oase, Amalien Passage; Engelsbur, Schelling str; Weinbauer, Fend str., Rolandseck, Viktoria str., Extrablatt, Leopold str; Pink Flamingo, Konigshof; Harry's New York Bar, 9 Falkenturm str. 9, Ost Friesische Teestube (tea room), Pundter Platz; Uhu, 138 Theresien str.; Alter Simpl, 57 Turken str., Marienkafer, Georgen/Schraudolph str.; Uni Reitschule, Konigin str.; Schellingsalon, Schelling str. (billiards).

MUSIC: Domicilie, Leopold str., next door, Maximilians; Schwabinger Podium, Wagner str; Allotria, Turken str. (both jazz); Rigan Apian/Herzog str. (rock); Favourite amongst the concert halls: Alabama Halle, 418 Schleissheimer str., Tel. 351 0852. New wave group, 'Herzschlag einer Stadt' - La Poupee, 7 Freilitzsch str., Ingrid's Insel, tropical mixed drinks; Kaisergarten, Kaiser str.; Cafe an der Uni, 24 Ludwig str., Cafe D'Accord, Kurfursten Platz/Nordend str.; Very good ice cream: Venezia, 31 Leopold str. and Rialto, 62 Leopold str. At Haidhausen: Cafe Haidhausen; Cafe Grossenwahn, new wave, 11 Lothringer str.; Greek food: Lyra, 5 Bazeille str. and Kytaro, 36 Innere Wiener; cosy: Zur Alten Kirche, 38 Kirchen str.; Ansacher Schlossl, Keller/Mich str.; Sedan, 7 Gravelotte str.; Cafe Giesing, Berg str. (small works of art by K. Wecker); JAM, 4 Rosenheimer str.; Vielharmonie, 20 Preysing str.(Jazz); Unterfahrt, 96 Kirchen str. The suburb of Neuhausen (U1) is almost rural, Cafe Ruffini, 22 Orff str., the best capuccino in Munich.

Young people's meeting place: Tageskino Cinema, Stiglmaier Platz. Disco: West Side, 11 Wendl Dietrich str. For brunch: Zoozie's Wittelsbacher Platz./Discos. P1, Prinzregenten str. 1; Charly M., 5 Maximilian str.; Cadillac, Super Funk, 1 Thekla str.; Typical beer halls: Salvatorkeller, 77 Hoch str; Augustiner Keller, 52 Arnulf str.; for Schunkeln, the Jodlerwirt, 4 Altenhof str.

FESTIVALS : Fasching 17th January to Maundy Thursday (February); the Starkbierzeit (strong beer time) March at the Nockherberg; Summer Festival Concerts-opera and theatre festival; Christ Kindl Markt (Christmas market) December.

ACCOMMODATION: Youth hostel: Winthier Platz, Tel. 089/131156, Guest house: 4 Miesing str.; for women only: 9 Goethe str., Tel. 55 58

91; International House, 87 Elizabeth str., Tel. 18 50 81; Camping: Thalkirchen, 49 Zentrallander str., Tel. 723 17 07; Obermenzing, 59 Lochhauser str., Tel. 811 22 35; Youth accommodation in Tents: Franz Schank str., Tel. 141 42 00; Hotels and pension information can be obtained at the tourist information office.

STUTTGART

Stuttgart has the industries of the future, is close to recreational areas and has the lowest number of unemployed and the highest growth rate. (Pop. 568,000).

BY ROAD: For quite a while Stuttgart has had is own expressway crossroads: the A8 from Munich/Karlsruhe and the A81 from Hamburg/Wurzburg/Singen and Switzerland. Some parking stations on the way into the city: in the Hauptstatter Strasse (from the south), the Konrad Adenauer Strasse (from the south and east), the Kriegsberg and Schloss Strasses-keep to the right of Heilbronner Str.(from the north and west). Other parking stations are found near the city centre which also has a parking area near the main railway station.

BY RAIL: For a long time the main railway station built of limestone blocks (1911-28) with its 56m high tower was recognised as one of the most important buildings of the railways. It offers all the necessary services and many shops. One of the two new, fast railway lines of the DB (German Railways) runs from here to Mannheim.
    When the Underground was constructed the main hall of the station was connected to the main shopping street, Konigs Strasse, by an underground passageway. Information Tel. 0711/ 29 9711.

BY AIR: The airport is 13km south of the city on the Filder Plateau. There are good connections to many of the european cities. The airport has been extended. Bus Line A runs between the city (cnr. Kronen/Lautenschlager Sts.) and the airport terminal, Tel. 790 1388.

TOURIST INFORMATION OFFICE is in Klett Passage under the square in front of the railway station, Tel. 2228240. Youth information at Jugendhaus Mitte, Hohe Str. 9, Tel. 29 79 36.

TOURIST NEWSPAPERS: 'Amtsblatt' and 'Stuttgarter Monatsspiegel'. Entertainment magazines are 'Live' and 'Ketchup'.

LOCAL TRANSPORT all comes under the one umbrella, various buses, trams, underground trains (the underground trams are better) and the city railway. (There are plans to extend the city railway right to the city centre). Tickets: 5 part blue tickets or 24 hour tickets which are valid for either Area A (near centre) or Area B.

CITY TOURS: 'Beautiful Stuttgart', May-September daily 10.00 a.m.-12 noon and 2.00-5.00 p.m. (from 14 DM). Bookings at the tourist information office. Expensive: Stuttgart by Night from 7.30 p.m.-1.30 a.m. (90DM, Wednesday, Thursday, Friday); interesting: Stadtebaurundfahrt (town buildings tour) April-October, Saturday 2.15 p.m.

POINTS OF INTEREST: The tour of the near city sights begins at the railway station. If you don't like crowds then don't go along Konigs str. with its shops and buskers, turn left instead to the green area which stretches from the Rosenstein Park in Bad Cannstatt, where the Wilhelma Zoo and former summer residence of the kings are, (tram 14) to the Schloss Park. In the top right section of the park is the most modern planetarium in Europe, 'Sternentheater' (Tuesday-Friday, 10.15 a.m., Saturday & Sunday 2.00, 4.00 & 6.00 p.m.) and in front of it is the Landes Pavilion with changing exhibitions. In the top left section of the Schloss gardens is the Wurttembergische Staatstheater where opera and theatre performances are held. On the other side of the busy Konrad Adenauer Alle is the newer, perhaps less spectacular, Staatsgalerie (state gallery) built from 1838-43 by Barth, and destroyed during the second world war and rebuilt by Stirling. It houses some important and interesting collections (Tuesday-Sunday 10.00 a.m.-5.00 p.m., Tuesday & Thursday until 8.00 p.m.). On the same side of the street is the Wilhelms Palais where the last king lived until 1918. To-day it houses a library, the archives and the city museum (Tuesday-Sunday 11.00 a.m.- 5.00 p.m.).

Back across Konrad Adenauer Alle is the neo-classical State Parliament House and the Neues Schloss which has been restored and furnished. To-day it is used by members of parliament as their offices and comes under the protection of the National Trust. In front of it is the symmetrical Schloss Platz with its Jubilaum column, framed in the west by the Konigsbau, shops and high arcades.

Schloss Platz is where it's all happening: you can relax on the grass, listen to the buskers, buy something from the small stands or watch the demonstrations. On the northern side of Schloss Platz is the Stuttgart Art Gallery and Wurttembergischen Kunstverein (Tuesday-Sunday 10.00 a.m.-5.00 p.m.).

To the south but also adjoining, is the city centre with its main pedestrian zone and the Altes (old) Schloss and Wurttemburgisches Landes Museum, which displays schwabish art and culture from roman times to the present (Tuesday-Sunday 10.00 a.m.-5.00 p.m.). Go through the small passage and you'll come to Schiller Platz with its memorial, the Stift church, the Fruchtkasten with roman lapidarium (Tuesday-Sunday 10.00 a.m.-4.00 p.m.) a celtic building, the Prinzenbau and market halls in Dorotheen str. where various markets are held. The

Renitenztheater cabaret is found at Konigs str. 17, Tel. 29 70 75. Go along Kirch str. or Schul str. and you'll come to the second market square and the Town Hall Square which is surrounded by shops. Unfortunately, there is not much left of the new gothic style building due to the war and the rebuilding.

There is an astronomical clock in the tower and the Breuninger spa baths are centrally located in Markt str. (Mineralbad Leuze, Karl Konigs Brucke, Tram 1/2/14.)

Along Markt strasse, opposite Leonhard Platz (Hauptstatter strasse) is not only St. Leonhard's church, but also the Bohnen Quarter which the establishment wanted to clean up and over which there have been many planning fights. Along the Charlotten strasse new super-structures have been built, in the centre (Weber, Brenner and Wagner strs.) the area has been cleaned up. The last town tower, the Schellenturm, is found in Weber str. and also Gustav Siegle's house which has been preserved as a memorial to the BASF founder.

WEST OF THE CITY CENTRE (from Schloss Platz go through the underground passage to Schloss str.) are the gardens in which is found the university, a bit further on the Singers Hall, where important concerts are held and also the multi-functional Schleyer Halle in Bad Cannstatt (S-Bahn, Bus 56) where the large concerts are held. Bad Cannstatt is interesting because of its architecture, shopping centre and McDonalds: the Calwer Arcade on Rotebuhl Platz.

IMPORTANT: The television tower built in 1956 with a viewing platform at 152.4m, Tram 15, Ruhbank. Nearby is the sports centre where, in summer, sporting clubs have open-air taverns. Return with the funicular from Degerloch, Karl Pfaff str. to Marien Platz. The Messe (exhibition halls) in Killesberg is next to Weissenhof Siedlung (Friedrich Ebert str.–Bus 43), with buildings by Le Corbusier, Mies van der Rohe and others. Also the Killesberg Park with its chairlift and open-air swimming pool.

Near the Liederhalle (singers hall) is the oldest cemetery in the town, the Hoppenlaufriedhof; in Bad Cannstatt apart from Rosenstein Park and the Kur Park, are memorials to Gottlieb Daimler (Taubenheim str. 13) the Uff Fredhof (cemetery–Waiblinger str. 66) as well as the Cannstatter Wason, on the Neckar River where a festival, similar to the Munich Oktoberfest is held every year.

A bit further on is the Neckar Stadium; in Rotenwald strasse (Bus 92) is the Birkenkopf which has been formed from the rubble of the war and which has a commemorative cross on top; a bit further along Wildpark str. is Schloss Solitude which can be reached with Bus 70 from Ruhbank or by the funicular from Hohenheim.

The Agricultural College is housed in a former schloss with its botanical and exotic gardens as well as agricultural museum (Wednesday-Sunday 2.00-5.00 p.m.). There is a garden swimming pool at Plieningen. A second super museum is the Daimler-Benz Museum in Unterturkeim (Monday-Friday 8.30 a.m.-4.30 p.m., Saturday & Sunday 10.00 a.m.-4.00 p.m., Tram 4/13, Bus 56).

MUSEUM TIPS: Linden Museum, Hegel Platz 1 (from Spring 86, Tuesday-Sunday 10.00 a.m.-5.00 p.m.); Natural History Museum in Schloss Rosenstein, Tram Mineralbader (Tuesday-Sunday 10.00 a.m.-4.00 p.m.); the Design Centre in the Landesgewerbe Amt, Kiene str. 18 (Tram Universitat, March-October Tuesday-Sunday 11,00 a.m.-6.00 p.m.); Galerie unter Turm, Eberhard str. 61 (Tuesday-Sunday 10.00 a.m.-5.00 p.m.); Porsche Museum, Zuffenhausen, Porche str. 42 (Monday-Friday 9.00 a.m.-12 noon & 1.30-4.00 p.m.); Winery Museum, Uhlbacher Platz (Saturday & Sunday 2.00-6.00 p.m.); German Playing-cards Museum, Schonbuch str. 32 (Tuesday-Friday 2.00-5.00 p.m., Sunday 10.00 a.m.-1.00 p.m.) or the Smallest Gallery in the World, Bolz str. 5, Tel. 74 42 06.

THEATRE: Vier Peh Podium, Esslingen, Flander str. 99, Tel. 375 426; Drei Groschen Theater, Am Bopser, Etzel str. 9, Gel. 60 6000; Culture centres: Theaterhaus, Ulmer str. 241, Tel. 420 021; L'aleph, Eberhard str. 22, Tel. 241 176.

PUB TIPS: Piano Bar Pianino, Konig str. 47,; Exil (New Wave) Marien Platz, Filder str. 62. Chic: Basta, Wagner str. 39; Treff Frohlich, intellectual, Schloss Str; Old Town: Eger, Wagner str. 30; Jenseitz Schwulen Cafe, Bebel str. 25; with a garden: Kochenbas, Immenhofer str. 33; small: La Concha, Wilhelms Platz; New wave: Tangente, Schloss str. 35; cosy: West Side, Rotenwald/Reinsburg Strs.; like a laundrette, Soho, Schwab str. 16a; handwoven: Zum Lehen, Lehen str. 13. Discos: Funky and large: AT, Konig str. 51; Muscland, Reinsburg str. 9; OZ, Buchsen str. 10; Razzle Dazzle: Perkins park, Stresemann str. 39; Popper: Maxim, Wilhelm str. 14; Special tip: Laboratorium, Wagenburg str. 147, more a pub with music; Jazz: Dixieland Hall, Marien str. 3b; Jazzkeller, Rotebuhl Platz.

Because Stuttgart is a wine town the 'wine village scene' at Markt & Schiller Squares from the end of August to the beginning of September is genuine. The Besenwirtschaften which sell the new wine aren't open all year round. There are more than 100 of them. Tip: Zaiss, Strumpfelbacher str., Unterturkheim; Karl Gohl, Epple str. 54, Degerloch and Karl Raff, Leonoren str. 5, also there.

ACCOMMODATION: Youth hostel: Hausmann str. 27, Tel. 0711/24 1583; Camping: Bad Cannstatt, near to Schleyer Halle. Information about hotels & pensions can be obtained at the tourist information office–cheaper in the suburbs.

BERLIN

You can compare the 'half city' of Berlin with any of the other lively capitals of Europe. (Pop. 1.87 Million).

BY CAR: Four transit motorways cross East Germany to Berlin–from Munich the E6 via Hof/Plauen; from Frankfurt the E70/E63/E6 via Bad Hersfeld (E6 near Jena); the E73/E8 from Cologne-Ruhr Area-Hannover via Helmstadt–all three cross the border at Dreilinden; the E15 from Hamburg (Border control Staaken/Heer strasse: Stoipe/Heilingensee). On the transit stretches the speed limit (100 km/h without exception) is strictly controlled, it is forbidden to drink and drive and it is also forbidden to leave the main road or to distribute printed matter. Park & ride from W. Schreiber Platz, Rathaus (town hall) Schoneberg, Bayerischer Platz U-Bahn (underground) Sudwest (southwest) or Jungfernheide am Tegeler Weg or Amrume Street north-east of Heer strasse.

BY RAIL: The main railway lines follow approximately the same routes through East Germany as the autobahns and are controlled by the East German Rail Authority (DR) (exchange traffic with West German carriages). The most important railway station in the western part of the city is Bahnhof Zoologscher Garten with only four tracks, at the south-west end of Tiergarten, in the centre of West Berlin. The quality and the speed of the train traffic doesn't come up to the same high standard as before the war (particularly to Hamburg). Information Tel. 312 1042.

BY AIR: West Berlin has two airports, Templehof and Tegel. Tegel is more important to-day. There are daily flights to 10 West German cities and to some european cities (airport bus No. 9.- Information Tel. 41011). The East Berlin airport, Schonefeld, has cheap flights to most east european cities, including Budapest.

TOURIST INFORMATION: before your trip write to IZB, Information Centre Berlin, Hardenberg Street 20, TEl. 0 30/31 0040 (accommodation bookings–Groups 3100 4172). There are several pamphlets available from them e.g. 'Worthwhile knowing about Berlin', 'Berlin for young people', etc. Main information office is at the Europa-Center, entry from Budapester Strasse 78, Tel. 78 23 031. Branch Office Tegel Airport.

TOURIST NEWSPAPERS: Very important in a town with 5500 Pubs, no set closing time and with an outstanding culture scene: Zitty, an illustrated magazine published every 2 weeks; even better is 'Berlin tut gut' available from the 'Verkehrsamt' (transport office); for tourists 'Berlin Program'.

LOCAL TRANSPORT: A U-Bahn network covers most areas and also the S-Bahn which was unexpectedly placed in the hands of the Senate in October 1983. Formerly, the S-Bahn in spite of low prices was not very popular among West Berliners who boycotted it because it was under East German control and the section in East Berlin had not been modernized since 1945, but this is now being remedied and the S1-3 lines are already open again. With this development, the Hamburger railway station and the Transport and Building museum came into western hands again after 40 years. After coming out of its 'Snow White Sleep' of 40 years it has been restored and will be opened in time for the 750 year celebration of the city (at the Ubergang Invaliden Strasse S-Bahn 3, open on weekends). There are plenty of buses in the city and also night buses-no extra charge-tickets 2 DM. Cheaper tourist tickets: for 2 days 16 DM, 4 days 32 DM, and even cheaper Sonderwochenkarte (special weekly ticket) for groups of 6 people 7 days 35DM.

POINTS OF INTEREST: All tours of the city start from Joachimstaler str., Kurfurstendamm and cost from 19 to 74 DM. A more interesting round trip is by boat, daily e.g. from S Wannsee to Kladow, to Glienicker Brucke, Spandau (Lindenufer) and Kohlhasenbruck. An interesting route is offered by the Reederei Reidel. Tel. 69 137 82/6 93 46 46: Starts around 9.00 a.m., Wichenbachbrucke on the Neukollner Schiffahrtskanal (canal). Change at the Kottheiser Brucke (bridge) for either Tegel or the Pfaueninsel (Peacock Island) with its castle. The trip travels through the whole city centre, the industrial suburbs and at last into the green parts of Berlin.

Other sights which you can reach on foot-the trip through the city centre, which is really two trips, starts at the Bahnhof Zoo (Zoo railway station). If you don't go into the zoo straight away (Hardenbergplatz-9.00 a.m. until evening) here is the first point of interest, a view of the city and the Kaiser Wilhelm Memorial church. Now walk along the Tauentzien str., firstly you'll see the Kunsthall (arts centre) (Tuesday-Sunday 10.00 a.m.-6.00 p.m.) and cinemas. Then have a quick look down the Ku'damm, a street which was once world renowned, keep going until you come to Wittenberg Square. Before you get there you will pass the KaDeWe Kaufhaus of the west (department store).

Turn right into Ansbacher str. and then right again to Lietzenburger str. which after a bit runs parallel to Schaper str. where the Freien Volkksbuhne is (open air theatre). Go along Joachimstaler str. which leads back to the Kurfurstendamm, and the Ku'dammeck, the Ku'dorf and the Cafe Kranzler.

Go along Pariser str. which is still in the pub quarter and turn right into Bleibtreu str., legendary because of the Cafe Bleibtreu (Stay True)(No. 45), across the road of course is the Cafe Untreu (Untrue); overall a lively street. Cross over Kant str. and turn right into Savigny Platz-small shops under the S-Bahn arcades. Turn into Knesebeck str.

and you come to the Renaissance Theatre, next to the extremely busy Ernst-Reuter Platz. Go along Hardenberg str. and the Technical University and the Academy of Arts are on the left and then go along Hardenberg str. back to the Bahnhof Zoo.

The other tour which starts from here goes around the zoo. Go south along Budapester str. to Hofjager Allee, then along Hofjagerallee to the str. des 17 Juni. You will see the Seigessaule (victory column) straight ahead. On the right of the str. des 17 Juni is the town park, Tiergarten, and on the left is the Schloss Bellevue which is the Berlin residence of the West German President.

The rebuilding of the town goes on monotonously all around and an attempt was made to have a spectacular range of architecture here. The result of this is the Hansa quarter which has also been the subject of considerable criticism. Berlin doesn't appear to be able to get away from the pompous new architecture and the little arguments e.g. the much discussed International Building Exhibition which gave Berlin such buildings as the 'Pregnant Oyster' (congress hall–on the left hand side of the Tiergarten), the much critized cultural centre (Kulturzentrum) near The Wall (Potsdamer str./Landwehrkanal) at the right end of the Tiergarten which includes the Matthai church, the Philharmonie, the National Library, the Museum of Prussian culture and the National Gallery (Potsdamer str. 50, Tuesday-Sunday 9.00 a.m.-5.00 p.m.).

With regard to architecture, particularly of the 1920s–compare Bruno Tauts Hufeisensiedlung (horseshoe surburb) on Britz, U Parchimer Allee, with the Bauhaus Archiv, (building archive), Tiergarten, Klingelhoefer str. 13 (Wednesday-Monday 11.00 a.m.-5.00 p.m.) Go along 17 June str. and you come to the Wall which goes in front of the Brandenburger Tor which is in East Berlin. You can get a better look at the 'Death Wall' which is covered by graffiti on the western side, from the 'Haus am Checkpoint Charlie', 61 Friedrich str. 44 (daily 9.00 a.m.-8.00 p.m.–highly recommended).

Left of the Brandenburger Tor is the place where everything started, the Deutsche Reichstag: It was here that the German Republic was proclaimed in 1918. To-day it contains an historical exhibition (Tuesday-Sunday 10.00 a.m.-5.00 p.m.). Cultural festivals have been held in front of The Wall. It was to the north of this square that Hitler planned to build his dream building with an a enormous dome, designed by his architect Speer.

Naturally, there are still other important parts of town: Firstly Kreuzberg, where now, as ever, the scene is composed of many alternative projects, pubs, cultural meeting places, and students. From Kreuzberg hill you get a view south to the overgrown Gleisdreiecks. You can also see Mehringdamm (road) which is good for a pub crawl in the evenings and Vicktoria Park.

An Area (U Kaiserdamm–Underground), S.Westkreuz (elevated railway) with comparatively large green areas starts behind the exhibition area with its radio tower 'Langer Lulatsch' and the

Kongresszentrum (congress centre). The Berlin forest begins behind this area at Wilmersdorf, firstly as the Teufelsberg, which is used as a toboggan run, then as the national park Teufelssee, then the Grunewald, a large woodland area bordered on the west by the Havel, a popular bathing area in summer, with the Grunewaldturm (tower) and the Jagdschloss (hunting lodge) Grunewald. North of the suburb of Charlottenburg with its schloss (U Sophie-Char.-Platz, S. Westend) are the Schinkel Pavillon (mausoleum) and Belvedere, as well as the schloss gardens and ornamental pond and also the museum of Prussian Culture, Department of Antiquities, Egyptian Museum and the National Gallery. (All open Saturday-Thursday 9.00 a.m.-5.00 p.m.) In the western part of Charlottenburg is the Olympic Stadium which was built for the 1936 Olympics (Platform U).

Some more green areas and contrasting impressions of Berlin are found in the northern parts of the city. There is the workers suburb of Wedding (U Osloer str.), bordered on the south by the Bernauer str., where until the wall was built people from the houses on the eastern side could flee to the western side of the street (U Voltastr) and Reinickendorf with its large industrial areas (Borsig Works, U/S Tegel) which is joined on its western side by the Tegelsee (lake) and framed by the green zone Jungfernheide in the south and the Berlin forest in the north. No. 20 Bus which leaves from S. Waldmannslust, will take you to Luebars in the rural north-eastern area of the western part of the city. A little south from there is Retortenstadt with its Maerkisches Quarter. If you go in the opposite direction, from U Tegel catch the No. 13 bus to Helligensee (lake) which is beautifully situated on the Havel. South of there is Spandau, which is famous for its Citadel completely surrounded by water (U Zitadelle).

OTHER IMPORTANT SIGHTS: the village areas of Alt-Britz, Gatow and Kladow; the Schoeneberger Rathaus (townhall) from where West Berlin is governed, John F. Kennedy Platz; the most important museums: next to the National Museum is the Botanical Gardens and Museum, Koenigin Luise str. 6 (Tuesday-Sunday 10.00 a.m.- 5.00 p.m.); the Preussischer Kulturbesitz at Charlottenburg's Dahlem houses several museums, Arnimallee 23 (Tuesday-Sunday 9.00 a.m.-5.00 p.m.) Art gallery, Sculpture gallery, Copper Etching gallery, Museum of Arts and Crafts, for East Asian Culture, Isalmic Culture, Indian Culture and for Deutsche Volkkunde. Important for frustrated locomotive drivers: the Verkehrs und Technik Museum, Trebiner str. 9 (Tuesday-Sunday 10.00 a.m.-6.00 p.m.); very good: Cinema Museum, Kreuzberg, Grossbeeren str. 27 (Wednesday, Friday, Saturday 8.30-10.30 p.m. Films) important: Anti-War Museum, Genter str. 9 (daily 4.00-8.00 p.m.); Berlin Museum, Linden str. 14 (Tuesday-Sunday 11.00 a.m.-6.00 p.m.); Brueke Museum, paintings by german expressionists, Bussardsteig 9.

ENTERTAINMENT TIPS: The Waldbuehne (open air theatre) behind the Olympic Stadium (S Pichelsberg, U Ruhleben); also the Old Berlin

Cabaret from the kaisers' time is reconstructed during the concert weeks (Konzertwochen); Kommunikationszentren (communications centre) Fabrik, Osloer Street 12; Forum Krezberg, Eisenbahn str. 21; Alternative projects: Mehringhof, Gneisenau Str 1; Administrative and workers groups in the UFA-Fabrik, Viktoria str. 13.

THEATRE: Grips Theater, Altonaer str. 20, Tel. 391 4004; Unart, Oranien str. 163, Tel. 614 2070. Cabarets: Stachelschweine, Europa Center, Tel 261 4795; Buegelbrett (ironing board), Hardenberg str. 12, Tel. 3129012.

CAFES: Schwarzes Cafe, Kant Stre. 148; Zillemarkt, Bleibtreu str. 48; Einstein, Kurfuestenstr. 58; Cafe Scheselong, Wilsnacker str. 61, Stresemann, St. str. 90.

MUSIC/DISCOS: Ballhaus Tiergarten, Perleberge str. 62; Go In, Bleibtreu str. 17; Quartier Latin, Potsdamer str. 99 opposite Potsdamer Abkommen; and the neu style of dance: Neue Welt, Hermannplatz (Roller Disco); Quasimodo, Kant str. 12a (Jazz); Max & Moritz, Oranien str. 162 (Old Berlin); Cassaleon, Hasenheide 69; very hard: Gift, Grossbeeren str and Domina Bar, Potsdamer str; Breitengrad, Mommen str (a meeting place of the stars). Yorkschloesschen, York str, 15; Nulpe, York str. 77. Flea Market: around the Bellevue Turm (tower) U Gleisdreieck. New In Places: Riemers, York str. where Wirtschaftswunder is playing often until early morning; Araxas, Kant str./Leibnitz str.; terrific food at the Alten Welt, Wissmann str./U Hermannpl.

ACCOMMODATION: A chain of youth accommodation is handled from the central IZB (see tourist information) it is best to check with them as the accommodation is often full. Camping: Koordination BCC, Geisberg str. 11, 30, Tel. 030/246071/72. Hotels and pensions information at the tourist office.

EAST BERLIN: The best actual information for a day trip to East Berlin is to be found in the 'Haupstadt Dispatcher' (newspaper) which is found in every city. Also in it are the programmes for the museums, culture centres, concerts and discos.

YUGOSLAVIA

The Socialist Federal Republic of Yugoslavia has an area of 255,804 sq. km. and is one of the most complex and culturally diverse countries in Europe but is sparsely populated (Pop. 22.4million).

Yugoslavia is divided into six provinces, Serbia (with the autonomous provinces of Kosovo and Vojvodina), Croatia, Slovenia, Bosnia, Herzegovina, Macedonia and Montenegro and these divisions attempt to cater for the differing geographical areas, different cultures and languages. In 1918/19 Yugoslavia officially came into being with the Act of Union but it had to fight the Germans for its freedom from 1941. It is independent from the Soviet Bloc.

It is very proud of its partisans a fact which you should keep in mind during your stay. There is a mountain chain running parallel to the coast which levels out in the central north-east of the land and becomes the Save Plain. In the south the mountains of Montenegro are connected to the mountains of Macedonia so that the main roads go up and down rather a lot, even though they mostly follow the Morava and Varda River valleys. Vojvodina is the only part which is quite flat.

ENTRY/FOREIGN EXCHANGE/CUSTOMS REGULATIONS: A valid passport is required and only 1,500 Dinar may be taken into or out of the country.

Duty Free Allowance:
200 cigarettes or 250 gm tobacco, 250 ml spirits and 1 litre wine. Be careful at customs as sometimes fellow travellers attempt to smuggle in goods by putting them into unsuspecting people's luggage!

Currency/Exchange Rate: The currency of the land is the Dinar which is rapidly depreciating:

You should change money daily as the inflation rate is constantly sending up prices and the rate may vary considerably.

TELEPHONE:
It's best to phone overseas from a post office.

Emergency Telephone Number: Police 92; Ambulance 94

EMBASSIES:
Australia: 13 Cika Ljubina, Belgrade, Tel. 624 655.
Canada: Kneza Milosa 75, Belgrade, Tel. 644 666.
N.Z.:   No Resident Representative–see Greece.
U.K.:   General Zdanova 46, Belgrade, Tel. 645055.
U.S.A.:   Kneza Milosa 50, Belgrade, Tel. 645655.

FOOD:

It is quite usual to buy something to eat and go into a park to eat it.

ACCOMMODATION:

Hotels and camping: Yugoslaviapublic, Knez Mihailova 10, Beograd;
International youth hostels: FSJ, Mose Pijade, 11 000, Beograd.

SPEED LIMITS:

In built up areas 60km/h;
outside built up areas 80-100 km/h; motorways 120km/hr.
Buy your petrol coupons from an automobile club before you arrive at
the border!Green insurance card is compulsory.

RAILWAYS:

Inexpensive tariffs.

AIRPORTS:

There are international airports at Belgrade and Zagreb, and 7 coastal
and 7 inland airports also have international connections.

BELGRADE–(BELGRAD)

The former capital of Serbia which, since the formation of Yugoslavia,
has also been its capital. Because of this some of the buildings and
squares (Trg Rebupica, Trg D. Ducovica, Trg Marksa Engelska) are truly
representative of the land. The old town suburb of 'Skardalija' has been
restored for the tourist trade, but a walk through the side streets will
give you a truer picture of how the town has deteriorated. In
comparison, the fort, Kalemegdan, at the junction of the Save and
Danube rivers with its victory column is a part of the town that is
worthwhile seeing. (Population 1.45 million).

BY ROAD: Belgrade is reached by the bumpy E 94. Only near and
around Zagreb is there a motorway where the cars and semitrailers can
speed along to the Balkans and the East.
    Several large parking areas are to be found near the Sava Centar,
where exhibitions and conferences are also held. Take the Novi Beograd
motorway exit and the information office is on the left before the river.

BY RAIL: It is very easy to reach Belgrade by train because the
international express trains branch off at Nice for Skopje and Athens
on the one hand, and Sofia-Istanbul on the other. As well, trains from
Munich-Zagreb and Vienna-Budapest come to Belgrade. The main

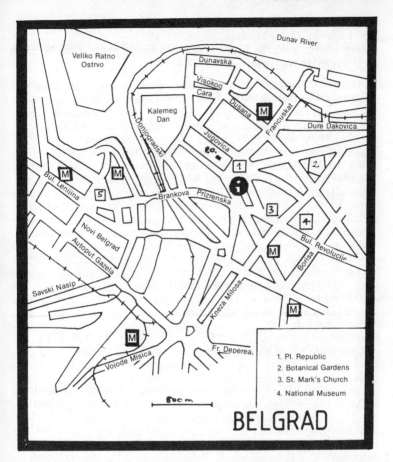

1. Pl. Republic
2. Botanical Gardens
3. St. Mark's Church
4. National Museum

BELGRAD

station which isn't under cover, can barely cope with all the traffic. Train and hotel information and the left luggage room are on the left.

Bus No. 34 which leaves from right in front of the main exit (purchase tickets on the right) goes directly to the Stanica Dunav (Danube railway station) which is even smaller. Tel. 76 38 80.

BY AIR: The international airport is in Surcin, 18 km from the city centre. Tel. 60 1424.

TOURIST INFORMATION: Head office in the subway under Terazije Square. Tel. 63 53 43. Town programme: Beogradscope.

LOCAL TRANSPORT: Buy your tickets at the kiosks. The most important forms of transport are bus, trolley bus and tram. Luckily, there is a route map available to tourists on which the main routes are drawn in. Sightseeing tours 9.30 a.m. from the Hotel Slavija, and 9.50 a.m. from the Hotel Moskva, Tel. 45 11 42.

There is a quay on the Danube from where the boats leave for trips on the river (Karadordeva 8, Tel. 62 22 79).

POINTS OF INTEREST: If you want to go on your own, then you should start in the old town quarter of Kalemegdan at the junction of the Sava and Danube rivers, the birth place of the city. From the railway station go along Nemanjina St., turn right into Kneza Milosa, go past the glass tower, Beogradanka, turn left at Marsala Tito st., go past the Hotel Europa, and the monumental Marx-Engels Square where big rallies are held, along Terazije st. to the Square of the Republic (the Yugoslavian tongue twisting Trg. Republike), the most important axis of the capital. A twisty, signposted way (Turisticki Put) goes from here through the small lanes and across the squares. The most important points on this path are the Bajrakli Mosque, Jevremova 11, the only remaining religious memorial of almost four centuries of rule by the Turks; the Republic Square with its memorials, museums and the palace of Queen Ljubica, Kn Sime Markovica 8; the cathedral in the same street, also the oldest cafe of the town; the lively students' square with most of the university buildings, and the Kalemegdan itself with the upper and lower forts, a lively park, a zoo and the distinctive Prince Eugen Gate, a first world war memorial, a tomb of one of the turkish sultans, turkish bath, and Victory Column–quite a lot by Belgrade Standards.

A few steps to the east of the city centre–Trg. Republike, Francuska st., Street of the 29th November–is the cultural centre of Skadarljia with its main street Skadarska. Its more a Soho or a Kings Cross than an artist colony. (Over priced taverns). In Bulevar Revolucije which leads off Marx-Engels Square, is the parliament house, Skupstina, and further along is St. Marks church, Tasmajdan–both have parks in front of them. And now there are only the new functional buildings left to see, e.g. the sports centre, Avezdara and the Hotel Metropol, and a few high buildings along the main street. The Cemetery of the Freedom Fighter (Ruzveltova–Tram 3) is also very impressive. The Marshal Tito Memorial Centre is a new complex near 'Hajd park', not far away is the Museum of the Fourth of July 1941 (It was here that Tito and his followers decided to revolt), Bulevar Oktobarske revolucije 10a. (Tuesday-Sunday 11.00a.m.-5.00 p.m.). At the '25th May', Boticeva 8, there is a spectacular collection of presents given to Tito. (Bus 34 goes to this area.)

DURING THE YEAR: Belgrade's Summer Culture Programme from July to September.

MUSEUM TIPS (Belgrade has a lot to offer in this area). National Museum, Vasina (Tuesday-Sunday 10.00 a.m.-5.00 p.m.); The Fresco Gallery displaying folk art from the middle ages of Yugoslavia, Cara Urosa 20 (Tuesday-Sunday 10.00 a.m.-5.00 p.m.); the museum of modern art, Usce, housed in a modern building on the new Belgrade side of the Sava. (Wednesday-Monday 10.00 a.m.-5.00 p.m.); Ethnological Museum, Studentski Trg 13 (Tuesday-Sunday 10.00 a.m.-5.00 p.m.); Museum of Immigrant Art, Vuka Karadzics 18 (Tuesday-Saturday 12 noon-7.00 p.m.); the Museum of the Revolution of the Yugoslavian People, Marx-Engels Square 11, (Tuesday-Sunday 10.00 a.m.-5.00 p.m.); Museum of the Illegal Party Printery, Banjicki Venac 12 (Tuesday-Sunday 10.00 a.m.-5.00 p.m.); The Railway Museum, Nemanjina 6, (Monday-Friday 9.00 a.m.-2.00 p.m.).

For relaxation perhaps a trip to the recreation centre, Ada Ciganlija (Bus 23, 31 or 33), or to the sports centre at Bad Kosutnjak (also camping. Bus 33), or to the beautifully located Tasmajdan Baths.

FOOD: Some cafeterias e.g. Luksor, Balkanska 7; Dusanov Grad, Terazije 4; Studentski Park, Bv Revolucije 106; Vuk, Vuka Karadzicaio near Kalemegdasi; Cafe-Bar Terazije; Gradska Kafana, Trg Republike 5; Pod Lipom, Makedonska 44.

ACCOMMODATION: Youth hostel: Miadost, Bulevar Jug. Narodne Armije 56a. Tel. 011/46 38 46, Tram 9 (13 Stops); Camping: Dunav, Batajnicki put 12 km. Tel 19 90 72, Kosutnjak, Kneza Viseslava 17, Tel. 555127, Nacional, Novi Beograd, Bezanijska kosa 1a, Tel. 69 35 09. Tip: All three places rent bungalows for 7-13 DM per person interesting for a somewhat longer stay and more people. Warning: Hotels are extremely expensive. The worst possible accommodation is offered by private people in the streets. During the day, see the tourist information office for information about rooms in private homes.

ENTERTAINMENT: In the evenings perhaps a visit to the student culture centre, Marsala Tita 48; concerts, folk dancing etc. are held at the Folk University Kolarac, Studentenplatz 5; National Theatre, Trg Republike; Pionier Sportpalace, Charlie Chaplin Street 39; or at the Sava Congress Centre.

YOUTH HOTELS: Jelica Milanovic, Brigada 8, Tel. 330100. Hotel Grand, Marsala Tita 31, Tel. 21 05 36.

IN THE AREA: There are very impressive Danube trips to the fort, Golubacki Grad, the Rajkova Caves and the stone age settlement, Lepenski Vir. In the north-west is the Fruska Gora National Park and the best that Europe has to offer: the train ride Beograd-Bar on the Adriatic Coast.

ZAGREB

The capital of Croatia, Zabreb, is richer in history and street life than Belgrade. For many it is the 'real' capital of Yugoslavia. Austrian and hungarian building styles are more pronounced here and a greater mixture of different cultures is evidenced in the streets of the old town. Zagreb lies not far from central Europe. It was always a town of opposites: even to-day there is a marked difference between the buildings of the old town north of the railway line and those in newer satellite suburbs south of the railway line; in the middle ages there was a big difference between the two towns, Kaptol, the seat of the bishop and Gradec, the seat of the king. (Pop. 667,000).

BY CAR: It is easy to get to Zagreb by car: The route is via Maribor from Vienna-Graz on the E93; or via Ljubljana from Munich, Salzburg, or Klagenfurt; or via Rijeka from the Gotthard or Brenner Passes, Milan, Verona or Triest. The main road goes through the southern suburbs of the new town. You can park near the concert hall (Hvratska bratske zajednice) or at the railway station.

BY RAIL: The through railway station is centrally situated, south of the lower town. A map of the town is to be found on platform 1 as well as a restaurant and a tourist information office. It all looks very austrian there, modern ground level shops, Tel. 38 181.

BY AIR: The airport is south-east of Zagreb at Pleso and buses run from there to the city centre. Information from the JAT airline office. Tel. 44 33 22.

TOURIST INFORMATION: The main office is at Trg Nikole Zrinjskog 14, Tel. 41 18 83. Ask for the 'Zagreb Program' there. Youth information: Studenski Centar, Savska Cesta 25 handles accommodation bookings Universiade '87 Office: Prol. Brigada 78, Tel. 041/536 790.

LOCAL TRANSPORT: There are buses and trams in the city. Groups of 10 people or more can take an inexpensive tram TT trip to see the city. In summer a lot of bus tours come here and you may be able to join one of them. Bookings: Kasse ZET, Maricev Prolaz. There is even a signposted tourist route (Touristenmagistrale, TM for short) which you can drive around. But it's better to go on foot as the distances in the upper town are only short.

POINTS OF INTEREST: There is a wide strip of parkland which runs from the lower town, Donji Grad, to the upper town, Gornji Grad, and south to part of the new town. The green strip is divided up into the Tomislav, Strossmayerov and Zrinjoskoga parks in which may be found

King Tomislav's memorial, the dreadful yellow Umjetnicki Pavilion and the Strossmayer Gallery which has paintings by the old masters (daily 10.00 a.m.-12 noon). On the left is probably the most important museum of the city, the Archaelogical Museum which contains everything the Croatians have collected over the ages. (Sunday-Friday 9.00 a.m.-1.00 p.m.).

Walk along Tr. Republike to the city centre. It was here that the masses gathered when this land was separated from the Austro-Hungarian Empire in 1918 and after gaining its freedom in May 1945. It still has a tremendous atmosphere in spite of the modern buildings. On the left (Illica street, Tomiceva) is the valley station of the famous cable car-a bit of Montmarte in Zagreb-which goes up to the upper town, Gornji Grad. At the top is the lookout tower, Lotrscak, from where a cannon is fired at exactly 12 o'clock every day. A flower market is also held on Radicev Trg Square. Also there is St. Mark's church which has Zagreb's and Croatia's Coats of Arms in mosaics in the roof. The over dimensioned design, sometimes surrounded by red flags, serves as a reminder of the communistic doctrines in this land. In the upper town, Gradec, there are a lot of things to see: churches, chapels, palaces, lanes and museums e.g. the Jesuit Monastery, St. Katherine's church, the Pfaffen Tower at the northern gate, and beautiful streets such as Demetrova and Strossmayer Promenade.

Go through the eastern stone gate to leave Gradec and go across Radieva lane and either down the steps, or across the Kravi bridge (bloody bridge) which serves as a reminder of the wars between the towns and you'll come to Kaptol. A colourful market is held on Dolac Square. Also on the square is the Petrica statue, a croatian fairytale character. But the piece de resistance is the 13th century cathedral which was renovated about 100 years ago in the new gothic style.

In the lower town area the classical Croatian National Theatre, on Marshall Tito Square is worth seeing. The theatre is the most impressive building in the town next to the cathedral. Also on the square: the fountain and on the second green strip of the lower town are some university buildings. Further east is Brace Kavurica, Boskoviceva, which was built between the wars. It is dominated by the Museum of the People's Revolution-(Tuesday-Sunday 9.00 a.m.-1.00 p.m. & 2.00-5.00 p.m.). A bit further on is Lenin Square with a very beautiful park and the Worker's Home where exhibitions and concerts are held.

The town hall (Skupstina Grada) is in the new town as well as the Worker's University to the south-west. Between the concrete towers, is a sporting and swimming centre. Another swimming pool is found at Dinamo Stadium, Maksimirska 128; the sports park Svetice also has a pool, and playing fields are found at Mladost, Horvanski Zavoj as well as a swimming pool and camping ground. Take the tram to the south-western terminus. Bundek jezero is a small lake on the Sava River, after the Slobode Bridge. To the left is the railway station which is not far from the botanical gardens. There is a zoo at Maksimir north west of the city (daily 8.00 a.m. to dark). The cemetery at Mirogoj to the north is very impressive.

In one of the smaller parks on Svacic Square is a brother of the Manneken Pis. . .(near the railway station on the left Haulikova Str.).

MUSEUM TIPS: The Ethnological Museum, Mazuranicev Trg. 14 (Tuesday-Sunday 9.00 a.m.-1.00 p.m. and Tuesday-Thursday 5.00-7.00 p.m.); the Primitive Gallery, Cirilometodska 3 (daily 10.00 a.m.-1.00 p.m. & 5.00-8.00 p.m.); Geological Museum & Planetarium, Demetrova 1 (Tuesday-Sunday 9.00 a.m.-12 noon); the Glyptothek of the Yugoslavs, the Academy of Science, Medvedgradska 2 (Sunday-Friday 8.00 a.m.-1.00 p.m.); the Hunting Museum, Nazorova 63, (Monday-Friday, Sunday 9.00 a.m.-1.30 p.m.); Memorial Museum of the 8th Zagreb Conference of the Communist Party, Pantovcak 178a (Tuesday-Sunday 10.00 a.m.-12 noon); the Museum of the First Communist Party Conference in Croatia, Prosinackih Zrtava 205 (Tuesday-Sunday 10.00 a.m.-12 noon); the Museum of Croatian History, Matoseva 8 (daily 10.00 a.m.-5.00 p.m.) and the Typhologische Museum for rehabilitation of the blind, Draskoviceva 80 (Monday-Friday 9.00 a.m.-3.00 p.m.).

FOOD: Self service cafetarias in Trg Republike or cheap shops at the railway station ground floor level. Restaurants: Kornat, Gajeva 9, Drina, Preradoviceva 11; central: Lovacki Rog. Ilica 14; with bar, Kaptolska Klet, Kaptol 5; Splendid, Zrinjevac 15; Kvarner, Trg Zrtava Fasizma; or the Prepusovec, Kraj Kasine, a favourite with the locals.

ENTERTAINMENT: In good weather go to the old town or to Republik Square where there is usually a lot happening. A disco restaurant/cafe is the Gradski Podrum, on the corner of Republik Square, Cesarca 2. Disco club: Saloon, Tuskanac 1a and the Kavana Neboder, on Republic Square. Folk, classical and sometimes pop. concerts are held at the Vatroslav Lisinka concert hall, Trnjanska bb, Tel. 53 98 39.

ACCOMMODATION: Youth hostel: Omladinski, Petrinjska 77, Tel. 041/44 14 05; Youth hotel, Petrinjska 73, Tel. 44 14 03;
Camping: Horvacanski Zavoj, bb, Tel. 518198; Private rooms: C Tourist, Tomislav Square 17, Tel. 411436; Generalturist Trg Zrinski 18, Tel. 44 52 99;
Pensions: Dvorac Brezovica, Brezovica bb, Tel. 52 18 88 (bungalows): Sunski Dvor, Prekrizje 2, Tel. 42 93 48.

EXCURSIONS: North of the city is Sljeme Hill from where you get a beautiful view in good weather (chairlift). At the top is Zagreb's T.V. tower. It's a pleasant walk down. Samobor is known for its therapeutic baths and castle ruins. Rude is a mining town from the middle ages. There is a good train service and also a motorway to Karlovac which was fortified in case of attack by the turks. Much of the former fortifications are now parkland, Dubovac fortress. Many yugoslavians visit Kumrovec where Tito was born.